Jean Croiset

Devotion to the Sacred Heart of Jesus

Jean Croiset

Devotion to the Sacred Heart of Jesus

ISBN/EAN: 9783743462991

Manufactured in Europe, USA, Canada, Australia, Japa

Cover: Foto ©ninafisch / pixelio.de

Manufactured and distributed by brebook publishing software (www.brebook.com)

Jean Croiset

Devotion to the Sacred Heart of Jesus

DEVOTION

TO THE

SACRED HEART OF JESUS.

By FATHER JOHN CROISET,

Of the Society of Jesus.

Translated from the Italian.

LONDON:

BURNS & LAMBERT, 17 & 18, PORTMAN STREET,
PORTMAN SQUARE.

1863.

THE AUTHOR'S PREFACE.

The deep and extraordinary interest taken by so many, in the devotion to the Sacred Heart of our Lord Jesus' Christ, the great fruits it has produced, and the singular esteem entertained for it, by persons of universally recognized merit, have led to the publication of this book. It is intended to instruct the faithful, and satisfy their pious desires. There might, perhaps, have been some reason to fear, at the very outset, that the mere title of Devotion to the Sacred Heart of Jesus Christ, however it might attract many persons to read this book, might also deter many others. Arrested by the first words, they might be led to form an inaccurate idea of the devotion. To remove this difficulty, it has been thought well to explain in the beginning, what is understood by devotion to the Sacred Heart of Jesus Christ. Experience has proved, that there is no one, who, after seeing in what it consists, does not agree, that it is reasonable, solid, and most useful, for our salvation, as well as for our perfection.

In the first part, are developed the motives, which should attract us to this devotion. In the second, are given the means of acquiring it. In the third, the practice of the Devotion is explained, and some of the exercises supplied, which are suited to it. And since the Devotion may be wholly reduced, to the perfect love of Jesus Christ, especially in the Adorable Eucharist; this perfect love is treated of, throughout the whole course of the work. The reason why the visit to the Blessed Sacrament, the august Sacrifice of our Altars, and Holy Communion, are spoken of at greater length, is, because, of all exercises of piety, there are none which bring us nearer to Jesus Christ, none more adapted to honour His Sacred Heart, and to inflame ours with an ardent love of Him.

It is hoped that the reflections here made, will help to convince many, of the reasons for practising these holy exercises, and teach them at the same time how to practise them with fruit. A portrait is then drawn of a soul that truly loves Jesus Christ, with a view of giving a true idea of real and solid piety.

The method of practising this Devotion is then given, by means of suitable exercises; and the work is closed by Meditations adapted to the Devotion. Those who know the singular merit and exalted virtue of Father La Colombière, and are aware that Almighty God especially selected him, to promote the Devotion to the Sacred Heart of Jesus, will be glad to find in various parts of this book, the thoughts and sentiments of this great servant of Jesus Christ upon this Devotion.

To lead Christians to the practice of this Devotion, it is unnecessary to adduce either authorities, revelations, or examples. It is enough to know, that it tends wholly to the perfect love of Jesus Christ. It has been thought well, however, to cite, in two or three parts of this book, such things as are found in the revelations of St. Gertrude and St. Mechtildis, bearing upon this Devotion. It would be nothing short of prevarication, were we to abstain, through fear of being considered too credulous, from pointing out the wonderful means, which Almighty God has made use of latterly, to renew the practice of this Devotion amongst the faithful. It cannot be denied, without condemning the sentiments of the entire Church, that there have existed at all times, pure and chosen souls, to whom God communicates Himself intimately. Although indeed, instances of this divine condescension and familiarity are most rare, nevertheless, there is not a century that does not furnish us with examples of it in some Saint. Those who have never received such favours, says St. Teresa, have sometimes a difficulty in believing in these extraordinary gifts: (St. Teresa in her Life, ch. 26.) But they should remember, that if, it be credulity to believe everything on such a subject, it is on the other hand, temerity to believe nothing. It is well here to state, that the revelations of St. Gertrude and of St Mechtildis, which we have quoted two or three times in this book, were examined by all the learned persons, who were then in Flanders, in France, in Italy, in Germany, and in the most celebrated universities. All were unanimous in asserting that they were full of the spirit of God, and that

He alone was the author of them. Learned Prelates and great Saints have esteemed and approved them. They have been cited with praise by celebrated Doctors. One of them has asserted, that, after the examination which has been made of them, he did not think, that a man of true wisdom and solid virtue, could fail to esteem them.*

The Spiritual Retreat of F. La Colombière has already made many pious souls acquainted, with the wonderful means, which Almighty God has employed, to inspire this Devotion. But, the person of whom that great servant of God speaks, "to whom" he says, "our Lord, communicates Himself most intimately," took always especial care to lead an obscure and hidden life, though honoured by God with those extraordinary graces, which we read of with admiration, in the lives of the greatest saints. We therefore exhort our readers to read the life of Sister Margaret Alacoque, Religious of the Visitation, by Monseigneur Languet, Bishop of Soissons, one of the greatest and most learned Prelates, that France has produced in these times. It was translated

---

* *Revelationes prædictis Fœminis factæ toti Orbi innotuerunt, et a piis, eruditisque viris jam olim fuerunt approbatæ; nam, et Sancti Patres passim eas citant in scriptis et libris suis . . . . Revelationes sanctæ Gertrudis ante et post mortem ipsius fuerunt a doctissimis, eruditissimisque viris summa cum diligentia examinatæ, quorum unus post accuratam illarum lectionem, scripsit sententiam hoc modo: Ego, inquit, in veritate divini luminis sentio, neminem qui Dei Spiritu sit illustratus, posse calumniari, aut impugnare ea quæ in hoc libro habentur, nam et Catholica sunt, et Sancta. Blos. Concl. Anim. fidel. C. 4. § 5. de Authent. Revelation.*

into Italian and printed at Venice. It will be seen in the person of that most virtuous virgin, that the arm of the Lord is not shortened, and that, even if it were true that the present age is (as some not very devout minds wish to persuade themselves) an age of no miracles, at all events there is not any age of the Church, in which great Saints do not appear.

NOTICE.

For the greater convenience of those who may use this book, it has been thought well to place all the Meditations at the end. Some ejaculatory prayers are appended to them. They may be employed to feed devotion during the day, according to the different necessities of different persons. They are taken from the Soliloquies, the Meditations, and the Manual of St. Augustin, and also from the works of St. Teresa.

DEVOTION TO THE
Sacred Heart of our Lord Jesus Christ.

FIRST PART.—MOTIVES.

Chapter I.

What is meant by Devotion to the Sacred Heart of our Lord Jesus Christ, and in what it consists.

THE particular object of this devotion is the immense love of the Son of God, which has induced Him to die for us, and to give Himself wholly to us in the Adorable Sacrament of the Altar, and this, although He foresaw all the ingratitude and outrages which He was to meet with in this state of a victim immolated till the end of ages; preferring rather to expose himself daily to the insults and contempt of mankind, than to fail in showing us, by the greatest of all wonders, to what an excess He loves us.

This is what has enkindled the piety and zeal of many. Reflecting on the little gratitude that is shown for such an excess of love, the little love that is felt for Jesus Christ, and the little value that is set upon His love for us, they have been unable to endure to see

Him daily so ill-treated, without protesting to Him their just grief and their excessive desire to repair, as far as they can, so much ingratitude and contempt, by their ardent love, by their profound respect, and by every sort of homage in their power. It is with this intention that certain days in the year have been chosen in order to make a more special recognition of the excessive love of Jesus Christ for us in the adorable Sacrament; and at the same time, to make Him some reparation of honour for all the indignities and all the contempt which He has received, and still receives daily, in this mystery of love. And certainly, this grief at the sight of the little love shown to Jesus Christ in this adorable mystery, this intense sorrow at seeing Him so ill-treated, these practices of devotion which are suggested by love alone, and which have no other aim but to repair, as far as possible, the outrages He there endures, are, without doubt, real proofs of an ardent love for Jesus Christ, and visible signs of a just gratitude.

It is easy to see that the object and principal motive of this devotion is, as we have already said, the immense love which Jesus Christ has for men, whilst they for the most part feel only contempt, or at least indifference, for Him.

The end we have in view is, first, to acknowledge and honour, as far as we are able, by our frequent adorations, by a return of love, by our thanksgivings, and by every sort of homage, the sentiments of love and tenderness which Jesus Christ has for us, in the adorable Eucharist, where He is so little known to men, or at least, so little loved, even by those who do know Him.

In the second place, we aim at repairing, by every means possible, the insults and outrages to which His love exposed Him, in the course of His mortal life, and to which the same love exposes Him still every day, in the most holy Sacrament of the Altar. So that this devotion wholly consists, properly speaking, in an ardent love of Jesus Christ, constantly residing amongst us in the adorable Eucharist, and in testifying this ardent love by our grief at seeing Him so little loved and so little honoured, and by the means we take to repair this contempt and this want of love.

But as we always require, in the practice even of the most spiritual devotions, certain material and sensible objects, which, by the strong impression they make upon us, engage our attention, and thus facilitate the exercise of these devotions, the Sacred Heart of Jesus has been chosen, as the sensible object that is most worthy of our respect, and the best suited at the same time to the end we have in view in this devotion.

Indeed, even if there had been no special reason for giving to these pious practices the name of Devotion to the Sacred Heart of Jesus, it would seem that nothing could better express the peculiar character of this devotion. For it is, in fact, but an exercise of divine love. Love is its object; love is its principal motive; and love is the end at which it aims. The heart of man, says St. Thomas, is in a manner the source and seat of love. Its natural movements follow and imitate the affections of the mind, and contribute not a little, by their strength or weakness, to foment or assuage its passions. It is on this account that the most tender sentiments of the soul are generally attributed to the heart. It is this also that makes the hearts of the Saints an object of such singular veneration.

From all that has been said, it is easy to understand what is meant by devotion to the Sacred Heart of Jesus. It means an ardent love for Jesus Christ at the remembrance of all the wonders He has wrought, to testify His love, especially in the Sacrament of the Eucharist, which is indeed the miracle of His love. It means a lively grief at the sight of the outrages committed by men against Jesus Christ in this adorable mystery. It means an ardent desire to omit nothing in order to make reparation, in every way we can, for all these insults. This is what is understood by devotion to the Sacred Heart of our Lord Jesus Christ. This is what it principally consists in, not exclusively, as some perhaps have supposed, in the loving and specially honouring that Heart of flesh, like our own, which forms a part of the adorable Body of Jesus Christ. Not that the Sacred Heart does not merit our adoration. It is enough to say that it is the Heart of Jesus Christ. If His Body and His precious Blood deserve all our respect, who does not see that His Sacred Heart claims our homage even more particularly? If we feel a devotion towards His Sacred Wounds, how much more powerfully should we be inflamed with devotion towards His Sacred Heart? This Divine Heart, regarded as a part of the adorable Body of Jesus Christ, is, properly speaking, the *material* object of this devotion. The immense love which Jesus Christ bears towards us is its form or motive principle. Now, as this love is purely spiritual, it was impossible that it could come under the cognizance of the senses. It was therefore necessary to find a symbol to express it. What more appropriate or more natural symbol of love could be found than the real Heart of Jesus?

It is for the same reason that the Church, when she wishes to give us a sensible representation of the sufferings of the Son of God, which are no less spiritual than His love, gives us the image of His Sacred Wounds. So that, as devotion to the Sacred Wounds is, in truth, a devotion to Jesus in his sufferings, so the devotion to the Sacred Heart of Jesus is, in truth, a more affectionate and more ardent devotion towards Jesus Christ in the adorable Sacrament, in consideration of the immense love He there testifies towards us, and with the intention of making reparation for the contempt which is manifested towards it. Assuredly, the Sacred Heart of Jesus Christ bears as close a relation, at least, to His love, as the Sacred Wounds bear to His sufferings. Now, if there has ever existed, in every age, so great a devotion to the Sacred Wounds of Jesus Christ, and if the Church, in her wish to inspire all her children with the love of Jesus Christ, continually places these Sacred Wounds before their eyes, how powerful necessarily must be the effect of the remembrance and representation of His Sacred Heart?

It will be seen, in the course of this work, that this devotion is not new, and that its practice is confirmed by the example of many great Saints. It has been sanctioned by various privileges. Clement X., by a Bull dated the 4th of October, 1674, granted great Indulgences to an association of the Sacred Heart of Jesus, in the Church of the Seminary at Constances, consecrated in honour of the Sacred Heart. Innocent XII. granted, by a special Brief, a plenary Indulgence in favour of the devotion to the Sacred Heart.*

It is not necessary to adduce here the numerous reasons which prove the solidity of this devotion. It is enough to say that the love which Jesus Christ has for us, and of which he gives us so marvellous a proof in the adorable Eucharist, is its principal motive; that to make reparation for the contempt with which this love has been treated is the principal end to which it is directed; that the Sacred Heart of Jesus, all on fire with this love, is its sensible object, and that a most ardent and tender love for the person of Jesus Christ ought to be its fruit.

---

* The reigning Pontiff, Clement XIII., at the request of many dioceses, provinces, and kingdoms, has allowed the feast to be celebrated with a proper Mass and Office. The devotion has in consequence rapidly spread over almost all Catholic countries.

Chapter II.

The means employed by Almighty God to promote this devotion.

Father la Colombiere, of the Society of Jesus, was one of the first whom Almighty God made use of to draw the faithful to this devotion. This great Servant of God was more illustrious for his glorious character of Confessor of Jesus Christ in England, than for the distinguished post which he held of Preacher to her Royal Highness the Duchess of York, now Queen of Great Britain. He is celebrated for his works, in which he unites solidity with elegance, and elegance with unction. But he is still more esteemed for his exalted virtue. He had bound himself by an express vow to aspire to it continually, and he attained to it in so short a time as to secure the admiration of all Catholics who knew him, and even of heretics. This great Servant of God conceived at once so true an idea of the solidity and importance of this devotion, and received from God such great graces by means of these holy practices, that he thought himself obliged to neglect nothing to make known this treasure, which belongs indeed to all, but which is known only to few. Let us hear what he has written on the subject himself in the Journal of his Spiritual Retreats, which he made in London, and the notes of which were published after his death.

"At the close of this Retreat," he says, "full of confidence in the mercy of God, I have resolved to procure, by every means possible, the execution of what was prescribed to me by my Adorable Master, regarding His most precious Body in the most holy Sacrament of the Altar, where I believe Him really and truly present. Full of the consolations which I receive and enjoy from the mercy of my God, though I cannot explain what they are, I have understood that Almighty God desired that I should serve Him, by procuring the accomplishment of His holy designs with regard to the devotion which He has suggested to a person to whom He communicates Himself very intimately, and for whose benefit He has been pleased to make use of my weakness. I have already inspired many persons in England with it, and I have written about it to France, and have begged a friend of mine to make it known where he is. It will be very useful there, and the number of chosen souls that are to be found in that Community makes me believe that its practice in that holy house will be very agreeable to God. Why cannot I, oh my God! be everywhere, and publish what Thou expectest from Thy servants and friends?

"Almighty God having manifested His designs to the person who, there is reason to believe, is according to His heart, from the great graces He has granted her, she consulted me regarding them, and I obliged her to put in writing what she had said to me. This I have myself written in the Journal of my Retreats, since Almighty God has deigned to make use of my weakness in the execution of this design.

"Being before the Blessed Sacrament," says this holy soul, "one day during the Octave of Corpus Christi, I received from God excessive marks of His love. As I felt moved with the desire of making Him some return and giving love for love, He said to me: 'Thou canst not make me a better return than by doing what I have so often asked of thee.' And disclosing to me His Divine Heart, 'Behold this Heart,' He said, 'which has loved men so much, and has spared nothing, even to consuming Itself, in order to show them Its love; and in return, I receive nothing but ingratitude from the greater number through the contempt, the irreverence, the sacrileges, and the coldness shown towards me in this Sacrament of love. But, what is more painful to me is, that these are hearts which are consecrated to Me. I therefore ask of thee, that the first Friday after the Octave of the Blessed Sacrament be dedicated to a particular festival in honour of My Heart, to make It a reparation of honour by an act of atonement, and by communicating on that day, in order to repair the indignities which It has received during the time of exposition on the Altars; and I promise thee that my Heart shall dilate Itself to pour abundantly the influences of Its divine love upon those who shall render It this honour.'

"But, oh Lord, why dost Thou address Thyself," said this person to Him, "to so miserable a creature, to so poor a sinner, that by her unworthiness she is calculated to hinder the accomplishment of Thy design, when Thou hast so many generous souls to execute Thy desires?"

"'Dost thou not know,' He said, 'that I make use of the weakest subjects to confound the strong? that it is generally in the most insignificant and the poor in spirit that I manifest my power, in order that they may attribute nothing to themselves?'

"Grant me then," I said to Him, "the means of doing what Thou commandest."

"He then added: 'Go to my servant N. and tell him from Me, that he must do all in his power to establish this devotion, and to give this satisfaction to My Divine Heart. That he must not lose courage at the difficulties he will meet with, for they will not be wanting. But he must bear in mind, that those who wholly distrust themselves, and confide entirely in me, are all-powerful.'"

F. la Colombière was a person of very nice discernment, and was not one who would believe anything lightly. But he had received too clear a proof of the exalted and solid virtue of the person that spoke to him to fear the least illusion in this matter. He therefore immediately set himself to the work which Almighty God had entrusted to him. But in order to accomplish it in the best manner that he could, he began it in his own person. He consecrated himself entirely to the Sacred Heart of Jesus. He offered to It everything in himself that he thought capable of honouring and pleasing It. The extraordinary graces which he received from this practice soon confirmed him in the idea he had formed of the importance and solidity of this devotion. No sooner did he begin to meditate on the tender love which Jesus Christ entertains for us in the Blessed Sacrament, where His sacred Heart is ever burning with love for men, and ever open to pour out upon them every kind of grace and benediction, than he felt deep grief at the thought of the horrible outrages which Jesus Christ has endured therein for so long a time from the malice of heretics, and from the extraordinary indifference which the greater number even of Catholics show for Jesus Christ in this august Sacrament. He was deeply moved at the remembrance of this forgetfulness, this contempt, and these outrages, and he was constrained to consecrate himself anew to the Sacred Heart, by that beautiful prayer which he calls An Offering to the Sacred Heart of Jesus. This prayer will be found at the end of this book. The departure of the Servant of God to England, his imprisonment, and the short time he survived his return to France, did not allow him to publish more regarding it. But God has not left His work imperfect. He himself inspired this devotion, which, as he had made known to St. Gertrude (Life of St. Gertrude, book iv. c. 4), He especially reserved for these latter times, in order to arouse by these means the tepidity and sloth of the faithful. By means of a little book composed as it were by chance, without art, without study, and without design, He has inspired with this devotion even persons who had never appreciated it, and who, at one time, without knowing in what it consisted, had thrown discredit upon it. Almighty God has made use of these persons in particular to diffuse it almost universally.

In less than a year then was this devotion happily established. The wisest directors, Doctors, and Prelates have pronounced its eulogium. Preachers have successfully inculcated it. Chapels have been erected in honour of the Sacred Heart of Jesus Christ. Pictures of It have been painted and engraved. Altars have been raised to It. The nuns of the Visitation, who, animated with the spirit of their holy Founder, have been the most zealous, or at least the first, in this undertaking, have had the consolation of hearing the Mass composed in honour of the Sacred Heart solemnly sung at Dijon, in the chapel which they have built to the Sacred Heart of Jesus. Their example has been followed with the greatest benefit by many other nuns. This solid devotion has spread and established itself with marvellous success over almost the whole of France. It has been carried into foreign kingdoms. It has passed even beyond the seas. It has been founded at Quebec, and has already penetrated by the help of missionaries into Syria, the Indies, and even China. In a word, the universal approbation this devotion has met with, the esteem entertained for it by persons of universally recognized merit and virtue, give us reason to hope that in future Jesus Christ will be less forgotten, better served, and much more loved.

Chapter III.

How just and reasonable is the devotion to the Sacred Heart of our Lord Jesus Christ.

The reasons which enforce the love of Jesus Christ are above any mere sentiment. Souls relish them according to their progress in grace. It seems as though to wish to seek the motives that should lead us to love Jesus Christ is, either to forget what we are, or to believe that we do not know who He is.

It might then appear useless to bring forward here the motives which should incline us to the devotion to the Sacred Heart of Jesus. This devotion is itself an exercise of the love we ought to have for Jesus Christ. But as all men are not always in the same dispositions, and grace is not always equal in all men, I have thought it well to make at least a few reflections on the three principal motives. They should be sufficient to convince any reasonable man.

We shall show in this and the two following chapters. 1. How just and reasonable is the devotion to the Sacred Heart of Jesus. 2. How useful it is both for our salvation and perfection. 3. What true sweetness there is in this devotion. In fact, whether we consider the sensible object of this devotion, which is the sacred Heart of Jesus, or confine ourselves to the principal and spiritual object, which is the immense love of Jesus Christ for men, with what respect, gratitude, and love should we not be filled!

I. *The excellence of the adorable Heart of our Lord Jesus Christ.*

The Heart of Jesus is holy with the sanctity of God Himself. Hence it follows, that all the movements of His Heart, owing to the dignity of the Person from whom they proceed, are actions of infinite price and value. For they are the actions of God Incarnate. It is therefore just that the Sacred Heart of Jesus Christ should be honoured with a peculiar worship. For in honouring It, we honour His Divine Person.

The veneration we bear the Saints renders their hearts so precious to us, that we look upon them as the most precious of their relics. What, then, must we think of the adorable Heart of Jesus Christ? Its claims to our love are not only higher in degree but different in kind. Where is the heart that was ever animated with dispositions so admirable, and so conformable to our true interests? Where shall we find one whose movements could be a source of so much good to us? It is in this divine Heart that all the designs of our salvation have been formed. It is through the love with which this Heart burns for us, that these same designs have been executed.

This sacred Heart, says a great servant of God, is the seat of all virtues, the source of all benedictions, the refuge of all holy souls. The virtues which may principally be honoured in It, are—first, a most ardent love for God His Father, joined to a most profound respect, and the greatest humility that has ever existed; in the second place, an infinite patience in sufferings, an excessive grief for the sins which He had taken upon Himself, the confidence of a most tender Son joined to the confusion of the greatest sinner; in the third place, a most lively compassion for our miseries, an immense love for us, notwithstanding these miseries, and with all these emotions, each of which was exercised in the highest degree possible, an unalterable equanimity, proceeding from so perfect a conformity to the will of God, that it could not be disturbed by any event, however contrary it might appear to His zeal, His humility, His love itself, and all the other dispositions He possessed.

This adorable Heart is still, as far as It can be, in the same sentiments. It is, above all, burning with love for man; always open to pour out on them every sort of grace and blessing; always full of compassion for our evils; always urged by the desire to make us partakers of Its treasures, and to give Itself to us;

always ready to receive us, and to be to us a refuge, an habitation, a Paradise even in this life.

For all this, He finds nothing in the heart of man but hardness, forgetfulness, contempt, ingratitude. Are not these motives to induce Christians to honour this Sacred Heart, and to repair so many insults and outrages, by manifest proofs of their love?

II. *The amiable qualities which are found in the Person of Jesus Christ.*

No one can apply himself to the knowledge of Jesus Christ, without finding in Him everything that is amiable in creatures, whether reasonable or devoid of reason. Every one has his own attraction to love. Some are drawn by great beauty, others by meekness. We see some who are drawn by the virtues in which they are themselves wanting, because they seem to them more admirable than those they possess. Others, again, have a greater liking for the qualities which agree with their own inclinations. Good qualities and true virtues command the love of all. But if there were on earth a person, says a great servant of God, in whom were united all motives for love, who could refuse to love him? Now, all agree that all these are to be found united, in a most excellent degree, in the adorable Person of Jesus Christ; and yet Jesus Christ is only loved by a very few.

The most celebrated beauty, says the Prophet, is nothing but a withered flower in comparison with that of our divine Saviour. It appeared to me, says St. Teresa, that the sun cast upon the earth but a pale light, after I had seen in an ecstasy, some rays of the beauty of Jesus Christ. The most perfect creatures in this world are those which have the fewest defects. The most splendid qualities in men are accompanied by so many imperfections, that whilst we are attracted on one side, we are repelled on the other. Jesus Christ alone is sovereignly perfect. Everything in Him is equally amiable.

There is nothing in Him, but what ought to win all hearts to Him. In Him, we find united all the advantages of nature, all the riches of grace and of glory, all the perfections of the Divinity. We discover abysses, a boundless space as it were, and an infinite extent of greatness. In a word, this God Incarnate who loves us so tenderly, and whom men love so little, is the object of the love, the homage, the adorations and the praises of the whole Court of heaven. It is He who has supreme authority to judge men and angels. The destiny and the eternal happiness of all creatures is in His hands; His dominion extends over all nature. All spirits tremble in His presence. They are obliged to adore Him, either by a voluntary submission of love, or by the forced endurance of the effects of His justice. He reigns absolutely in the order of grace and in glory. The whole world, visible and invisible, is under His feet. Is He not, then, an object worthy of the homage of mankind? Does not this Man-God, with all His titles and all the glory He possesses, and loving us as He does, deserve that we should love Him?

But what still more powerfully attracts our love in our Divine Saviour, is, that He unites all these rare qualities, these magnificent titles, this eminent sovereignty, with so great a meekness, and tenderness for us, that it is carried even to excess. His meekness is so amiable, that He charmed even His mortal enemies. He was led, says the Prophet (Isaiah liii. 9), as a *sheep to the slaughter:* and He was dumb as a *lamb before his shearer*, and *he did not open His mouth*. He compares Himself sometimes to a father, who cannot contain his joy at the return of a prodigal son (St. Luke xv. 11); sometimes to a shepherd, who, having found his sheep that was lost, puts it upon his shoulders, and calls together his friends and neighbours, that they may rejoice because he has found it (St. Luke xv. 5). *Hath no man condemned thee?* He says to the adulterous woman; *Neither will I condemn thee: go and now sin no more* (St. John viii. 10). He exercises no less meekness towards us every day. It is extraordinary what precautions it is necessary to take in the world, to avoid offending a friend. Men are so sensitive, that often a single expression of ill-humour is enough to make them forget twenty, thirty, forty years of service. A single word, spoken unseasonably, sometimes breaks the strongest friendship.

It is not so with Jesus Christ. It seems incredible, but nevertheless it is beyond dispute, that we cannot possibly have a friend more grateful than He is. We must not imagine that He is capable of breaking friendship with us for a slight ingratitude. He sees all our weaknesses, and bears with incredible goodness all the miseries of those He loves. He forgets them, and appears not to perceive them. His compassion goes so far as to give comfort to those souls who are too much afflicted at them. He does not desire that our fear of displeasing Him should go so far as to disturb us and torment our minds. He would have us avoid the smallest faults; but He does not even wish that we should be disquieted at great ones: He desires that joy, liberty and peace of heart should be the eternal portion of those that truly love Him.

The least of these qualities, in one of the great ones of the world, would be enough to win the hearts of all those under him. The mere account of any of these virtues in a prince whom we have never seen, and are never likely to see, makes an impression on our hearts, and makes him beloved, even by strangers. Jesus Christ is the only one in whom all these splendid qualities, all these virtues, and whatever we can picture to ourselves as great, excellent and amiable, are to be found united. How is it, then, that so many motives for inspiring love do not succeed in making us truly love Jesus Christ? It often requires so little in the world to gain our hearts. We give away our heart, and are prodigal of it for ever so little. Shalt Thou alone, oh my God, have no part in it?

Can we reflect a little on these things, and not feel an ardent love of Jesus Christ? Can we fail to have at least a lively grief at loving Him so little? We owe Him our hearts, by so many titles. Can we refuse Him, then, this heart, if we add to all these titles the immense benefits with which He has presented us, and the ardour and excessive tenderness with which He has loved and does love us still, never ceasing to give us daily manifest proofs of the immense love He has for us?

III. *The sensible proofs of the immense love that Jesus Christ has for us.*

Of all marks of love, there is none that moves the heart of men so deeply as benefits. Either because there is nothing that marks more strongly the affection of the person who loves; or because nothing is so gratifying to our nature, ever inclined, as it is, to seek its own interest, as a love which is of service to us. Jesus Christ has used this means also, in order to oblige us to love Him. He has presented us, He has loaded us with a thousand blessings, the least consideration of which far exceeds all that we can merit, hope for, or desire. All are continually receiving His benefits. All agree in acknowledging the excess of His love, of which these benefits are themselves such striking proofs. And yet, how few are there who are gained by His benefits, or feel themselves touched by His love!

By dint of hearing the Creation, the Incarnation, and Redemption constantly spoken of, we become accustomed to these words, and to the things they signify: and yet, there is no one so unreasonable as not to be at once transported with love, for any one from whom he knew he had received the hundredth part of the least of these favours. As our soul depends much on the senses in its operations, we were naturally little moved by the thought of a purely spiritual being. Hence it is, that, before the Incarnation of the Word, notwithstanding the prodigies wrought by Almighty God in favour of His people, there was always a greater admixture of fear in their love. But now, this God has rendered Himself, so to speak, more sensible to us, by becoming man. This Man-God has done more than all that we could possibly have conceived, to oblige all men to love Him. Had He never formed the design to redeem us, He would have been no less holy, powerful, or happy. He has, however, had our salvation so much at heart, that it might have been supposed, seeing all that He has done, and the manner in which He has done it, that all His happiness depended upon ours. When he might have redeemed us at very little cost, He has chosen to merit for us the grace of salvation by His death, and by the most disgraceful and cruel death, the death of the Cross. When He might have applied His merits to us in a thousand ways, He has chosen the most wonderful abasement, which has astonished heaven and all nations, as the means of doing so. All this has been done in order to move our hearts, which are naturally grateful for the least benefit, and the smallest mark of friendship. Birth under circumstances of the greatest poverty, a laborious and obscure life, a Passion loaded with insults, an infamous and painful death, are wonders that overpower us: and they are all the effects of the love which Jesus has for us.

Have we ever well conceived the greatness of the benefit of our Redemption? and if so, is it possible that we should be only ordinarily grateful for such a benefit? The sin of our first Parent has, indeed, drawn down upon us great evils, and has deprived us of great benefits. But can we look upon Jesus Christ in the manger, upon the Cross, or in the Blessed Eucharist, without acknowledging that our losses have been repaired with advantage? That the blessings which we have gained by our Redemption are at least equivalent to the privileges which man enjoyed in his state of innocence.

The character of universal Redeemer is no less powerful a motive to oblige us to love Him. All were dead, says the Apostle, by the sin of Adam, and Jesus Christ has died for all. No one has been able to preserve himself from the contagion of so great an evil. The whole world has felt the effect of so powerful a remedy. Our loving Saviour has given all His blood, for the infidel who knows him not, and for the heretic who will not believe in Him, as well as for those who, whilst they believe in Him, yet refuse to love Him. How infinite is the value of His Blood! How great a Saviour; and how abundant a Redemption! Jesus Christ has not been satisfied with paying the debts we had contracted. He has prevented all those which we might have contracted in future. He has paid, so to speak, in advance, before they have been incurred. To this we must add those powerful helps, those great graces, those signal favours which He heaps on faithful souls, and by which He sweetens and renders palatable every thing that is bitter and painful in our existence.

My God! Didst Thou but grant us the grace to understand this excess of mercy, could it be possible that we should not be moved, and love Jesus Christ with our whole hearts? Our Blessed Saviour is, indeed, most worthy of our love, for having redeemed us by so difficult a means. But is He not still more amiable, for having done so, though compelled to it only by His immense charity, and by the desire He had to oblige us to love Him, by such striking proofs of His most ardent love?

We are utterly unworthy of being redeemed at so high a price. Nevertheless, Jesus Christ Himself has so valued us, that He has spontaneously offered this excessive Redemption for us. And after all this, shall we not love Him?

But we must remember that, however great and ineffable is all that our Lord has done for our salvation, the love which has led Him to do it is still greater than all, because it is infinite—and as if this love could not be satisfied, so long as there remained a miracle it had not wrought, He institutes the adorable Sacrament of the Altar, the sum of all His wonders. He truly lives with us until the end of the world. He gives Himself to us, under the appearances of bread and wine. He makes His flesh and blood the nourishment of our souls, in order to unite Himself more closely to us, or rather to unite us more closely to Him. Can we then be possessed of reason, and not be deeply moved at the mere recital of this marvel? Can we still retain any feeling of humanity, and not be all inflamed with love for Jesus Christ, at the sight of such a benefit? A God feels tenderness for man, takes delight in him, and is solicitous about him! A God desires to unite Himself to us, and desires it to such an extent as to annihilate and immolate Himself daily, and to wish that we should feed upon Him every day, without being in the least changed, either by the indifference, the disgust, or the contempt of those who never receive Him, or by the coldness and the faults of those who receive Him often! Finally, He remains upon our Altars, shut up within the Tabernacle, and this every day, and at all hours of the day. Are not these manifest proofs of the love which Jesus Christ has for us? Are they not motives powerful enough to oblige us to love Him? Ungrateful as we are, since it is for us alone that all these wonders have been wrought, what are we to think? Does not Jesus Christ, dwelling on our Altars, deserve to be honoured by us? Does He not shew us love sufficient to merit a return of love? Woe and anathema to him, who, after all this, does not love Jesus Christ.

To say the truth, said a great servant of God, could any thing shake my faith in the Blessed Eucharist, I should not doubt of the infinite power which Almighty God displays therein, but rather of the excessive love which God shows towards us. How what was bread, becomes flesh, without ceasing to appear bread : how the Body of Jesus Christ is at the same time in several places: how He can be contained in an almost indivisible space : to all these wonders I have nothing to answer, but that God can do all things. But if I am asked, how can it be, that God can love a creature so weak and miserable as man ; and that He can love him ardently and to such an excess: that He can love him as He has loved him : I confess that I have no other answer to give, but that this is a truth which is above my comprehension : that the love which Jesus Christ bears us, is an excessive love, an ineffable love, an incomprehensible love, a love which ought to cause admiration and surprise in every reasonable man.

I do not know what power these reflections may have in moving the faithful at the present day. But they have so deeply moved even the most savage and barbarous nations, that they have been heard to cry out, at the mere recital of some of these wonders: What a good God is the God of the Christians! He is a great benefactor, and He is worthy of love! Who can help loving a God, who loves us so passionately? These reflections, and the desire of making some return to a Saviour, who loves us with so much tenderness, and of shewing Him some gratitude, have filled cloisters with religious, and deserts with vast numbers of holy solitaries who dedicated and consecrated themselves to the praise and love of Jesus Christ.

However reasonable such a mark of gratitude may be, it is not required of all. They are exhorted, not entirely to forget Jesus Christ, who has wrought the greatest of miracles, only to satisfy His excessive desire of remaining with them ; to have a little more feeling for the outrages which the excessive love of Jesus Christ, for them, causes Him to endure ; in fine, to be at least as grateful to Jesus Christ, who loves them so constantly, and who has done for them more wonders than they can comprehend; to be as grateful to Him as they are towards men, who are ready to sacrifice their best friends to the least of their own interests.

Now a devotion which tends only to inspire this gratitude to Jesus Christ, and is in itself, properly speaking, only a continual exercise of a perfectly grateful love, is it not a reasonable devotion ? Is it not just to seek to gain some love for Jesus Christ, especially at a time when He is so little loved ? There is little love for Him in the world, which has little sense of His benefits, in which His counsels are so little followed, and His maxims so greatly disparaged. There is little love for Him at a time, in which there is nothing but indifference for His Person, and all the gratitude and respect which are shown Him, may be generally reduced to a few prayers and ceremonies, which degenerate through custom into mere affectation, at a time when His Divine presence causes weariness, and His precious Body, disgust.

IV. *The extreme ingratitude of men towards Jesus Christ.*

However incredible may appear the love which the Son of God shows us in the Adorable Eucharist, there is something else yet more surprising. It is the ingratitude with which we repay so great a love. It is marvellous, indeed, that Jesus Christ should take delight in loving man. But it is most unaccountable that man should not love Jesus Christ, and that no motive, no benefit, no excess of love can inspire him with the least feeling of gratitude. Jesus Christ may perhaps have some reason for loving men. They are His work. In them He loves His own gifts. In loving them He loves Himself. But can we have any reason for not loving Jesus Christ, for loving Him only in a small degree, for loving anything together with Him? Is there anything, then, in Him, that keeps you from Him? Has He not yet done sufficient to merit our love? Should we ever have dared to desire, or ever have been able to imagine, all that He has deigned to do, in this adorable mystery, in order to gain our hearts? And yet all this has not been enough to oblige men to have an ardent love for Jesus Christ.

What advantage has Jesus Christ derived from so wonderful an abasement? It might in some sense be said that all the other mysteries, the effects of His love, have been accompanied by circumstances so glorious, and prodigies so striking, as to show clearly, that in taking care of our interests, He did not entirely overlook His own glory. But in this most amiable Sacrament, it seems as if Jesus Christ had altogether forgotten all these advantages, and that it was His love alone that engaged Him therein. Ought not, then, so wonderful an excess of love to excite an excessive love in the hearts of all men. Alas! it is quite the contrary. It seems as though Jesus Christ would have been more loved had He loved us less. I shudder with horror, oh my God! at the mere thought of the indignities and outrages which the impiety of wicked Christians, and the fury of heretics, have committed against this august Sacrament. With what horrible sacrileges have not our Altars and our Churches been profaned? With what repeated insults, impiety and infamy, has not the Body of Jesus Christ been treated? Can any

Christian reflect on such impiety, without conceiving an ardent desire to repair by every possible means these cruel outrages? Is it possible, then, that he should live without giving it a thought?

If, amidst the impiety which Jesus Christ meets with at the hands of heretics, He at least were honoured and ardently loved by the faithful, we might in some degree console ourselves for the outrages of the one, by the love and sincere homage of the other. But alas! where are we to look for that crowd of adorers, earnestly bent on honouring Jesus Christ in our Churches? Are not our Churches deserted? Can there be greater coldness and indifference than what is shown towards Jesus Christ in the Blessed Sacrament? The scanty number that are to be seen in our Churches during the greater part of the day, are they not a visible proof of the forgetfulness and want of love of almost all Christians? Those who approach our Altars most frequently, familiarise themselves with these most august mysteries. It may be said, that there are Priests, whose familiarity with Jesus Christ goes so far as to grow into indifference and contempt. How many amongst them are there, who, by offering Him daily, increase in love for Him? How many who celebrate these divine mysteries, like persons who truly believe in them?

We perhaps think that Jesus Christ is insensible to such bad treatment. But can we ourselves think on the treatment which He receives, and be insensible, and not seek to make reparation by every means in our power? How can anyone reflect a little on these truths, and not dedicate himself wholly to the love of this Man-God, who alone has a right to the hearts of all. If we do not love Him, it must either be that we do not know Him, or that we are worse than that wicked demon spoken of in the life of St. Catherine of Genoa, who did not complain of the flames that consumed him, nor of the other pains which he endured, but only of being devoid of love,—of that love which so many souls know nothing of, or refuse to exercise, to their eternal loss.

Let us remember, that the Sacred Heart of Jesus in the Blessed Sacrament has still, as far as can be, the same sentiments It always had. It is always inflamed with love for man, always sensibly touched by our misfortunes, always urged by the desire to make us partakers of Its treasures and to give Itself to us, always disposed to receive us, and to serve as a dwelling and a paradise for us, even in this life, and above all, as a refuge at the hour of death. And, for all this, what sentiments of gratitude does He find in the hearts of men? what solicitude? what love? He loves, and He is not loved. We do not even know His love, because we do not condescend to receive the gifts by which He would show it to us, nor listen to the tender and secret declarations that He would make of it to our hearts. Is not this a motive powerful enough to touch the hearts of all who are at all reasonable, and who have some little tenderness for Jesus Christ? Our loving Saviour, in instituting this Sacrament of love, foresaw clearly all the ingratitude of mankind. He felt by anticipation in His Sacred Heart, all the grief which it was to cause Him. Yet all this could not keep Him at a distance, nor prevent Him from showing us the excess of His love, in the institution of this adorable mystery.

Is it not just, amidst so much incredulity and coldness, so many profanations and outrages, that this God of love should find at least some friends of His Sacred Heart, who should be pained by the little love felt for Him, feel the injuries offered Him, be faithful and assiduous in adoring Him in the holy Eucharist, and neglect nothing in order to repair, by their love, by their adorations, and by every kind of homage, all the outrages to which the excess of His love daily exposes Him, in this august Sacrament?

This is the end which we aim at in this devotion, in honouring this Sacred Heart, which ought to be infinitely dearer to us than our own. The act of atonement and of oblation, the visits to the Blessed Sacrament, the prayers, the Communions, and all the other practices, tend only to render us more grateful and more faithful, by giving us an ardent love for Jesus Christ. There is no devotion, then, more just or reasonable. We shall see, in like manner, that there is no devotion more useful for our salvation and perfection.

Chapter IV.

How useful this devotion is for our salvation and our perfection.

If Jesus Christ has wrought so many miracles to oblige us to love Him, what favours will He not do to those whom He sees anxious to show Him their gratitude and ardent love? He has loved us with tenderness, says St. Bernard, and has loaded us with gifts, when we did not love Him, when even we did not wish that He should love us. "Dilexit non existentes, sed et resistentes." (St. Bern.) What gifts and graces will He not heap upon those who love Him, and who are so touched by seeing Him so little loved?

It has been shown clearly enough, that the devotion to the Sacred Heart of Jesus is a proof, or rather, a continual exercise of an ardent love for Jesus Christ. It consists, moreover, in the practice of the holiest exercises of our religion. It unites in itself such power and tenderness, that it obtains all things from God. Indeed, if Jesus Christ grants such great graces to those who have a devotion to the instruments of His

Passion, and to His Sacred Wounds, what favours will He not bestow on those who have a tender devotion towards His Sacred Heart? Reasons have been adduced in the Preface of this book, to lead any prudent man not to refuse his belief to the revelations of St. Mechtildis. Hear what this Saint says on the subject which we are speaking of. (Sp. Works of St. Mechtildis, book ii. ch. 18.) "I saw one day," she says, "the Son of God. He held in His hands His own Heart, which was brighter than the sun, and shed rays of light from every part. It was then that our loving Saviour made known to me, that, from the plenitude of that Divine Heart issue all the graces which God pours continually upon men, according to the capacity of each." The same Saint testified, shortly before her death, that having one day earnestly begged of our Lord a great grace, for a person who had asked her to do so (book iv. chap. 14), Jesus Christ said to her: "My child, tell the person for whom you pray, that whatever she wishes for, she must seek in my Heart. Let her ask Me for all things in this Heart, like a son who knows no other artifice but what love suggests, and who asks of his father whatever he wants."

Almighty God having made known to that person of whom we spoke in the second chapter, and for whom Fr. la Colombière had so much veneration, the great graces that He had annexed to the practice of this devotion gave her to understand that it was by a last effort, so to speak, of His love for men, that He had resolved to discover to them the treasures of His Sacred Heart, and inspire them with this devotion, which is calculated to make the love of Jesus Christ spring up in the hearts of the most insensible, and to inflame those of the least fervent. "Publish everywhere," said our loving Saviour, "insinuate, recommend this devotion to persons in the world, as a sure and easy means to obtain from Me a true love of God;

to ecclesiastics and religious persons, as an effectual means of attaining to the perfection of their state; to those who labour for the salvation of their neighbours, as a means of touching the most obdurate souls; and finally to all the faithful, as one of the most solid and suitable devotions by which to gain the victory over the strongest passions, to restore peace and union in the most disunited families, to rid themselves of the most inveterate imperfections, to obtain a most tender and ardent love of Me, and finally to arrive in a short time, and by an easy method, at the most sublime perfection."

St. Bernard, full of these sentiments, always speaks of the Sacred Heart of Jesus as the treasury of all graces, and the inexhaustible fountain of all blessings (St. Bern. Pass., tract i. ch. 3). "Oh most sweet Jesus," he cries, "what riches dost Thou enclose in Thy Heart, and how easy is it for us to enrich ourselves, possessing as we do, in the adorable Eucharist, this infinite treasure." "In this adorable Heart," says St. Peter Damian, "we find all the weapons necessary for our defence, all the remedies suited to the cure of our diseases, all the most powerful aids against the assaults of our enemies, all the sweetest consolations to alleviate our sufferings, all the purest delights to fill our souls with joy. Cor Christi cœleste gazophilacium et erarium est" (St. Peter Damian, Excell. of St. John Evang., serm. 1). "Are you afflicted? do your enemies persecute you? does the remembrance of your past sins trouble you? do you feel your heart agitated by disquiet, by fear, or by passions? Come and prostrate yourself at the foot of the Altar. Throw yourself, as it were, into the arms of Jesus Christ. Enter even into His Heart. He is the asylum and refuge of holy souls, and a place of shelter where our soul is in perfect security. Cor Christi asylum perfugii in tentationibus and tribulationibus" (Blosi Consol. of the faithful soul). "The

Sacred Heart of Jesus," says the devout Lanspergius, "is not only the seat of all the virtues, but it is also the fountain of graces by which these virtues are acquired and preserved. Have a tender devotion to this loving Heart, which is so full of love and mercy. Through It ask for all that you wish to obtain and offer of all your actions. For this Sacred Heart is the treasury of all supernatural gifts. It is, so to speak, the way by which we unite ourselves more closely with God, and by which God communicates Himself more lovingly to us. You have in this Sacred Heart all the graces, all the virtues of which you stand in need, and you need not fear to exhaust this infinite treasure. Have recourse to It in all your necessities. Be faithful in the holy practices of a devotion so reasonable and so useful, and you will soon perceive its effects. Ad venerationem cordis piissimi Jesu, amore ac misericordia exuberantissimi studeas te ipsum excitare, ac sedula devotione ipsum frequentare. Per ipsum petenda petas, et exercitia tua offeras quia charismatum omnium est apotheca et ostium, per quod nos ad Deum, et ipse ad nos accedit . . . . . Gratiam quoque ejus, et virtutes, ac prorsus quid-quid fuerit tibi (quod mensuram excedit) salutare, videaris tibi ex gratioso Corde attrahere . . . . Ad quod in necessitate confugias, unde consolationem quoque et omne auxilium haurias" (Lanspergius, Shafts of Divine Love to the Sacred Heart of Jesus). We find also an illustrious example of this in the life of St. Mechtildis. The Son of God, in an apparition to her, commanded her ardently to love and to honour as much as possible His Sacred Heart in the Blessed Sacrament. He gave her His Heart as a pledge of His love, and as her place of refuge in life, and all her consolation in death. From that time the Saint felt within herself an extraordinary devotion towards the Sacred Heart, and received from It so many graces, that she used to say, that were she to write down all the gifts and favours she had received by means of this devotion, there would be no book, however large, that would suffice to contain them. The happy results which have been already experienced, and are still daily experienced, by those who have this devotion at heart, sufficiently confirms the sentiments of these beloved friends of God.

"I am resolved," says the author of the Interior Christian (book v. ch. 23), "to depend in future only on Divine Providence, without seeking either consolation or support in creatures. I should be like an infant, which, without disquiet or fear, reposes sweetly in the arms of its mother, whilst it receives from her a thousand caresses and endearments. I confess that it is thus our Lord treats me. For, without seeking elsewhere wherewith to nourish and enrich my soul, I find in His Sacred Heart all the helps and graces of which I stand in need, and I find them in so great abundance, and I am so liberally enriched with them, that I am sometimes filled with astonishment, and dread my own negligence in receiving such great graces from this Sacred Heart with so little trouble of my own."

But, even though we could not adduce in favour of this devotion either authority, or example, or special revelation, and even though Jesus Christ had not expressed Himself so clearly and so frequently on the subject, would it require much reasoning to convince a Christian that there is nothing more solid or more advantageous for our salvation and for our perfection, than a devotion which has no motive but the purest love of Jesus Christ; the end of which is to repair, as far as possible, all the indignities which Jesus Christ suffers in the adorable Eucharist, and all the practices of which tend to make Jesus Christ honoured and ardently loved?

Can this adorable Saviour, Who has done so much to gain the hearts of men, refuse anything to those who themselves ask of Him a place in His Heart? If Jesus Christ allows Himself to be given even to those who do not love Him, and would have Himself carried to dying persons who never condescended to visit Him in their lifetime, and who have been insensible both to the manifest marks of love which He gave them and to the cruel outrages He received in the adorable Eucharist: in fine, to persons who have perhaps themselves ill-treated Him, what will He not do for faithful servants who, sensibly touched at seeing their dear Lord so little loved, so rarely visited, so cruelly outraged, make Him atonement, from time to time, for all the insults He receives, and neglect nothing to repair so many offences, by their frequent visits, their adorations, their homages, and chiefly their ardent love? Is it not, then, plain that there is nothing more reasonable, more useful, than the practice of this devotion? Can it be necessary to use many words in order to persuade Christians to practise it?

Chapter V.

How much true sweetness there is in the devotion to the Sacred Heart of Jesus.

ALTHOUGH all exercises of devotion are capable of filling the soul with interior consolation, and all good works are accompanied by an unspeakable delight and joy, which is inseparable from the testimony of a good conscience, and which surpasses all other pleasures, it is however certain that Jesus Christ never grants so many even sensible favours as in the practices of devotion which tend only to honour Him in the most blessed Sacrament. The lives of the Saints are filled with examples of this truth. When did a St. Francis, a St. Ignatius, a St. Teresa, a St. Philip Neri, a St. Aloysius Gonzaga, and numberless others feel their hearts more inflamed with love, than when they approached this august Sacrament? What sighs of love issued from their hearts, what sweet tears streamed from their eyes in the celebration or in the participation of this adorable mystery! With what consolations, with what torrents of delight, were they not replenished! For indeed Jesus Christ is nowhere more liberal than in this august Sacrament; so nowhere does He make us feel more abundantly the sweetness of His presence. In the other mysteries He gives us His graces. In this, the first grace He bestows on us, is to give Himself really and truly to us. Joy is ever the attendant of a banquet. Jesus Christ prepares a banquet daily for us in the adorable Eucharist. Can we be surprised if He treats His friends therein with so much sweetness and love?

As the devotion to the Sacred Heart of Jesus Christ makes us true and faithful adorers of Jesus Christ, in the most blessed Sacrament, so it also procures for us the greatest favours. It might be said, that our Lord measures the singular favours He grants therein, by the number of insults He has received: and that, as there is no mystery in which He has received so many outrages, so there is none in which He fills with sweeter consolations those who neglect nothing to repair these indignities. The motive of this holy practice being so pure and so pleasing to Jesus Christ, we need not wonder if, as He is the best and holiest of all Masters, He gives so much consolation to His faithful and grateful servants, especially at a time when He meets with so little gratitude, so little true love, in those even, who make a profession of loving Him.

As it is impossible to have this devotion at heart, without having, at the same time, much love for Jesus Christ, it is very difficult to practise it without feeling that sweetness and those interior consolations, which are, for the most part, inseparable from the exercise of pure love. And as the mere sight of the wounds of Jesus Christ inspires a feeling of confidence in His mercy, the mere remembrance of His Sacred Heart inspires a joy and sweetness, that may be felt, but cannot be expressed. It is strange, that we approach Jesus Christ, and are well received by Him as often as we visit Him, and yet do not feel even the pleasure, that we ordinarily feel, when we are well received by the great ones of this world. Our little love for Jesus Christ, our great imperfections, our little faith, and a variety of other failings are the unhappy cause of this misfortune, which is far greater than we think. But as none of these failings are to be found in the practice of true devotion to the Sacred Heart of Jesus Christ, we may say that these singular favours should be, as it seems, inseparable from the exercise of this devotion.

This has been happily experienced hitherto by all who have been known to be devoted to the Sacred Heart of Jesus. It is still experienced every day, by those who imitate them. It is this leads us to say, that it seems as if Jesus Christ could not refuse His tenderest endearments to the friends of His Sacred Heart. It has been observed, that those Saints who have had most devotion and tenderness towards the Sacred Heart, have all been loaded with the most signal favours. They seldom speak of the devotion to the Sacred Heart of Jesus, without using terms which shew clearly the extraordinary graces and the interior sweetness with which they were replenished. "It is a good thing, it is a sweet thing," cries out St. Bernard, "to dwell in this Sacred Heart! 'O quam bonum, quam jucundum habitare in Corde hoc! exultabimus et loetabimur in Te, memores Cordis Tui.' It is enough for me," he continues, " to call to mind Thy Sacred Heart, oh sweet Jesus, to be filled with joy."

By means of this devotion did St. Gertrude and St. Mechtildis receive great favours from Jesus Christ.

St. Clare asserted, that it was to the tender devotion which she bore to the Sacred Heart of Jesus, that she owed, so to speak, that extraordinary sweetness which filled her soul every time that she presented herself before the Blessed Sacrament. St. Catherine of Siena felt herself all inflamed with the love of Jesus as soon as she thought of His adorable Heart. Jesus Christ, when appearing once to St. Mechtildis, addressed to her these beautiful words: "My daughter, if you wish for the pardon of all your negligences in my service, have a tender devotion towards My Heart. For it is the treasury of all the graces, which I continually bestow upon you. It is the fountain of all those interior consolations and ineffable delights with which I replenish My faithful friends."

Fr. la Colombière expressed himself in a similar manner. Although Almighty God had conducted him for a long time in the paths of the most sublime perfection, not by means of sensible consolations, but only by means of a lively faith, and very great trials, it seemed as if the Divine Spirit changed His direction of him, when He inspired him with the practice of this devotion. Hear how this Servant of God expresses himself, on this point, in one part of his Retreats: "My heart is dilated and feels delights that I can indeed taste and receive from the mercy of my God, but not explain. Thou art infinitely good, oh my God, to communicate Thyself with so much mercy to the most ungrateful of Thy creatures, and the most unworthy of Thy servants. Be Thou blessed and praised for it eternally. I understood that God willed that I should serve Him, by procuring the fulfilment of His desires, regarding the devotion which He has suggested to a person, to whom He communicates Himself with great familiarity. Why cannot I, oh my God, be everywhere and publish what Thou requirest from Thy servants and Thy friends?" And in another place: "Cease," he cries, "cease, oh my supreme and loving Lord, to load me with Thy favours, I know how unworthy I am of them : Thou wilt accustom me to serve Thee through interest, or Thou wilt oblige me to do something extravagant. What would I not do, didst Thou not oblige me to obey my Director, in order to merit a moment of that sweetness which Thou impartest to me? Foolish man that I am! why do I say merit? Pardon me the word, my most loving Father! I am confounded by the excess of Thy goodness: I know not what I say. Can I merit the graces and ineffable consolations with which Thou preventest and replenishest me? No, my God: Thou alone, by Thy sufferings, dost obtain for me from Thy Father all the favours that I receive. Be Thou eternally blessed for them. Load me with sorrows and miseries to give me some share in Thine. I shall not believe that Thou lovest me, unless Thou wilt grant me to suffer much and for a long time."

Thus did this great man express himself in the excess of sweetness and interior consolation which he experienced, in the exercise of a tender devotion to the Sacred Heart of our Lord Jesus Christ.

CHAPTER VI.

Of the devotion that the Saints have had to the Sacred Heart of Jesus Christ.

As the example of the Saints is at the same time a powerful motive to attract us to a devotion, which they themselves have practised, and a particular instruction to teach us how to practise it; it is very much to the purpose to mention here the sentiments of those who have had the greatest tenderness, and the most generous feelings, towards the Sacred Heart of Jesus Christ.

St. Clare, inflamed with love for Jesus Christ, and desiring to make Him some return, thought no exercise more suitable to prove her gratitude, than to salute and adore, many times every day, the Sacred Heart of Jesus, in the most Blessed Sacrament, and by means of this devotion, as we read in her life, her soul was filled with the sweetest delight, and the most special favours. " Nullo non die Cor Christi salutabat, ac venerabatur, quo in pietatis exercitio non modicis voluptatibus perfundebatur." (Liran. Imit. of J. C. in His Passion, b. v. ch. 6.)

The Prayer of St. Gertrude to the Sacred Heart of Jesus, which will be found towards the end of this book, is a proof of the esteem in which the Saint held this devotion; and the historian of her life, describing her happy death, says, that this blessed soul took its flight to Heaven, and reposed in the sanctuary of the Divinity, I mean, he adds, in the Adorable Heart of Jesus, which her Divine Spouse had opened to her, by an excess of love: " Beata illa anima expirans, in cœlum ad suavissimum Cor Jesu evolavit." (Corn. a Lap. ch. 3).

St. Mechtildis had so high a sense of this devotion, that she scarcely ever spoke but of the adorable Heart of Jesus, and of the singular favours which she received every day through this devotion. This loving Saviour gave His Heart to her Himself, as a pledge of His love, and to serve her as an asylum where she might always find tranquillity in life, peace and unspeakable consolation at the hour of death : " Ecce ego do tibi cor meum in pignus amoris et in locum refugii, ut semper, maximeque in hora mortis tuæ consolationem et requiem in illo invenias." (Corn. a Lap. p. ii. ch. 3. vers. 13).

St. Catherine, of Siena, had this devotion singularly at heart: she made an entire donation of her heart to her Divine Spouse, and obtained in exchange the

Heart of Jesus, protesting that in future, she neither desired to live nor to act, but according to the movements and inclinations of the Heart of Jesus Christ. "S. Catharina Senensis pro corde suo petiit et obtinuit Cor Christi, ut illo vegetaretur, viveret et ageret quæcumque agebat" (Com. cap. 4, verse 9, Cant. Cantic).

If you are anxious about my health, said St. Elzear to St. Delphina; if you desire to hear of me, often go to visit our loving Saviour in the blessed Sacrament, enter into His Sacred Heart, and you will hear of me, for you will always find me there, for there is my usual habitation. "Hic enim habito" (Vita S. El.).

But the words of St. Bernard not only discover to us, what were the beautiful sentiments that animated this Saint towards the adorable Heart, they also show us that the Devotion to the Sacred Heart of Jesus is not a devotion, merely of our own days. Oh most sweet Jesus, he cries, what riches dost Thou contain in Thy Heart! How can it possibly be, that men have but a slight sense of the loss they suffer, by their forgetfulness and indifference towards this loving Heart? For myself, says this great Saint, I will neglect nothing to secure and possess It; I will consecrate to it in future all my thoughts; Its sentiments and Its desires shall be mine; in fine, I will give all to acquire so precious a treasure. But why need I acquire it, he adds, since it is truly mine? Yes, I say it with confidence, Jesus is mine, since He is my head, and does not what belongs to the head belong also to the members? This Sacred Heart, then, shall be in future the temple in which I will unceasingly adore Him, the victim that I will offer continually, the altar on which my sacrifices shall be offered, on which the same flames of divine love, with which His Heart burns, shall consume mine: in this Sacred Heart I shall find a model to regulate the movements of my own, a treasure whence to satisfy all that I owe to the divine justice, and a place of security, where, safe from shipwreck and storms, I shall say with David—I have found my heart to pray to my God. Yes, I have found this Heart in the adorable Eucharist; I have there found the Heart of my sovereign, my good friend, my brother. This Heart is no other than the Heart of my loving Redeemer. After this, who shall ever hinder me from praying with confidence, and obtaining what I have asked? Let us go, my brethren, let us enter this loving Heart, never again to depart from It. My God, he continues, if so great consolation be felt at the mere remembrance of Thy Sacred Heart, what will it be to love it with tenderness, to enter therein and dwell there continually? Draw me entirely into this holy Heart, oh my loving Jesus, open to me this Heart which has so many attractions for me. But what! does not Thy opened side offer me a place of entrance, and the very wound of this Sacred Heart, does it not invite me to enter therein? "Bonus thesaurus, bona margarita cor Tuum, bone Jesu! quis hanc margaritam abjiciet quin potiùs dabo omnia, omnes cogitationes et affectus mentis commutabo et comparabo illam mihi, jactans omne cogitatum meum in corde Domini (St. Bernard Pass. ch. 3).

To this should be added, what the celebrated Lanspergius, well known by his works, so full of unction and solid piety, has left us on this subject. Take great care, he says, to excite yourself continually by frequent acts of constant devotion, to honour the loving Heart of Jesus, so full of love and mercy for you. It is by means of It, that you must ask for all you would obtain. By means of It, and in It, you must offer to the Eternal Father all that you do. For this Sacred Heart is the treasury of all supernatural gifts and graces. It is, as it were, the way by which we unite ourselves more closely to God, and by which Almighty God communicates Himself more liberally to us. I advise you, therefore, to place, wherever you pass most frequently, some devout picture, representing the Sacred Heart of Jesus. The sight of it will serve continually to remind you of your holy practices of devotion towards this adorable Heart, and will move you to love Him more and more. When you feel yourself touched with a more tender devotion, you may kiss the picture, as though you were kissing the Sacred Heart of our Lord Jesus Christ. To this Sacred Heart, you must continually endeavour to unite your own, wishing to have no other desires or sentiments, but those of Jesus Christ, persuading yourself that His spirit and His Sacred Heart passes, so to speak, into yours, and that of two hearts there becomes only one. Appropriate to yourself from this loving Heart all the graces imaginable; you will never exhaust It. It is useful; nay, it is necessary to honour with singular devotion the Sacred Heart of our Lord Jesus Christ. It is your refuge; you must fly to It in all your necessities, to draw from It the consolation and all the helps which you need. Even though all men should abandon and forget you, Jesus will be your one faithful friend. He will always keep you in His Heart. Trust in Him: rest upon Him. Others may and will deceive you. The Sacred Heart of Jesus is the only one that loves you sincerely. He alone will never deceive you. Such is what Lanspergius says in the chapter entitled Exercise of Devotion to the Sacred Heart of Jesus. In it are two beautiful prayers to the Sacred Heart of Jesus and Mary, which will be found in the last part of this book. " Ad venerationem Cordis piissimi Jesu, amore ac misericordia exuberantissimi studeas te ipsum excitare, ac sedula devotione ipsum frequentare, illud osculando et mente introeundo. Per ipsum petenda petas, et exercitia tua offeras, quia charismatum omnium est apotheca et ostium, per quod nos ad Deum, et ipse ad nos accedit. Itaque figuram aliquam Dominici Cordis ponas in loco aliquo, quem sæpius transire habeas, qua sæpius exercitii tui et amoris tui excitandi in Deum admonearis: hanc intuens memor sis exilii, miseræque captivitatis in peccatis. Posses etiam, urgente devotione interna, figuram hanc, idest Cor Domini Jesu osculari, et animo tuo persuadere, quasi verum deificum Cor Domini Jesu sub labiis habeas osculandum, in quod Cor, tuum imprimere gestias, atque spiritum tuum immergere, absorberique, desideres, videarisque tibi ex gratioso Corde ipsius attrahere in cor tuum spiritum ejus, gratiam quoque et virtutes, ac prorsus quid quid fuerit tibi (quod mensuram excedit) salutem. His enim omnibus Cor Jesu exuberantissime scatet. Expedit autem et valde pium est, Cor Domini Jesu devote honorari, ad quod in omni necessitate confugias, unde consolationem quoque, et omne auxilium haurias. Nam ubi cunctorum te mortalium corda deseruerint, ubi imposuerint tibi, securus esto, hoc fidelissimum cor te non decipiet, nec derelinquet." (Lansperg. Divine love and Apostolic Perfection. Exercise of devotion to the Sacred Heart of Jesus, p. 129.)

The author of the book entitled The Interior Christian, a person of solid and exalted piety, whose work is full of the spirit of Jesus Christ, has told what was his own practice, and what a high idea he entertained of the solidity and importance of this devotion. "The Sacred Heart of Jesus," he says, in the seventh chapter of the fourth book, "is the centre to which we must tend. When our soul is distracted and dissipated, we must conduct it tranquilly to the Heart of Jesus Christ, and offer to the Eternal Father the holy dispositions of this adorable Heart, and unite the little we do with what is done by Jesus Christ with infinite perfection. In this manner, whilst doing nothing ourselves, we do much by means of Jesus Christ. Let the Sacred Heart of Jesus be henceforward your

Oratory, devout soul. In It, and by means of It, offer all your prayers to God the Father; if you wish them to be accepted, This is the school which you must frequent if you would learn the sublime science of God, and be instructed in its lessons so directly opposed to the maxims and false opinions of the world. This must be your treasury from which you are to draw all that you may require in order to become rich—purity, pure love, fidelity. But the most precious and the most abundant riches this treasury contains are, humiliations, sufferings, and an ardent love of the greatest poverty. The esteem and love of these things is so precious a gift that it is only to be found in its original source, the Heart of a God made man. All other hearts, however holy and noble, possess it in a greater or less degree; only as they seek it with more or less diligence in this treasury, the Heart of Jesus Christ."

In fine, it has been observed, not only that all the Saints of the Church, who have seemed to be favoured with the highest graces, have had a most ardent and tender love for Jesus Christ, but also that there is not one, so to say, of those who have had this exceeding love for Jesus Christ, that has not had a singular devotion to His Sacred Heart.

Those who have read the life of St. Francis of Assisi, the works of St. Thomas, and those of St. Teresa, the lives of St. Bonaventure, St. Ignatius, St. Francis Xavier, St. Philip Neri, St. Francis of Sales, and St. Aloysius Gonzaga, will have noticed the tender devotion of these Saints towards the Heart of Jesus Christ. And to shew that this is still familiar to all those chosen souls, who burn with a most fervent charity for our loving Redeemer, it will suffice to read the life of the great servant of God, Armelle Nicolas, who died not long since, in the odour of sanctity. In her life, entitled The Triumph of Divine Love, she says: "As soon as any affliction befel me, from creatures, I had recourse to my loving Saviour, Who immediately filled me with the sweetest consolations; you would have said, that He was afraid lest I should suffer any uneasiness, so solicitous was He to console me in all my sorrows. Frequently, also, He shewed me His opened Heart, that I might hide myself therein, and at the same moment, I found myself enclosed in this Sacred Heart, in such security, that all the efforts of hell seemed to me but weakness. For a length of time I could not regard myself as in any other place than in this Sacred Heart, so that I used to say to my friends, 'If you wish to find me, seek for me nowhere but in the Heart of my Divine Saviour, for I shall not quit it either by day or night. This is my retreat and place of refuge against all my enemies.'"

END OF THE FIRST PART.

SECOND PART.—MEANS.

CHAPTER I.

The dispositions requisite for a tender devotion to the Sacred Heart of our Lord Jesus Christ.

ALL the dispositions requisite for this devotion may be reduced to four: a great horror of sin; a lively faith; a great desire to love Jesus Christ; and interior recollection.

I. FIRST DISPOSITION.—*A great horror of Sin.*

As the end of the devotion to the Sacred Heart of Jesus is nothing but a most ardent and tender love for Jesus Christ, it is clear, that to possess this devotion, we must be in the state of grace, and have an extreme horror for every kind of sin. As the Sacred Heart is the fountain of purity, not only will nothing defiled be permitted to enter therein, but only what is most pure, and most capable of pleasing Him. Whatever may be said or done for His love and glory, unless accompanied by innocence of life, is a dishonour to Him. The court of Jesus Christ is composed only of the most pure souls; His Heart cannot endure sin; one single hair disarranged, that is to say, the smallest failing, the least stain, gives Him a sort of horror.

But, on the contrary, how ready an approach have innocence and purity to the Sacred Heart. Jesus loved St. John, because, as the Church sings, his singular chastity had made him worthy of being loved with a singular love. He was loved in the highest degree, says St. Cyril (St. Cyril. Alex. Comment. on

St. John's Gospel, b. xii), because he possessed extreme purity of heart. Souls that aspire to true devotion to the Sacred Heart of Jesus Christ, are souls that aspire to the quality of favourites of our adorable Saviour. The practice of this devotion consists, properly speaking, only in a more tender, a more familiar love of Jesus Christ than that which is entertained for Him by the greater number of the faithful. As soon as a soul becomes careless about committing deliberate venial sins, and intends only to preserve herself from those which are mortal, she is not only in great danger of speedily losing her innocence, and the grace of God, but she cannot hope to enjoy that inexplicable sweetness with which Jesus Christ usually fills those who love Him truly and without reserve.

It is plain, then, that at the same time that we undertake to be devout to the Sacred Heart of Jesus Christ, we must resolve to neglect nothing in order to acquire a purity of heart, far higher than that of Christians of ordinary virtue. Indeed, the practices of this devotion to the Sacred Heart of Jesus Christ are, themselves, most suitable means for acquiring this special purity.

II. SECOND DISPOSITION.—*A Lively Faith.*

The second disposition is a lively faith. A languid faith never produces a high degree of love. The reason why Jesus Christ is so little loved, although all agree that He is worthy of love, is because the great wonders, by which He makes His love known to us, are not believed as they ought to be.

What exertions are made to give a proper reception to any one who is thought powerful at court? What attention, what modesty, what respect, are shown in the presence of a person who is believed to be a king, even though disguised in the rags of the poorest beggar! What should we not do, then, in the presence of Jesus

Christ upon our Altars? What attention, what respect, but, above all, what love should we not manifest in the presence of so loving a Redeemer, our King, and our Judge, concealed under the lowly appearance of bread, did we but sincerely believe Him to be present; or at least, did we but believe it with a lively faith? The bones of a Saint inspire great respect; the mere reading of his virtues creates in us a veneration and love for his person, because we have no doubt of the truth of what we have heard, or read, and yet the Body and Blood of Jesus Christ, who is living on our Altars, even the sight of the prodigies He works in order to shew us His excessive love, hardly inspire us with any respect, much less love! We never find the time long when we are with a person whom we love. How is it, then, that we find a quarter of an hour before the Blessed Sacrament so tedious? We find a play too short, though it may have lasted several hours. A Mass in which Jesus Christ is really and truly offered in sacrifice for our sins, seems to us insupportably long, if it last half an hour; and yet we are persuaded that the Play is but a fiction, the actors are not what they appear, and the whole performance is useless to us; whilst on the other hand, we profess to believe, that in the sacrifice of our Altars the selfsame Victim is offered Who offered Himself on Calvary, and that nothing can be more useful to us than this most august sacrifice. "In divino hoc sacrificio, quod in missa peragitur, idem ille Christus continetur et incruente immolatur, qui in ara crucis semel, semetipsum cruente obtulit, una enim, eademque est hostia." (Council of Trent, sess. xxii, chap 2.)

Jesus Christ dwells in the midst of us in the same manner as He dwelt at Nazareth amidst His relatives. He was there without being known by them, and without working in their favour, the miracles that He wrought elsewhere. Our blindness and evil dispositions prevent Him from letting us experience the wonderful operations with which He favours those whom He finds well disposed. Why is it, that we deplore so much the misfortune of the Jews? Why do we feel so much indignation at their ill treatment of our Blessed Lord, whom they refused to acknowledge? Doubtless, because we believe the truth of this article of faith. Why is it, then, that we have so little feeling either for the neglect shown to Jesus Christ in the most Blessed Sacrament, where He is visited by so few, or for the outrages He there endures, from the very persons who profess to believe in Him? Certainly because the faith of Christians on this point is very weak. It is necessary, then, to have a lively faith, in order to have this ardent love for Jesus Christ in the most Blessed Sacrament, and to be touched by a sense of the insults to which the excess of His love for us exposes Him; and to acquire, in fine, a true devotion to the Sacred Heart of Jesus Christ. In order to this, we must lead a pure and innocent life. We must animate our faith by our assiduity, and especially by our profound respect when we present ourselves before the most Blessed Sacrament, and by every sort of good works. We must pray much, and often ask of God this lively faith. We must, in a word, act like persons who believe, and we shall soon feel ourselves animated with this lively faith.

III. THIRD DISPOSITION.—*A great desire of having an ardent love of Jesus Christ.*

The third disposition is a great desire of having an ardent love of Jesus Christ. It is impossible to have a lively faith and live in innocence without being at the same time inflamed with a most ardent love of Jesus Christ, or at least with an ardent desire of loving Him. This desire of having an ardent love of Jesus Christ is a disposition absolutely necessary for acquiring the devotion to the Sacred Heart, which is itself a continual exercise of this ardent love. Jesus Christ never gives this love but to those who earnestly desire it. The capacity of our heart is measured by the greatness of its desires. All the Saints agree that the best disposition for acquiring a tender love of Jesus Christ is to have a great desire to love Him. *Blessed*, says the Son of God, *are they that hunger and thirst after justice, for they shall have their fill.* A heart must necessarily be purified by this ardent desire to be in a condition to be enkindled by the pure flames of divine love. This ardent desire not only disposes our heart to be inflamed with love for Jesus Christ; it also obliges our loving Saviour to enkindle in our hearts this sacred fire. Let us desire truly to love Him. Such a desire, we may say, is always efficacious. It is unheard of that Jesus Christ ever refused it His love.

Can we ask for anything more reasonable? Is it possible for any easier condition to be required? There is no Christian that does not pretend to have at least a wish to love Jesus Christ. But how then is it, if this desire be so suitable a disposition for acquiring an ardent love for Jesus Christ, that so few have an ardent love of Him, though all flatter themselves they possess this disposition, and Jesus Christ is always ready to give His love to those who are well disposed? It is because our heart is filled with self-love, and what we call a desire of loving Jesus Christ is nothing but a mere speculation, a barren knowledge of the obligation we are under of loving Him. It is an act of the intellect, not of the will. This knowledge, which is common to all who have any sense of the benefits which they have received from Him, passes for a true desire in the minds of many who, provided they have some specious pretext for deceiving themselves, readily persuade themselves that they are in a good state of conscience. To convince ourselves that we have not a true desire of loving Jesus Christ, we have only to compare this pretended desire with any other desire which really influences us. How anxious we are, what efforts we make, when we love anything passionately! We are wholly occupied by the desire, we think of it, we speak of it at all times, we are continually taking measures and seeking means, we even lose our sleep in order to ensure its accomplishment. And what similar effect has ever been produced in us by the desire we pretend to have of loving Jesus Christ? Has the fear of not acquiring this love ever cost us much labour? Does the thought of it occupy us much? The truth is that we do not love Jesus Christ, and we are deceived when we flatter ourselves that we have a great desire of loving Him. The true desire of loving our divine Saviour approaches too nearly to true love, not to produce the same effects. It is in vain that we make use of all the artifices of self-love. It will never be true that we have a great desire to love Jesus Christ, as long as we love Him so little. There is great danger that these sort of fruitless desires, which we sometimes feel, of loving Jesus Christ, may be little sparks of an almost extinguished fire, and real signs of the tepidity in which we live. If we have not this ardent love for Jesus Christ, let us make, at least once in our life, some serious reflection on the obligation we are under of loving Him, and it is certain, that it will at least give rise to a true desire of being inflamed with this ardent love.

IV. FOURTH DISPOSITION.—*Interior Recollection.*

The fourth disposition necessary for this devotion, if we would taste its sweetness, and draw from it all its advantages, is interior recollection. Almighty God does not make Himself heard in a confusion: *Non in commotione Dominus.* A heart open to every object, a mind constantly scattered abroad, and incessantly occupied with a variety of superfluous cares and useless thoughts, is not in a state to hear the voice of Him Who communicates Himself and speaks to the heart in solitude : *Ducam eam in solitudinem, et loquar ad cor ejus.*

Perfect devotion to the Sacred Heart of Jesus Christ is a continual exercise of the love of Jesus Christ. It cannot, then, exist without this recollection. Jesus Christ communicates Himself to the soul in a particular manner by means of this devotion. It is necessary, then, that she should be at peace, free from embarrassment and from the tumult of external things; in a state to hear the voice of her loving Saviour and taste the special graces which He bestows on a heart, free from all that can disquiet it, and prepared to be occupied with God alone.

This interior recollection is so completely the foundation-stone of the spiritual edifice in our souls, that without it, it is impossible to advance in perfection. It may be said that all the graces which a soul, not yet established on this foundation, receives from God are but characters formed in water, or letters imprinted on sand. The reason is this. To advance in perfection we must unite ourselves more and more closely with God. Now, without interior recollection, we cannot unite ourselves with God; for He makes His dwelling only amidst the peace of the mind, and the retirement of a soul that is not dissipated by various objects, nor disturbed by the perplexity of exterior occupations. St. Gregory observes, that when Jesus Christ wishes to inflame a soul with His divine love, one of the first graces He gives her, is a great attraction to interior recollection.

It may be said, that the most ordinary source of our imperfections is the want of recollection and attention to ourselves. This is what stops so many in the path of piety. This it is which causes the soul to find scarcely any relish in the holiest exercises of devotion.

No one who had but little recollection has ever been very devout. Whence is it, said a holy man, that so many religious, so many devout persons who have good desires, and who seem to do all that is necessary to become holy, nevertheless draw so little fruit from their prayers, communions, spiritual reading; and that, after having practised all the exterior exercises of spiritual life for so many years, they appear to have drawn scarcely any profit from them? How is it that directors, who guide others in the path of perfection, remain themselves subject to their ordinary imperfections? that men of zeal, labourers who give themselves with so much ardour to the salvation of souls, persons who are entirely occupied in good works, still have passions so strong, are always subject to the same failings, experience scarcely any facility in prayer, and pass their whole life in a sort of languor, without ever tasting the ineffable sweetness of peace of heart, always in disquiet; persons whom the thought of death terrifies, and the least misfortune depresses? All this comes from their negligence in guarding their heart and preserving it in recollection. These persons leave the care of their interior, and give themselves too much to the exterior. Hence it follows that they fail to perceive a number of failings, inconsiderate words, caprices, irregular affections, purely natural actions. This would not happen if they were attentive in regulating their interior, and a little more careful in their actions, so as to prevent the passions which there find their nourishment from daily gaining strength, and this with the greater danger from their being masked under an appearance of zeal and of virtue.

It must therefore be acknowledged, that interior recollection is so necessary for having a perfect love of Jesus Christ and advancing in the spiritual life, that we make progress therein only in proportion as we give ourselves to it. It was by this that St. Ignatius, St.

Francis of Sales, St. Teresa, St. Francis Xavier, St. Aloysius Gonzaga attained the height of perfection. If we do not take care to keep ourselves recollected during our actions, we shall draw little fruit from them, however excellent they may be in themselves. Let us keep silence if we wish to hear the voice of Jesus Christ. Let us keep our mind at a distance from the tumult and embarassment of exterior concerns, that we may be at liberty to converse with Him longer, and to love Him tenderly and ardently.

The devil, who knows well the great advantages that a soul derives from this interior peace, and this custody of the heart, will omit nothing to make her lose this recollection. As he despairs of inducing her to leave off her exercises of devotion and her good works, he makes use of these good works themselves, to lead her to dissipate herself abroad, and go forth, so to speak, from that retreat, where she was safe from his persecutions. A soul, attracted by the satisfaction which is found in this crowd of external actions, led away by the specious pretext of doing much for God, becomes dissipated, and loses imperceptibly that union with God, and the sweetness of His presence, without which she labours much and yet advances little. A dissipated soul is like a lost and wandering sheep, which is speedily devoured by the wolf. We think that we shall find it easy again to enter into ourselves. But, besides that the presence of God is a grace, which is not always at our disposal, the soul is no longer in a state to free herself from numberless external objects that occupy her. She has lost the relish for spiritual things, by the too long sojourn she has made, so to speak, in a foreign country. The remorse and uneasiness she feels, whenever she fixes her attention on herself, make this interior recollection a torment to her. She is dissipated, and in the end she loves the dissipation. Good God! what a loss is it for a soul to spread herself continually abroad on external things! What inspirations, what graces does she render useless! Of what favours does she deprive herself, by the want of recollection!

If we would escape this misfortune, we must take great care to keep ourselves always in the presence of God, and to preserve the spirit of recollection in all our exterior occupations. When the mind is working, the heart must be in repose—immovable in its centre, which is the will of God. From this it must never separate itself. To acquire this interior recollection (for, though it is a gift of God, it is never refused to those who desire it with ardour, and take means to obtain it), we must accustom ourselves to make many reflections on the motives which should actuate us in all we do. Before beginning an action, let us always take a glance to see if it is well ordered, if it is pleasing to God, and if we are doing it for Him. During the action, let us from time to time raise our heart to God, and renew the purity of our intention. A sign that we are doing an action for God is, that we leave it easily, continue it without uneasiness or regret, and are not annoyed when we are interrupted in it. But the surest and most effectual practice to preserve interior recollection in our principal exterior actions is, to represent to ourselves Jesus Christ as He laboured. Let us represent to ourselves with what modesty and exactness He worked when He was upon earth; how He applied Himself to perform perfectly all that He did; and with what meekness, with what tranquillity He accomplished it. What a difference between His manner of working and ours! If what we have to do is displeasing to us, what specious reasons do we not allege to exempt ourselves from it! What pretexts do we make use of to put it off! With what tepidity and indifference do we perform it? If it suits our inclinations, we feel a degree of joy that soon causes dissipation in our soul. The mere thought of not succeeding, renders us uneasy and melancholy. Let us then propose to ourselves Jesus Christ as a model. We must look at Him continually, if we wish to keep ourselves in interior recollection and to advance in His love.

When it is said, that in order to preserve ourselves in interior recollection, we must not be too much taken up with external things, it is not meant that exterior employments which are of obligation are an impediment to interior recollection. We may be very recollected whilst in action. The greatest saints, who have had most intimate communication with God, and who have consequently been most recollected, have been most actively employed in external actions. Such were the Apostles and apostolic men who have been employed in the salvation of their neighbour. It is therefore a mistake to suppose that the greatest exterior occupations are obstacles to interior recollection. Provided it be Almighty God who places us in these employments, these same employments are the most suitable means to keep us continually united with God. All that is necessary is, that we only lend, as it were, our mind to these external things, and do not give them our heart.

We must absolutely choose one of these two things, said a great servant of God, either to become an interior man, or to lead a tepid and almost useless life. If we are not very careful to preserve our interior recollection, so far shall we be from fulfilling the designs of God, that we shall not even know them, and we shall never arrive, either at the degree of sanctity our state requires, or at perfection.

A man that is not recollected, wanders about without finding rest anywhere. He seeks after all kinds of objects, without feeling satisfied with any. Whereas, if by giving himself to recollection he entered into himself, he would there find God. He would feel a satisfaction in God, who by His presence would fill him with so great an abundance of His gifts, that he would no longer go to find elsewhere wherewith to satisfy his desires. This is what may be seen every day, in interior persons. We imagine that the love they have for retirement, and the pain they feel in diffusing themselves outwardly, is an effect of melancholy. But it is not so. They taste Almighty God within themselves; and the ineffable sweetness with which they are filled, makes them feel the diversions and pleasures which are met with in the world so insipid and nauseous, that they have a horror of them. When we have once felt what Almighty God is, and relished spiritual things, everything connected with flesh and blood becomes insipid.

What wonderful advantages are derived from the interior life, by those who have once established themselves in it! It may be said, that they alone relish Almighty God, and feel the true sweetness of virtue. I do not know whether it be the effect of interior recollection, or the reward of the care they take to keep themselves constantly united with God; but it is certain that an interior man possesses faith, hope and charity in so sublime a degree, that nothing is capable of shaking him in his belief; he finds himself insensibly superior to all human fears. He is always in the same state of mind, always immovable in God. He takes occasion to raise his heart to God, from everything he sees and hears. He sees only God in creatures, in the same manner as, when we have looked for a long time upon the sun, we imagine that we behold it in everything we look upon afterwards.

Nor are we to suppose that recollection makes persons idle, and favours negligence. A man that is truly interior works more, does more good, and renders more service to the Church in a day, than many others who are not interior can render it in many years, even if they possessed greater natural abilities. Not only because dissipation is an obstacle to the fruits of zeal, but because the man who is not recollected, and yet labours much, labours indeed for God; whereas, in the case of one who is recollected, it is God Himself who, by means of that recollection, works for man. That is to say, a person who does not live in recollection, may have God for the motive of his actions, but humour, self-love and nature have generally the greater share in his good works. On the contrary, a recollected person, always attentive to himself and to God, always on the watch against the caprices of nature and the artifices of self-love, works for God alone, and according to the impression and the direction of the Spirit of God.

The difference that is to be seen between an interior man and one who is not so, should be enough of itself to give us an esteem for recollection. We see in a man that is little recollected, an air of dissipation, which obscures the most striking actions of virtue, and which has in it something so repulsive, that it lessens the esteem we had conceived for his piety, and causes his words to have little or no unction. On the contrary, what an impression does that air of modesty, meekness and peace, which are visible on the countenance of a truly interior person—that reserve, silence, and continual guard over himself, make upon our minds? Does not all this inspire veneration and love for virtue? It is very difficult to be long recollected, without being really devout. For it is a certain fact, that the want of devotion generally springs from the want of recollection. The means of acquiring this interior recollection, and of preserving this precious gift, is, to be very careful—1st. To avoid too great eagerness in what we do, and not to undertake anything which may prevent us from fulfilling, with entire liberty of spirit, our usual exercises of devotion. 2nd. Never to distract our heart with unnecessary occupations, so as to render it barren for prayer. 3rd. So to watch over ourselves, and keep ourselves so disposed, as to be always ready for prayer. 4th. To make ourselves masters of our actions, by raising ourselves, as it were, above our employments, keeping our hearts free from the embarassment and tumult that are generally caused in souls, by works of zeal, application to study, the care of a family, commerce with the world, the perplexity of business, and never considering the employments of our state, but as means to arrive at our last end. 5th. Retirement and silence are powerful means for gaining recollection. It is very difficult for a person who talks much to be very interior. 6th. Interior recollection is not only the sign of great purity of heart, it is also its reward. *Blessed are the clean of heart, for they shall see God;* that is to say, they shall walk continually in His presence. 7th. To make this exercise of the presence of God easier to us, we may take some sign that may remind us of it, as the striking of the clock, the beginning and end of every action, every time we enter our room or leave it, the sight of a picture, the arrival of a person, and similar circumstances. 8th. Reserve and modesty in all we do, are excellent means for becoming interior, especially if we are careful to propose to ourselves for a model, the modesty and meekness of Jesus Christ. 9th. Frequent reflection is a great help to anyone that wishes to become interior: to consider from time to time, that God is within us, or rather that we are in Him; that wherever we are, He sees us, He hears us, He is close to us,—at prayer, at work, at table, in society; to make acts of faith in the presence of God; to be modest, alone as well as in company. Finally, interior recollection is a gift of God. We must often ask this gift, and ask it as a necessary disposition for having an ardent love of Jesus Christ. This motive gives an efficacy to all our prayers. Devotion to the Saints who have excelled most in interior life, may be of great use for obtaining interior recollection. Such are the Queen of all the Saints, St. Joseph, St. Anne, St. Joachim, St. John Baptist, and in particular, St. Aloysius Gonzaga.

Chapter II.

Obstacles which prevent us from gathering all the fruit we ought, from the devotion to the Sacred Heart of Jesus Christ.

As the devotion to the Sacred Heart of Jesus Christ is useful, easy, reasonable, and solid, in the highest degree, there are few persons of solid virtue who do not relish it and practise it. But all do not feel that ardent love for Jesus Christ, nor that true sweetness which He imparts to those who love Him, though these special favours are the fruit of devotion to His Sacred Heart. Whatever impedes the progress of souls in perfection, is an obstacle to the signal graces which this devotion procures us. These obstacles, which few are found to overcome, dry up, as it were, the fountain of these great graces, and are the reason why Almighty God communicates Himself only to a few. We have been in the habit of complaining that we scarcely ever taste, in our practices of devotion, that heavenly sweetness which the saints enjoyed, and which, though not necessarily a part of sanctity, helps very much to make Saints. We experience nothing but dryness, tepidity, and disgust, in our exercises of piety: we have no consolation, no sweetness in prayer, no sentiment of devotion, either at holy Communion or Mass. We feel coldness and weariness in all that ought to be our greatest delight and our deepest interest. Upon this, what do we do? We try to console ourselves by the thought that sanctity does not consist in sensible devotion. But whilst we are so tepid and imperfect, we have reason to fear that it is in punishment of our want of fidelity, that Almighty God does not allow us to experience that interior sweetness, and those spiritual consolations, which would help very much to make us more courageous and more perfect.

The path of perfection is not different now, from that in which the Saints have walked. They all acknowledge, that it is not possible to conceive greater pleasure than is felt in the service of God. They tell us that therein the soul is replenished with so great sweetness, that the greatest austerities and labours are delightful to her. She does not know what it is to feel disgust or melancholy. What appears most frightful, causes in her a joy so pure and perfect, that the most terrible misfortunes of life cannot trouble it. They assure us that even the most severe trials which Almighty God sends them, have their sweetness and consolation; that sin alone can destroy the peace they enjoy; that Almighty God inspires them with so much confidence in His mercy, that their own failings do not disturb their peace.

These are not the sentiments of a few only. It is what all the true servants of God, of every rank, of every nation, and in all states of life, have experienced. It is what they have confirmed at the moment of death, that moment of the greatest sincerity. What motive can we possibly have for imagining that persons so wise, of a probity and virtue so universally recognized, should have wished to deceive us or themselves. With so many irreproachable witnesses, who all speak from experience, and with the greatest unanimity, can any reasonable person doubt the truth of a fact so well established? Whence is it, then, that amongst so many who at the present day profess piety, and seem to walk in the footsteps of these Saints, so few are to be found who receive the same graces? Without doubt, it is because there are very few whose virtue is really solid. Sanctity does not, it is true, consist in these feelings of sensible devotion; but it is no less certain that this interior joy, that peace which all the misfortunes of life cannot disturb, that perfect submission to God's will, that sweet confidence in His mercy, which is what is meant by this sensible devotion, has been the portion of all the Saints, and is still of all the true servants of God.

We have now seen what true sweetness there is in the devotion to the Sacred Heart of Jesus Christ. The fruit of this devotion is a most ardent and tender love for Jesus Christ, accompanied by that interior joy, that sweetness, that unalterable peace, which surpass all thought, and are so many gifts inseparable from the perfect love of Jesus Christ. We are now to show what are the obstacles which hinder us from deriving this fruit from it. They may be reduced to four: great tepidity in the service of God; a great fund of self-love; a secret pride; and certain passions, that we have not taken care to mortify in the beginning of our conversion. From these four heads, as from four fatal sources, proceed all those failings and imperfections, which keep so many souls back in the path of piety, destroy the most noble designs, and the most generous resolutions, and finally, render the most holy practices of devotion fruitless.

I. FIRST OBSTACLE.—*Tepidity.*

As the devotion to the Sacred Heart of Jesus Christ is a continual exercise of ardent love, it is very plain that tepidity is one of its greatest obstacles, and hinders all its fruit. Though the Son of God has an infinite hatred of sin, He has not a horror of the sinner. He calls him, He seeks him, and has compassion on him. But His Divine Heart cannot endure a tepid soul. *I would thou wert cold or hot,* says our Blessed Saviour to us, *but because thou art lukewarm, I will begin to vomit thee out of my mouth.* The Heart of Jesus Christ looks for pure souls, who are capable of His love. His Sacred Heart is always liberal. It seeks souls that are in a state to receive Its favours, and to reach the degree of perfection for which He destines them. This is what is not to be found in a soul that lives in tepidity. A tepid soul is in a state of blindness, caused by the passions that tyrannize over her; by the continual dissipation in which she lives, and which prevents her from entering into herself; by the multitude of sins that she commits, and by the subtraction of heavenly graces, which her resistance draws upon her. This blindness leads to the formation of a false conscience, under cover of which, as if in security, a soul whilst frequenting the Sacraments, may remain for many years in considerable sins. They are hidden from her, or disguised by passion, because she has neither the will, nor the courage to correct herself of them.

We sometimes see religious persons, or seculars who make a profession of piety, nourish secret aversions, envenomed jealousies, dangerous affections, a spirit of bitterness or murmuring against their superiors, a fund of self-love and pride, that diffuses itself over almost all their actions, and other failings of a like nature. In the midst of these they live tranquilly, falsely persuading, or trying to persuade themselves, that there is nothing very sinful in all this, and seeking reasons to excuse faults, which Almighty God condemns as grievous sins, and which they themselves will condemn at the hour of death, when passion will not prevent their seeing things as they really are.

What makes this state still more perilous, and obliges Jesus Christ to reject a tepid soul, is, that she is in a certain way, beyond hope, for tepidity is scarcely ever cured. As the sins which a tepid soul commits, are not of that gross and scandalous kind, that horrify a soul which has a little fear remaining, but are purely interior and do not pass beyond the heart, they easily escape the notice of a conscience that is not over particular, and of a soul that pays little attention to herself. Hence, as she does not know the greatness of her malady, she does not take the trouble to remedy it. Whereas, a great sinner, as he easily knows his sins, is in a better state to feel their weight and conceive a horror of them. And in this sense our Lord says, it is better to be cold than lukewarm.

The most solid practices of devotion are useless to a soul that is in this unhappy state, either because the little profit she derives from the holiest exercises of piety takes from her the desire of making use of them, or because, in consequence of her being used to these holy exercises, they have less effect upon her. The great and terrible truths of salvation, which terrify by their novelty, and shake with their force the greatest sinners, make scarcely any impression on her, in consequence of her having gone over them so frequently and with so little profit. As soon as a soul gives herself up to tepidity, she no longer thinks of anything but herself. She continually seeks after what can give her pleasure. She has a delicacy that sometimes surpasses that of the most sensual persons: a love of self, which not being weakened by foreign objects, is the stronger from being shut up in herself alone, and is entirely applied in forming for herself an easy and tranquil life. A soul in this state, insensible to the most striking truths of eternity, is still more insensible to the manifest proofs of the love of Jesus Christ for us. She is too far removed from the necessary dispositions for devotion to the Sacred Heart of Jesus, to draw any profit from it.

The marks by which we may know if we are in the dangerous state of tepidity, are: 1. Great negligence in all spiritual exercises; prayer without attention, confessions without amendment, communions without preparation and without fruit. 2. The continual dissipation of a mind which is scarcely ever attentive to itself or to God, but which continually diffuses itself over all kinds of objects, and occupies itself in a thousand trifles. 3. A bad habit of performing her actions without any interior spirit, but either through caprice or habit, scarcely doing anything in which passion, self-love or human respect have not some share. 4. Sloth in acquiring the virtues belonging to her state. 5. A disgust for spiritual things, and especially an indifference for great virtues. The yoke of Jesus Christ begins to appear heavy; the exercises of piety become burdensome; the maxims of the Gospel regarding the hatred of self, the love of crosses and humiliations, the necessity of doing violence to oneself, of walking by the narrow way, seem impracticable. The continual exercise of modesty, mortification and interior recollection is found insupportable, the life of persons of solid virtue is regarded as unhappy, and the practice of virtue almost impossible. The 6th effect of tepidity is an insensibility of conscience for lesser sins. We no longer feel remorse for our ordinary infidelities, or relapses, and we allow ourselves to commit all sorts of venial sins deliberately.

But how much is it to be feared that this want of tenderness of conscience—this facility in continually falling into the same faults, and in confessing them without amendment—this negligence—this contempt for small things—this indifference for the greater virtues—this inconstancy in the exercises of piety—this perpetual alternation between fervour and relaxation, may be visible signs of a dying faith, of an almost extinguished charity? How much is it to be feared that this unhappy state of tepidity may lead us imperceptibly into that of hardness of heart and insensibility? It is the more dangerous, as it is less perceived, and as its consequences are less feared. And yet, nothing is more common. Such persons as do not relish the devotion to the Sacred Heart of Jesus Christ, those who draw no fruit from its practice, have great reason to fear that this is the obstacle which occasions their disgust, and hinders them from profiting by the holiest exercises of piety.

As the fatal cause of this unhappy state of tepidity is generally to be found in a great fund of self-love, the means recommended in the following chapter, for subduing, or, at least, mortifying self-love, will serve as a remedy for tepidity, since true mortification is inseparable from fervour. What has been said of tepidity is partly drawn from the Spiritual Retreat, according to the spirit and method of Ignatius, composed by F. Nepveu, of the Society of Jesus. It may be useful to add the following reflections:

1. It is extraordinary that there should be any religious persons, who, after having been generous, in leaving great things for God, should prefer afterwards in religion to be deprived of the greater graces of God, rather than abandon some trifles which constantly retard their progress in the way of piety. For faults, however slight, when they are committed with advertence, are a continual impediment to that joy and ineffable sweetness, which are experienced by those who serve God with fervour.

2. It is no less extraordinary that persons who have made such great sacrifices to secure their salvation and merit a happy and tranquil death, for want of a little generosity die with disquiet and full of regret, after having so long and so greatly feared to die.

3. What is it that keeps us back? It is not possible but that, in religion, we should frequently have good desires. But it is astonishing that we fail to execute them through a kind of sloth, of which worldly persons would not believe us capable. We had begun so well to serve God: did we intend then to deceive men? If God was really the motive of our conversion,

whence is it, that though the same motive continues, we do not persevere?

4. It is certain either the Saints have done too much, or we do not do enough to become Saints. But some may say we must be Saints, to live as the Saints have lived. Let us rather say: we must become Saints; and it is only by living like the Saints, that we can hope to become so.

5. We are not easily tired, we do not find the time too long, when amassing riches to leave to others, or when occupied in procuring ourselves a vain reputation in the world. But to acquire eternal felicity in heaven, we think we have always time enough. A person with fine natural gifts, great talents and a lively disposition, some may say, cannot make up his mind to lead a perfect life. But when did the finest natural qualities, which have always been great helps to attain the most exalted virtue, become obstacles to sanctity?

6. What an error it is to imagine that there can be any age or condition unsuited to the practice of the highest virtues! What will these persons say when they shall be shown a multitude of Saints of every age, of every rank, who have become great Saints in every state, and in all sorts of employments? Not only will the example of these Saints one day form our accusation, we shall be ourselves our own condemnation. Whilst we attempt to excuse our tepidity, and our negligence, by alleging our age, our employments and our condition, it will be shown to us, that at the same age, in the same employments, and the same condition, we have suffered and laboured more for the world, than Almighty God required of us to labour in order to gain heaven.

7. There is no one who would venture to say, or who would believe, that after spending ten years in the study of human sciences, he would think himself fortunate if he knew as much as he had learned in the

first six months after he began his studies. Yet we find persons who make profession of piety, persons whose chief employment is to become perfect, who, after ten and twenty years of study and practice in the sublime science of salvation, are not ashamed to say, and are not displeased if others believe, that they would think themselves very happy, if they were as fervent, as mortified and as holy, as they were after the first six months of their perfect conversion. It is true that they manage to stupify themselves, as it were, by exterior dissipation, and the insipid pleasures of a tepid life : but, sooner or later, they will arrive at the end of their life, and what sentiments will they have at the hour of death?

8. Are we well convinced of the great truths of our religion? If we do not believe, we do too much. But if we believe, certainly we do too little. What is it that is at stake? So much is said of the importance of salvation, of the value of the soul, of eternity. Is it true that I am in the world only in order to save my soul? that Jesus Christ became man only to show us that this is the only business of mankind, that it alone deserves our application, alone demands our whole application, and depends on our application? Is it true that if this affair succeeds ill all is lost? that to put oneself in danger of succeeding ill in this, is to risk all; and that to live in tepidity, is to place ourselves in a kind of necessity of succeeding ill? Is it true that this is the affair of eternity? Can Almighty God have been deceived in saying that all the rest is of no consequence? Can He have employed His care and His providence without sufficient purpose, in referring all things to this one end? Is God then of so little consequence, that it can be an indifferent matter to us whether we lose Him? Why so many tears, so many and such bitter regrets in hell, if the good, which the damned have lost, deserved so little

effort to secure it? Why shudder at the very thought of eternity, if it matters so little whether we be eternally unhappy? But do we show any great apprehension of this misfortune, if we take so little trouble to avoid it? Are we taking much trouble if we continue in the tepidity and indifference in which we live?

9. If we were careful to make these reflections frequently, we should be ashamed to lead a tepid life, and to be so backward in God's service. We should soon take the resolution of loving Jesus Christ. But alas! after we have made these reflections, and have been moved by them, the moment afterwards we seek to distract ourselves, as if we were sorry to have made them, and to have been touched by them. *" Compared to a man* (says St. James ii. 23) *beholding his own countenance in a glass. For he beheld himself, and went his way, and presently forgot what manner of man he was."*

II. SECOND OBSTACLE.—*Self-love.*

It is a most certain fact, that there are very few who do not act through self-love. All the difference that there is between spiritual persons and those who are not so is, that in the one, self-love acts without disguise, whilst in the others, it is less perceptible and more masked. Any one who would take the trouble to make a few reflections, on the true motives of the greater part of his actions, which appear the least defective, would discover numberless windings and turnings of a secret self-love which forms their principal motive and destroys all their fruit. We relish and approve of only such practices of virtue as we find easy. The specious pretext of preserving our health, which we imagine to be so necessary for the glory of God, takes up our whole mind with a thousand little cares. We are careful of ourselves. Most kinds of mortification appear to us to be either indiscreet, or not suited to our age or our

F

state. The thoughts and desires which God gives us, from time to time, of attending seriously to our perfection, we treat as illusions.

We wish to persuade ourselves that God does not require from us so high a sanctity, though He has granted us very great graces, or has placed us in a state that requires us to be great saints. We flatter ourselves that we have a true desire of leaving all things as soon as the will of God shall be manifested to us. In vain does God make Himself heard in the depth of our heart by His inspirations, in vain does He speak to us by means of a director or spiritual father, or by means of the reflections we make, of the lights we receive, of the examples we see, and which we ourselves are ready to praise. The voice of God is not recognized when it is opposed to self-love. The reason is, that it is not the will of God that we take as the rule of our life, but our inclination and self-love. We would fain make these the rule of the will of God.

Whence comes it that there are some persons who are never more uneasy, more melancholy, more full of resentment, or ill-humoured, than when they are more recollected, and seem to be applying more particularly to their perfection? It is because the lights they then receive in prayer, and the inspirations which God gives them, disturb them from their not being able to reconcile them with the self-love that fills their minds. It seems as though they expected that the path of perfection should present no difficulty, or that God should heap upon them sweetness and interior consolations before they have taken the first step in the way to perfection. As the life of such persons seems well regulated, and their conduct irreproachable, they go on unhappily crawling and languishing during their whole life in this state, without ever correcting a single failing.

It would be better for us, if we may say so, not to

have certain virtues with the possession of which we comfort ourselves. We should at least acknowledge our indigence and misery. But the little virtue we possess serves only to render us daily more imperfect. We content ourselves with a composed exterior, a natural or affected modesty, an apparent virtue, which is rather the effect of education than of grace; and as we see that we are secure from the reproaches which those whose lives are ill-regulated draw upon themselves, we imagine that we have a great fund of virtue, because we do not allow many faults to appear.

We form to ourselves a plan of devotion according to our humour, our natural inclination, and our caprice. We find many inexperienced or yielding directors who approve this system upon which our whole life turns, and thus we become insensible to the examples, the reflections, and the truths which move the greatest sinners. We need not wonder, if, being so full of self-love, we are always seeking our ease in trifles. We cannot bear to want anything, under the pretext that we are willing to leave all. If we deprive ourselves of anything, we generally do it in order that we may deceive ourselves by this pretended mortification, and enjoy in quiet many other things which are dearer to us, and of which we are unwilling to deprive ourselves. We mostly act either from nature or inclination. We feel tenderness only for those with whom we sympathise. We refuse nothing to our senses, and if we mortify them in anything, it is only in what gives us the least difficulty, or when such mortification does us honour. We are willing to do good works, but we wish to choose what we will do. Hence it follows that we feel nothing but disgust for the slightest obligations which our state imposes on us, whilst we find great attraction in more painful occupations, either because they are of our own choice, or because they put us under the necessity of exempting ourselves from the ordinary obligations of our state. We consider sickness in others as a visitation, and as a gift of God; but, as soon as Almighty God grants us this gift, we become uneasy, melancholy, impatient, and anxious. It is not that sickness is the cause of this. But we show in sickness what we really are, because we have then no longer the motives or the means which health afforded us for disguising our self-love.

From the same source, too, proceed those barren desires and chimerical projects which form the food of a spirit naturally proud, and which give nourishment to self-love. We propose to ourselves certain plans of life which we intend to carry out at certain times; and, as if our conversion and sanctification were secure, we take no further trouble about correcting our imperfections. Though we are convinced that mortification is absolutely necessary if we would be holy, we refuse the crosses that present themselves under the pretext that they are too small. We sigh after greater crosses, only because we see them at a greater distance. We satisfy ourselves in the meantime with these idle imaginations. We are at rest, confiding in this composed exterior, in these good works which please us, and in the practices of devotion in which we are most exact. We are intoxicated, as it were, with the vain and insipid praises of those who flatter us. We are full of the idea of some virtue which we possess only in name. At length we find ourselves, at the close of a long life, devoid of merit, and often without any sentiment, more praiseworthy than a vain and barren desire of being then as virtuous as we were at the beginning of our conversion.

Such are the effects of self-love, and few are exempt from it. We are to be pitied for nourishing within ourselves an enemy dangerous in proportion as he is crafty, and to be dreaded in proportion as we distrust him less. Now it is certain that Jesus Christ will never recognize as the true friends of His Heart those who love only their own ease, and who are so cautious about labouring for Him. This is what He has expressly said in giving us the description of His true servants. In vain, says He, will any one flatter himself that he is My disciple, because he has left for My love his goods, his parents, his friends, if he does not also renounce himself : *adhuc autem et animam suam.* We must do violence to ourselves, make war against our passions, stifle or at least mortify our self-love in everything, in order to be truly His disciples. There is no true love of Jesus Christ where there is no true mortification.

III. THIRD OBSTACLE.—*A Secret Pride.*

Secret pride is no less an obstacle to the love of Jesus Christ. It seems that there cannot be a greater obstacle to our perfection, and consequently to an ardent love of Jesus Christ, than the spirit of vanity, from which there are so very few who preserve themselves. Our other enemies we weaken and overcome by the practice of virtue ; whereas, it is in the very practice of virtue itself, that this enemy finds its strength. Our very victories are weapons which the devil makes use of, to vanquish us, by taking occasion from them to inspire us with pride. We may say, that of all vices, there is none that has kept so many souls back in the path of piety, or that has plunged so many from the highest perfection into tepidity, and even into sin. From this spirit of vanity proceed the inordinate desire that we have to be seen, and the excessive eagerness we feel to succeed in all that we undertake.

In vain do we torment ourselves, to assure ourselves that in all this we are seeking nothing but the glory of God. We have but to listen to our conscience, to be convinced that we seek nothing but our own glory. That excessive uneasiness which the fear of not succeeding causes in us; that sadness and discouragement we experience after a failure; that joy and satisfaction we feel at the sight of the honours and praises we receive, are clear proofs of the spirit of vanity that urges us to act.

This same spirit also mixes itself up with the practice of the highest virtues: we wish to be highly mortified, to be obliging, courteous, civil, charitable, and we may add, to give great edification to our neighbour, by appearing so. From the same source spring almost all our defects. We fill our minds insensibly with the idea of a pretended merit, which we do not possess, and which this idea alone would make us lose, did we really possess it. We love to recount our adventures. We have always some circumstance of our life ready, as an example of the subject on which we are speaking. One would say, that it is no longer any failing to praise ourselves continually, when we already bear a good reputation. We wish to possess the esteem and the hearts of all. Hence it is that we prefer to omit our obligations, rather than disoblige another; and what is still more extraordinary, we try to cover this ambition and vanity by the specious pretext of civility, charity, and condescension. We falsely persuade ourselves that we must act thus, in order to make virtue less difficult to others. We wish to please both God and men. By this means, we very often fail to please men, and we always displease God.

From the same source spring that delicacy regarding the point of honour, those little coolnesses in friendship, those regrets which approach so nearly to envy, if they have not all its malignity; that secret pain which is caused by the success of others. We always find some accident to which the greater part of their good fortune is attributed. We try to lower them. We speak coldly of them. We consider anyone who speaks in their praise, either tiresome or a flatterer. Whence proceeds all this? From our being filled with vanity and pride. We feel resentment at the least disagreeable word, or at the least sign of contempt. We think ourselves at liberty to omit certain acts of civility towards others; but we do not pardon them, if they fail in what we consider due to us. By a still more ridiculous illusion, we imagine that we owe it to the honour of God, Whom we serve, and of that exalted virtue which we flatter ourselves we possess, to display before the world our spirit, our talents, our good qualities, natural and supernatural. If anyone after this does not show us all the esteem and veneration that we expected, this is enough to make us at once consider him as imperfect, or as one who has no regard for merit, or esteem for virtue.

Nor are these yet all the effects of this secret ambition. We love fame, applause and praise for all we do. We see some who labour much for God, but who are always saying how much they do. They are always uncomfortable, hurried, fatigued and oppressed; one would say that they are inviting everyone to have compassion on them, in their labours. The truth is, that vanity has a great part in so much labour. We think ourselves very important and necessary; and we wish to appear so. Pride comes in, even in the very actions that belong to humility. We love to distinguish ourselves in the practice of certain virtues, and even in the exercise of good works. But all this alacrity is not for God alone, it is also to secure our own distinction. Finally, that excessive sadness and discouragement which we feel after a relapse into our former failings, is not the effect of tenderness of conscience, as some imagine. It is the effect of a secret pride, which makes us think ourselves more holy than we really are.

In a word, we pass for spiritual persons, we even think ourselves such, and yet we are influenced merely by human prudence, disguised under the name of good sense. We refer all to the rule of this pretended good sense which we have framed for ourselves, in order that we may deceive ourselves without scruple. It is by this false rule that we judge even of spiritual things, of divine operations, and of the marvels of grace. We approve of nothing but what suits our ideas. The graces which God bestows either upon ourselves or others, we use according to the maxims of human prudence, and by an extraordinary blindness which is the chastisement of proud spirits, we think that we are following reason and good sense, the further we remove from the spirit of God.

Are we astonished, then, with all this, that we have neither spiritual consolations nor sentiments of devotion, after ten or twenty years spent by us in the exercise of virtue and the practice of good works ? Do we lament that we make no progress, that we are always imperfect, that the use of the Sacraments is of little profit to us, that we do not know what sensible devotion is ? That secret pride which we nourish in the depth of our heart, dries up, as it were, the fountain of the greatest graces. It is this that causes persons so wise in appearance, so regular, so circumspect, who have lived with so much honour, and have been proposed as the model of those who are called wealthy in the world—*viri divitiarum*, and who, from appearances, ought to be loaded with spiritual riches, to find themselves at death with their hands empty of good works. This self-love, this little ambition, this secret pride, have robbed them of all, and corrupted everything. This is the worm that withers the loftiest oaks; this is the leaven that, sooner or later, corrupts the whole mass, or at least inflates it, and fills it with nothing but wind.

It is evident that the love of Jesus Christ cannot exist at the same time with a vice so opposed to it. How can our blessed Saviour, who would have the first of the beatitudes, the foundation of the spiritual life, and the first step to be taken in the path of virtue, to be that spirit of humility which He Himself has chosen, in preference to all the other virtues as His own special characteristic;—how can He be greatly loved by those who so little resemble Him? This sincere humility of mind and heart is the distinctive character of Jesus Christ. It is impossible, then, to be animated by His spirit, and to dwell in His Heart, unless we are truly animated by this spirit of humility.

IV. FOURTH OBSTACLE.—*Some Unmortified Passion.*

The fourth obstacle, and the fourth source of those defects which hinder and destroy the love of Jesus Christ, and consequently the devotion to His Sacred Heart, are certain unmortified passions to which we are attached, and which, sooner or later, are the fatal cause of some great misfortune.

The greater number of persons who wish to give themselves to God, and who consequently declare a mortal war against all vices, proceed in this war something in the same way as Saul did, in the war he undertook by the order of God against Amalech—*Vade, percute Amalech, et demolire universa ejus; non parcas ei, et non concupiscas ex rebus ipsius aliquid. Now, therefore, go and smite Amalech, and utterly destroy all that he hath; spare him not, nor covet anything that is his* (1 Kings xv. 3). Almighty God had ordered Saul to exterminate all the Amalekites, and destroy whatever belonged to them, without sparing anything. Saul exterminated the people, but, moved with compassion, he pardoned the king, and reserved for sacrifice whatever he found most precious on the field: *et pepercit Saul Agag . . . et universis quæ pulchra erant, nec voluerunt disperdere ea; quidquid vero vile fuit et reprobum, hoc demoliti sunt. And Saul spared Agag . . . and all that was beautiful, and would not destroy them, but everything that was vile and good for nothing, that they destroyed. The Lord hath rejected thee from being king.* But this disobedience cost Saul his kingdom, and was the cause of his reprobation and ruin : *abjecit te Dominus ne sis Rex.*

Many follow the example of Saul in the war they undertake against their vices. May God preserve them from a similar fate. We are well convinced that God wills that we should make a sacrifice to Him of all our passions, and that He cannot endure that we should spare any vice. But we consent to this only in appearance. We destroy, so to speak, all our enemies, but there is some predominant passion that we spare. There is always something particularly dear and precious that we do not touch. That we may deceive ourselves without scruple, we leave a place in our heart always with some good motive, for one of our enemies. We extinguish in ourselves the spirit of the world, but we like to see it still living in its followers. We dress ourselves with all modesty, but we wish a daughter to be attired in the extreme of unchristian fashions. We do not gamble, but we are recklessly extravagant in the entertainments which we give. We moderate our impetuosity and our anger, but we spare a secret ambition and some secret jealousy which we cannot resolve to overcome. We mortify that constant dissipation which is so unbecoming in persons who make profession of loving Jesus Christ in a special manner, but we will not deprive ourselves of the liberty of spending whole hours in visits and useless conversations. Under the pretence that we must make ourselves agreeable to all, to gain all to Jesus Christ, and that we must make virtue easy, sweet, and amiable, we insensibly get into the habit of doing everything just like others, and reserve only the name and appearance of virtue.

Others, a little more generous, break the strongest links that kept them attached to the world. They leave their parents and their property. They even give up their liberty in a certain way, and submit to the yoke of religious obedience. But they do not take pains to break the smaller links, that is to say, to free themselves from a variety of little affections, which fail not to stop them, and retard their progress in the way of perfection. What does it matter, that the fetters which keep us bound to creatures are slight, if there are many of them? A single chain, however small, suffices to hinder us from advancing a single step when we will not break it.

Finally, there are some who are generous enough to resolve to overcome all. They even make some efforts to do so. But they do not touch their natural disposition or that failing which suits their inclinations best. This one enemy left unconquered, this single passion not mortified, this single chain unbroken, makes them go on creeping all their lives, and hinders them from arriving at the high perfection to which they were called—*pro eo ergo abjecit te Dominus ne sis Rex. The Lord hath rejected thee from being king.* A small opening is enough to destroy a ship, and to bring to ruin in course of time the most splendid edifice. A spark suffices to cause a great conflagration. Death is often the consequence of a trifling sickness neglected. A single ill drawn stroke of the pencil is enough to discredit a picture, otherwise well executed.

We are surprised sometimes to see persons who have grown old in exercises of piety, men of consummate spirituality and highly mortified, who still retain very great imperfections which they themselves condemn in others, and of which, however, they never correct themselves. This arises from their familiarising themselves, as it were, with their own failings. They have spared them from their youth; they allow their natural disposition to act. They easily become impatient; they continually praise themselves always with some good motive, and under some grand pretext. They neglect to become perfect when they are young, and they find themselves most imperfect when they are old.

Such are the great obstacles to the love of Jesus Christ, and consequently to the devotion to His Sacred Heart. Such are the sources of the many imperfections that are noticed in persons who seem the most spiritual; imperfections, however, which do great injury to true piety, by the false idea they give of devotion. True piety always condemns these defects. The true love of Jesus Christ cannot exist together with these imperfections, this secret pride, this self-love. The effects of these three fatal sources are not to be found in those who possess this true love. And yet, without this pure and true love of Jesus Christ, there is no solid devotion, no perfect virtue.

"My God!" exclaimed a great servant of God, "what confusion and disorder is this? At one time we are cheerful, at another sad; to-day we are kind to every one, to-morrow we are like a hedge-hog, that no one can touch without being pricked." This is a clear proof of a want of virtue. It is a sign that nature still reigns in us, that our passions are not mortified. A truly virtuous man is always the same. Is there no danger, if we sometimes do good, of our doing it rather through humour than from virtue?

CHAPTER III.

The means of overcoming the obstacles, that hinder us from gathering the fruit we ought, from the devotion to the Sacred Heart of Jesus Christ.

It is certain that tepidity, self-love, secret pride, or any other passion that we have not taken care to mortify, are the chief springs of our imperfections, and the greatest obstacles to our gathering the fruit we ought, from the devotion to the Sacred Heart of Jesus Christ. We have only a weak and languishing charity. We cherish within us our most formidable enemies. Without us are the devil who tempts us, the world which attracts us, objects which dazzle us, occasions which surround us, examples which draw us away. If, then, we are not always on our guard, and do not keep the doors of our senses closed against all these enemies who besiege us, they will speedily make themselves masters of our heart. "It is extraordinary," says a great servant of God, "how many enemies we have to fight against. From the moment we form the resolution of becoming saints, they seem to be all let loose: the devil with his artifices, nature with the resistance it makes to our good desires, the praises of the good, the scoffs of the wicked, the solicitations of the tepid, the example of those who pass for devout, but are not so. If God visit us, we have to fear vanity; if He withdraw Himself, timidity. Discouragement may succeed the greatest fervour. Our friends tempt us by means of the condescension which we show towards them: the indifferent by the fear we have of displeasing them. Indiscretion is to be feared in fervour, sensuality in moderation, and self-love in everything. What then are we to do? For sanctity does not consist in being faithful for a day or a year, but in persevering and advancing until death. We must make use of those means which all the Saints, together with Jesus Christ Himself, assure us to be most suitable for weakening and destroying that self-love and secret pride which are the source of all these impediments. These means are mortification and humility. We must resolve on one of two things, either never to have a perfect love for Jesus Christ, or to be truly humble and perfectly mortified.

I. FIRST MEANS.—*True Mortification.*

Mortification is so necessary for the perfect love of Jesus Christ, that it is the first lesson that Jesus Christ Himself gives to those who wish to be His disciples. Without it, we can have no hope of ever being disciples of Jesus Christ. *If any man will come after Me,* says our loving Saviour, *let him deny himself, take up his cross, and follow Me; and whosoever doth not carry his cross, and hate his own life, cannot be My disciple, and is not worthy of Me.* For this reason all the Saints agree in considering that there is no stronger proof of real piety than perfect mortification. Is he a very mortified person? asked St. Ignatius, when the virtue of some one was praised by others. He would give them to understand that true mortification is inseparable from true piety, not only because no virtue can long exist without constant and general mortification, but also, because, without mortification, there is no such thing as true virtue.

There are two sorts of mortifications: one exterior, which consists in the maceration of the body; the other interior, which is properly the mortification of the mind and heart. Both are necessary for attaining perfection. One cannot exist long without the other. Fasts, watchings, hair-shirts, and other bodily mortifications are powerful means to become truly spiritual and truly perfect; and when they are used with discretion, help marvellously to strengthen nature, always weak for good and prone to evil; to repress the assaults and escape the snares of our common enemy, and finally to obtain from the Father of mercies, the helps that are necessary for all the just, and especially for beginners.

It is true that sanctity does not consist in exterior penances, and that they are not incompatible with hypocrisy. But it is not so with interior mortification. This is always a mark of true piety. It is, therefore, still more necessary than exterior mortification, and no one can reasonably abstain from it. We must do ourselves this violence continually, in order to gain heaven. All are not able to fast, or to wear a hair-shirt, but there is no one who cannot be silent, at a time when passion moves him to answer, or vanity to speak. There is no one who cannot mortify his natural disposition, his desires, his passions. It is in this that interior mortification chiefly consists. By it we weaken our self-love, reduce it to reason, and free ourselves from our imperfections. It is in vain that we flatter ourselves we love Jesus Christ, if we are not mortified. All the sublimest sentiments of piety, all the practices of devotion are to be suspected, if not accompanied by this perfect mortification. We wonder to see ourselves so imperfect, and after so many practices of piety, so many communions, to feel the various passions that continually agitate our heart. Do we not see that it is the want of perfect mortification which is the source of all these disorders? It is necessary, then, if we would weaken and destroy this self-love, by which all the passions are fed, to resolve upon generous and constant mortification.

It is not enough to mortify ourselves for a certain time, and in some things. We must, if possible, mortify ourselves in all things and at all times, though with prudence and discretion. A single irregular gratification which you allow to nature has more effect in making her haughty and rebellious, than a hundred victories that you may have gained over her will have in weakening her. A truce with enemies of this kind is a victory for them. My brethren, says St. Bernard, what is lopped off, sprouts again; what is extinguished, rekindles; what is slumbering, wakes up again. To preserve the interior spirit of devotion we must prevent our soul from diffusing itself abroad. We must surround it on all sides, as the Prophet says, with a hedge of thorns. Now this we neglect to do; and hence our tepidity, our relaxation, and all our indevotion. If we mortify nature in one thing, we immediately repay it by some other satisfaction which we allow it. If we are recollected in a retreat, as soon as it is over, we open all the doors of our senses to objects that will dissipate us. The exercise of this interior mortification, so habitual to all the Saints, is familiar to all those who have a true desire of perfection. We have but to attend to the suggestions of the Spirit of God. The love of Jesus Christ is so ingenious on this point, that the diligence and the methods of mortification, with which it at once inspires the most ignorant persons, surpass the ideas of the most learned, and may almost be called miraculous. There is nothing that does not afford them an opportunity of mortifying their natural inclinations. There is no time, or place, that does not seem suited to mortify themselves, without ever departing from the rules of real good sense. It suffices that they have a great wish to see or to speak, to oblige them to cast down their eyes, and be silent. The desire to hear news, or to know all that happens, is to them a constant motive for mortification. This mortification is the more meritorious in proportion, as it is less extraordinary, and has God for its sole witness. A happy remark, a witty pleasantry, may do us honour in society, but it may also form the subject of a pleasing sacrifice. There is scarcely an hour of the day which does not offer some opportunity of mortification. Whether we are sitting or standing, we can easily find a less comfortable place or position, without anything appearing exteriorly. If we are repeatedly interrupted in some very serious occupation, we can reply as often with as much mildness and civility as if we had not been occupied at all. The patience of a person of solid virtue, may find great exercise in the ill-temper of any one about him; the imperfections of a servant, or the ingratitude of one who is under obligations to him. Finally, inconveniences of place, season, or persons, borne in such a manner, as if we did not perceive them, are, it is true, small opportunities of fying ourselves—but mortification in these little things is no little matter. It is of great merit; and it may be said that the greatest graces, and the most exalted sanctity, depend generally on the generosity which we show in mortifying ourselves in these little things. It is not a small mortification to omit none of the duties of a community, and to conform oneself in all things to community life, without having any regard to our own inclinations, our employments, or age. This kind of mortification is the more valuable in proportion, as it is less exposed to vanity, and more conformable to the spirit of Jesus Christ.

But if we did not find in external things so many occasions for mortifying ourselves, they are always to be found within ourselves. We cannot be for a long time modest, recollected, reserved, without great mortication. Honesty, meekness and civility may be the effect of education, but they are generally the marks of one who is habitually mortified. Without this virtue how can we be in peace, and always the same, do always perfectly what we do, and be always content with what God wills?

II.—SECOND MEANS.—*Sincere Humility*.

The second means is sincere humility. Jesus Christ, says St. Augustin, does not say to us, learn of Me to work miracles, but learn of Me, because I am meek and humble of heart, to give us to understand, that, without humility, there is no true piety. We are sufficiently convinced of the necessity of this virtue; all the difficulty consists in knowing what is true humility. Many think they are truly humble, as soon as they have a low opinion of themselves. But they deceive themselves, if they are not at the same time well pleased, that others should entertain the same opinion of them. It is not enough that we acknowledge ourselves to possess no virtue or merit. We must believe it. We must be pleased that others believe it. The first step to be taken in gaining this virtue, is to beg it earnestly of God. The next is firmly to convince ourselves, by means of serious and frequent reflection on ourselves, of our poverty and our own imperfections. The remembrance of what we have been, and the thought of what we may be, serve greatly to humble us. The truly virtuous think little of others, and occupy themselves solely with their own imperfections. The truly humble are scandalized at nothing, because they know their own weakness so well. They see themselves so near the precipice, and they are so much afraid of falling, that they are not surprised if others fall. The less we speak of ourselves, the more closely we conform ourselves to true humility. Those affected discourses, by which we wish to make it appear that we have little esteem for ourselves, have no effect usually but to gain us praise. The most certain mark of sincere humility is to have a special love for those who despise us: never to avoid any humiliations that present themselves to us; not to take pleasure in vain thoughts and vain projects for the future, which only serve to nourish a secret pride within us; never to speak to our own advantage; never to complain and not to allow others to complain of anything Almighty God allows to happen to us; to excuse the failings of our neighbour; never to be troubled at our own relapses; to defer to others in all things; never to undertake anything but with diffidence in ourselves, and to have little esteem for what we do. Finally, to pray much, and to speak little.

Any one who is convinced that he is very miserable, is not offended if he is despised: he sees that it is only just. A humble man, whatever bad treatment he may receive, thinks that justice is done him. Men do not esteem me; they are right, they agree in this with God, and with the Angels. Whoever has deserved hell,

thinks that contempt is his due. It is not meant by
this, that we are obliged to receive a humiliation with
sensible pleasure. Contempt is naturally disagreeable.
But not to complain, to be silent under contempt, to
thank God for it, and to pray to Him for those whom
He makes use of to humble us, whatever repugnance
nature may feel in submitting, are certain marks of
sincere humility, without which there is no virtue.
We have enemies, says St. Paul, within and without
us, who spread snares for us on every side. The love
of humility, of abjection, of a hidden and obscure life,
is a powerful remedy against so many evils. There is
no peace but in the forgetfulness of ourselves. If we
wish to become perfect, we must resolve to forget even
our own spiritual interests, and to seek only the pure
glory of God.

III. THIRD MEANS.—*The joy and true sweetness which are
inseparable from the exercise of true mortification and of
sincere humility.*

There is no devotion, without universal, generous,
and constant mortification. There is none without
sincere humility. But is it possible to speak of humility and continual mortification, without terrifying persons who perhaps have some desire to gain an ardent
love of Jesus Christ? Do they not immediately tremble
at the thought of so uncomfortable a condition?

Who can look upon a life full of crosses, without
feeling horror? To thwart our natural inclinations in
everything, to deny our senses every satisfaction that
is not absolutely necessary, to live in retirement and
silence, without seeking the esteem of men, taking
pleasure in their praises, or feeling regret at their contempt,—is not this, we may say, to lead a very unhappy
life? All, however, who live in this manner, declare
that they are perfectly happy. The world says that
this kind of life is insupportable; but Jesus Christ

Himself says that it is sweet and easy, full of joy and consolation. The world—that is to say, those who know nothing about this life—say one thing; and all who have experienced it, say quite the contrary. St. Francis of Sales calls this sort of life the sweetness of sweetnesses. St. Ephrem, whilst practising a most mortified life, cried out, full of consolation, "It is enough, my God, it is enough! Do not load me with Thy benefits. Moderate Thy liberality, if Thou wouldst not have me die, for the ineffable sweetness which I taste in Thy service is enough to cause my death." "I am in a country," says St. Francis Xavier, writing from Japan to his brethren in Europe, "where I am in want of all the conveniences of life. But nevertheless, I feel so much interior consolation, that there is danger of my losing my sight through weeping with joy." Can so many thousands of Saints, whom we acknowledge to have been so wise and so sincere, have agreed to say exactly opposite to what they thought and experienced?

But if we are so unhappy, as worldly persons think, in this exercise of continual mortification, how is it that those we see to be most mortified are always the most contented? How is it that we find no persons on earth perfectly contented, perfectly happy, but those who are most mortified? If this mortified life does not itself produce this unalterable joy, by what artifice do these persons preserve themselves until death, in a sweetness and tranquillity which no misfortune of life can ever disturb? If they merely feign it, how is it that persons of the world, who know so well the art of dissimulation, have never as yet been able to conceal their uneasiness and their regrets, though they pass the greater part of their life in pleasure and amusement? Virtue alone, says St. Augustin, though it seems austere, gives true pleasure. There is no perfect felicity in this world, except for virtuous persons, who seriously labour at their sanctification. Exempt as they are from the disturbance of those cruel passions which tyrannise over the wicked, they experience more sweetness in their life, and less regret. Perfectly submissive to God's will, they enjoy a calm and profound peace which the world cannot give. This sweet tranquillity of conscience is the ordinary result of virtue. The more we belong to God, the more do we enjoy it. The more we keep back from God, the less do we participate in this sweetness.

What might we not say of the secret unction by which Almighty God lightens the yoke of His law ; of those happy moments in which He makes Himself heard by just souls ; of that sweet hope, which makes them feel in anticipation the joys of heaven ; of those rays of light, which show them so clearly the vanity of the world ; of those tears of consolation, which they sometimes shed at the foot of the crucifix, when they experience a purer and more exquisite joy than the most delightful pleasures of the world can afford? This joy and this interior sweetness, which surpasses all imagination, is a hidden mystery to tepid souls. It is for them an unknown language. But give me, says St. Augustin, a fervent soul, one truly humble and mortified, a heart full of the love of Jesus Christ; such a one will understand what I say. "*Da amantem et sentiet quod dico.*" It is true, that to be perfect, it is not necessary to be altogether insensible to the misfortunes of life. Disasters may cause some agitation to the just, but they do not overpower him. He has always in his virtues a strong rock of support. In the broad way in which the imperfect walk, even though it had no crosses of its own, everything would contribute to raise them up around. Whereas, in the path followed by those who have an ardent love of Jesus Christ, whatever crosses there are, heaven and earth conspire, as it were, to sweeten them. The Son of God Himself carries them with us, to lighten their weight. Finally, the mere thought of death is enough of itself to alarm the happiest worldlings, whereas it serves but to console and rejoice the virtuous. Was there ever anyone at the point of death, at that moment when so correct a judgment is formed of everything, who was sorry for having practised mortification, or for having led a perfect life? Or rather, is there anyone, on the contrary, who has not felt a deep regret for not having done so?

Perfect mortification must assuredly have charms that we know not, because we are not perfectly mortified. Our weakness lets us do only enough to feel the difficulty, but not enough to taste the sweetness. It seems as though we mistrusted what is told us by the virtuous, and what Jesus Christ Himself promises us. We would have Him pay us in advance. We forget that in this, it is only the first step that is difficult. All the difficulty lies in resolving to mortify ourselves. Taste, says the Prophet, and see. In this matter, the eye is deceived; we must judge by the taste alone. Those who had seen the land of promise only from afar, were frightened, and said that it devoured its inhabitants. But those who had been there, said quite the contrary, and declared that it was a land flowing with milk and honey. Let us make this perfect sacrifice for a fortnight, at least. A thing must be indeed of little value, if it is not worth the trial. If, after a fortnight of continual and perfect mortification, we do not taste that sweetness which others experience, I am content, said a great servant of God, that it should be said, that the life of those who truly love Jesus Christ is irksome, and that the yoke of our Lord is heavy.

Is it not strange, that men should require so much to convince them that they can be happy in the exercise of constant mortification, when they see daily so many persons pensive and uneasy amidst the greatest dissipation? If there are sufferings which are unseen, is it impossible that there should be a hidden sweetness? There is such, certainly, and it depends on ourselves to experience it.

Fr. la Colombière had made a vow, with the leave of his superiors, to observe all his rules, and he had bound himself in particular to a continual mortification in all things. What will those to whom the three essential vows of religion seem an insupportable burden, think of this great servant of God? Would they not consider him unhappy? But see what he himself has written in his Spiritual Retreats, in which, as is commonly the practice of persons of solid virtue, who are resolved on making constant progress in the way of perfection, he has noted the sentiments given him by God, and the graces which He granted him, in order to remind himself to thank Him for them, and to encourage himself to love Him more every day.

"On the sixth day," he says, "making a consideration on the particular vow I have made, I was filled with gratitude to God, who has granted me the grace to make this vow. I had never had time to consider it thoroughly. I felt great joy in seeing myself bound thus by a thousand chains to do the will of God. The thought of this obligation is so far from alarming me, that it fills me with joy. It seems to me, that, in place of being a slave, I have entered into the kingdom of liberty and peace."

"When I am quite alone," he says elsewhere, "I feel, by the infinite mercy of God, a liberty of heart that causes me incomparable joy. I feel myself attached to nothing, at least at the time. This does not hinder me from feeling every day the emotions of almost all the passions. But a moment's reflection serves to calm them.

"I have often felt great interior joy in the thought

that I was in God's service. I have felt that this was worth more than all the favour of kings. The occupations of worldly persons appeared to me most contemptible, compared with what is done for God. I feel myself exalted above all the kings of the earth by the honour of belonging to God.

"I feel continually a greater desire to apply to the observance of my rules. I feel the greatest delight in practising them. The more exact I am in them, the more I seem to enter into perfect liberty. It is certain that this does not cause me any uneasiness. On the contrary, this yoke makes me, as it were, much lighter. I look on this as the greatest grace I have ever received in my life."

It cannot be doubted that this great servant of God practised continual mortification in all things after making an express vow to do so. Thus he was seen in his last illness, when his infirmity would allow him to leave his bed, passing many hours of the day on a seat without any kind of support, persevering in this manner until death in the practice of universal mortification. This mortified life filled him with such consolation and so great interior joy, that he confesses that it may indeed be felt, but cannot possibly be described.

"The sight of Jesus Christ," he says, "makes the cross so pleasant to me, that it seems as if I could not be happy without it. I look with respect on those whom God visits with humiliations and adversities, of what kind soever they be. They are without doubt His favourites. To humble myself I have only to compare myself with them whilst I am in prosperity."

"The following words," he continues, "never come into my mind, but light, peace, liberty, meekness, and love enter in, as it seems to me, at the same time with them: 'Simplicity,' 'confidence,' 'humility,' 'self-abandonment,' 'absence of all reserve,' 'the will of God,' 'my rules.'"

The experience of this great servant of God shows us, that not only have the Saints who have preceded us found so much sweetness in the exercise of universal and constant mortification, but that even those with whom we live experience the same, as soon as they have the generosity to mortify themselves continually.

CHAPTER IV.

The particular means of acquiring this perfect love of Jesus Christ, and this tender devotion to His Sacred Heart.

FIRST MEANS.—*Prayer.*

BESIDES the obstacles that we must avoid, and the dispositions in which we must find ourselves, in order to acquire this perfect love of Jesus Christ, and this tender devotion to His Sacred Heart, it is well to suggest here the means that are most appropriate for this end.

Now, the first means to obtain this ardent love of Jesus Christ, and this tender devotion to His Sacred Heart, is Prayer. We may well wonder that Christians are not, as it were, all powerful; that they have not all they desire, since they have an infallible means of obtaining all they ask, and this means consists only in asking.

There is nothing to which Jesus Christ has so solemnly and so repeatedly bound Himself as to hear our prayers. But of all prayers there can be none more pleasing to Him than that by which we ask Him for His love. He has strictly bound Himself to grant this love to all who should ask Him for it. But we may add, that even though He had not engaged Himself to it, the request itself would oblige Him to it.

Jesus Christ has done all that we can imagine, nay more, to oblige us to love Him. It rests with Him to give us this love. Who will dare believe that He will refuse it to us if we ask Him for it? But our esteem for this love must be indeed small, since we trouble ourselves so little about it, and ask for it so seldom. You wonder that you have not an ardent love for Jesus Christ, though this love is so just and so conformable to reason. There would be greater reason for astonishment if you did love Him, seeing that this love is the greatest of all His gifts, and that yet you do not even condescend to ask it. Of all the means of obtaining the love of Jesus Christ, there is none more efficacious than prayer. There is none more easy. For who can excuse himself from praying? Still there is none, as it appears, that is more neglected. It might be said, that the most powerful motive by which Jesus Christ seeks to oblige us to make use of this means keeps us from it. *Credite, quia accipistis.* Be sure that you will be heard. But, my God, is not this the very thing that is dreaded? "Timebam, ne me citò exaudires." "I was afraid that you would hear my prayer too soon" (St. Aug. Confess., book i.). We fear, unhappy as we are, that didst Thou but once hear us, Thy love would induce us to become more virtuous, more recollected, more devout, and more holy than we wish to be. We fear that if we had an ardent love for Thee, we should feel nothing but disgust for all that we have loved, and that we still love. In a word, we seem to fear that we shall not be able to help loving Thee. But regard not, oh my Saviour, these sentiments that arise within us, and which we detest as soon as we perceive them. Give us only Thy love with thy grace, and we shall be rich enough. How soon shall we, disgusted with everything else, if, opening to us Thy Sacred Heart, Thou allowest us but once to taste the sweetness that is experienced in loving Thee. Let us pray and often ask for this love. It is impossible to ask for it earnestly and constantly without obtaining it. We fear, perhaps, to be importunate or excessive in our requests, to offend

Jesus Christ by our indiscretion or our importunity. But, on the contrary, the reason why we obtain so little from God is because we do not ask much. We are too limited in our desires, and too languid in our prayers. Jesus Christ has given us in the Gospel the parable of the man, who obtained what he asked, merely by his importunity, in order to teach us that, if we wish to obtain what we ask, we must become importunate. We obtain little, because we ask too little, and because we do not beg earnestly for the little we ask for. We must ask Him for nothing less than His love; but it must be a tender, ardent, generous, and perfect love, and we must ask for it earnestly and with importunity. As He has so solemnly engaged Himself to refuse us nothing that we ask in His Name, He cannot refuse to hear us without breaking His promise. Most frequently we do not know what we ask. But we should do an injury to Jesus Christ, and falsify our own belief, if, when we ask Him for His love, we were to doubt His hearing us, more especially if we ask it with earnestness and sincerity. I believe, indeed, that Jesus Christ, to punish us, or to humble us, and in any case to increase our merit, will leave us certain defects and imperfections, from which we entreat Him to deliver us. But no one will ever persuade me that, after we have asked Him sincerely and earnestly for an ardent love of Him, He will refuse it to us. On the contrary, He will grant us more than we asked. Thou hast brought this divine fire on earth, oh Lord, and what dost Thou desire but that it be enkindled? *Ignem veni mittere in terram, et quid volo, nisi ut accendatur?* (Luke xii.) With whom does it rest wholly to inflame me with it? Give me, then, if it please Thee, give me Thy love, oh Lord. This shall be in future my constant prayer. I will make it morning and night, when at rest and when at work. I will make it every hour, and will never cease to say: Give me but Thy love, oh Lord, with Thy grace, and I am rich enough; I ask no more.

II. SECOND MEANS.—*Frequent Communion.*

The second means is the frequent use of the Sacraments, and frequent Communion. It is enough to know what Holy Communion is, to understand that there is no more certain means of becoming inflamed with love for Jesus Christ than to communicate frequently. It is not possible, says the Wise Man, to carry fire in one's bosom, and not be set on fire by it. Divine love has enkindled a furnace, so to speak, on our Altars in the adorable Eucharist. It is by approaching to this sacred fire that all the Saints have been inflamed with a most ardent and tender love for Jesus Christ. The love which burned within them after Communion appeared even in their countenance. How often have they been forced, in the depth of winter, to seek the cool air in order to moderate the ardour of divine love? The name or the picture of Jesus Christ was enough to make them fall into raptures and ecstacies. It cannot be doubted that the great love which the first faithful had for Jesus Christ was the effect of Holy Communion, which they received daily. All who render themselves worthy, by the innocence of their life and the exercise of true piety, to communicate frequently, experience still every day, in this point, the admirable effects of frequent Communion. They love Jesus Christ more and more. Their love increases in proportion as they nourish themselves more frequently with this Bread of Angels. So far are they from becoming disgusted with the frequent use of it, that, on the contrary, their hunger sensibly increases, as the love they have for Jesus Christ grows more ardent.

All the other Sacraments are effects of the love which the Son of God has for men. There is not one that is not capable of instilling into our hearts a true love for our divine Saviour. But the Sacrament of the Altar, says St. Bernard, is the love of loves. Sacramentum Altaris est amor amorum. It is the effect of the greatest love, that Jesus Christ can have for man; and at the same time, the most fruitful source of the tender and ardent love that men ought to have for Jesus Christ. Everything in this mystery contributes to inspire and increase this ardent love: the gift, the manner of giving it, and the end for which it is given. Jesus Christ gives us therein His adorable Body, and His precious Blood, to be our food. What shall have power to light up this divine fire in the hearts of men, if this heavenly food cannot do it? But the loving manner in which Jesus Christ makes us this gift obliges us less powerfully to love Him. Our Divine Saviour, the expected of the people of Israel, the desired of nations, the desire of the eternal hills, allowed His coming into the world to be wished for, for so many thousand years. But here He Himself asks men, entreats of them, and even does violence to them to make them receive Him. Oblige them, says He, in the Gospel, oblige them to partake of the banquet that I have prepared for them: *compelle intrare.* Love is impatient. It is an enemy of delay. It does not know what it is to hesitate or to be cautious. What has our loving Saviour in view, in so much earnestness? He desires to be loved by men. He gives them His Body and Blood to gain their hearts. He makes Himself their food only to gain possession of their heart, to rob them of it, without their being, so to say, able to prevent it. The chief intention you should have in communicating, says St. Francis of Sales (Introduction to a Devout Life, part ii. ch. 2), should be to increase and strengthen yourself in the love of God, for you ought to receive through love what love alone gives you. " Nowhere," continues this great Saint, is our Saviour more loving or more tender than here. He here annihilates Himself, as it were, and becomes our food, in order to regenerate our souls, by uniting us most closely to Himself.

We look with admiration on the fervour of those pure souls, who never approach the Altars, without feeling a sensible increase of love for Jesus Christ, and being wholly inflamed with it.* But it is far more marvellous that Communions should be so frequent, and yet these marvels of so rare an occurrence. Your sins, your relapses, your weaknesses, give you uneasiness. You wish to correct yourself, to overcome that repugnance, that tepidity, to break that link which is the only thing that keeps you back in the path of piety. You wish to have an ardent love for Jesus Christ. You allow that only those who love Him perfectly are perfectly happy; and, yet, after so very many Communions, you are still so imperfect, so tepid, you have no greater love for Jesus Christ.

For a year, for ten years perhaps, you have said Mass every day. You have received the Body and Blood of Jesus Christ more than three thousand times in your life; and yet, for a year, for ten years, you have been fighting against some imagination, some fancy, you say, which hinders you from belonging entirely to God, and from tasting that peace and sweetness which are enjoyed in His service. Perhaps even your love for Jesus Christ is less. "Ah! my God," exclaimed a great servant of God, "are they heretics or infidels that speak thus" (Fr. la Colombière, Reflex. Chret). How is it possible that a Christian who feeds so often on the Body of Jesus Christ should desire anything in vain? Who will ever believe that a God, offered as the price of the graces that are sought, will not be able to obtain them? That Jesus Christ, who has instituted this mystery only in order that He may

* This extraordinary ardour of divine love is marvellous only because it is so rare.

be loved, will refuse His love to those to whom He gives Himself without reserve or restriction! If, then, unhappily we find that by communicating every week, or even oftener, or by celebrating Mass daily, we derive no profit from this adorable Sacrament, do not amend, misuse Holy Communion, do not love Jesus Christ more, always feel the same tepidity and weaknesses, are we therefore to leave off Communion? Must we give up saying Mass daily? No; but we must regulate our life and free ourselves from the vices and failings that hinder us from profiting by it. The evil does not spring from communicating too frequently, but from communicating ill. Suppose that no sort of food did you good, because you took it when you should not, what would you do in such a case? Would you abstain altogether from eating, or would you adopt every necessary precaution in order to derive benefit from what you eat? Suppose that some one formed the extraordinary resolution of preventing the food which he took at his meals from digesting in his stomach. He falls ill; the physicians are consulted. Will any one of them be found to advise that the sick man take no more food? He must eat; but he must do it with the necessary precautions. He must be less indiscreet and imprudent. If he did not eat, the food would not indeed corrupt in his stomach, it is true; but he would die of weakness. This imprudent and culpable resolution would not hinder digestion, but it would soon exhaust the remains of his strength, and you would soon see him fall in the course of twenty-four hours into a mortal weakness. He would not die of indigestion, but of hunger. In a word, it would be folly to take from him what supports his life, in order to deliver him from what makes him ill. It is easy to apply this example to those who do not draw any profit from Communion. These persons have great reason to fear that they are ill-directed, that their conscience is in a bad state, that their faith is too weak, and that their confessions are without sincerity, without sorrow, or without resolution of amendment. If you are ill-disposed, correct yourself at once, in order that you may communicate often .If you are imperfect, communicate often, in order that you may amend. The Son of God calls this adorable mystery our daily bread, to show what frequent use we should make of it. He calls the poor and the blind to His banquet, in order to teach us that, however poor we may be, and whatever infirmities we labour under, if we be still living, we must have no difficulty in eating this bread of life.

The little fruit that the greater number of persons, especially Priests, draw from frequent Communion, gives rise sometimes to a doubt, whether it be advisable to communicate so frequently. But this doubt cannot be better answered than by quoting here what St. Francis of Sales has said on this subject.

"I do not wish," says the Saint (Introd. to a Devout Life, pt. ii. ch. 20), "either to blame or to praise those who, not being Priests, communicate every day. But I advise all, and exhort them as earnestly as I can, to communicate every eight days, provided they have no affection to sin." These are the very words of St. Augustin, he continues. He neither praises nor blames absolutely those who communicate every day, but leaves the matter to the prudence of the director. For as the disposition necessary for communicating so frequently is so very rare, it is not well to advise it generally. But inasmuch as this disposition, however rare, may be found in many persons of solid virtue, it is not well on the other hand to forbid it generally to all.

As it would be imprudence to recommend so frequent a use of the holy Eucharist to all indifferently, so it would be no less imprudence to blame those who make frequent use of it, by the advice of a wise director. The answer of St. Catherine of Sienna, on this subject, is to the purpose. You tell me that I ought not to communicate so often, because St. Augustin neither praises nor blames those who do so every day. Since St. Augustin, she answers, does not blame it, do not do so yourself. You see Philothea, that St. Augustin exhorts and strongly recommends to communicate every Sunday. Do so then, as far as you can. For since, as I suppose, you have no affection either to mortal or venial sin, you have the disposition required by St. Augustin. Nay, you have more; for not only have you no affection for sinning, but you have no affection for sin. You should therefore communicate every Sunday, and even oftener, if your spiritual Father judge it proper.

If worldly persons, adds the Saint, in the following chapter (Int. to a Devout Life, pt. ii. ch. 21.) should ask you why you communicate so frequently, tell them it is to learn to love God, to purify yourself from your imperfections, to free yourself from your miseries, to console yourself in your afflictions, to gain strength in your weaknesses. Tell them that two kinds of persons should communicate frequently; the perfect, because being well disposed, they would do wrong not to approach the source of perfection and sanctity, and the imperfect, in order that they may amend and become perfect; the strong, that they may not become weak, and the weak that they may become strong; the sick in order that they may be cured, and those who are well that they may not become ill. That, as regards yourself, as you are imperfect, weak and infirm, you require frequently to communicate with Him who is your perfection, your strength, your medicine. Tell them, that persons in the world who have not much to do, should do so no less frequently, because they need greater helps, and that those who labour much and undergo great fatigue, should take solid food and eat frequently. Tell them that you communicate often in

H

order to learn to do it well, for what we seldom do, we never do well.

Communicate often, Philothea, and as often as you can with the advice of your director. Hares become white in our mountains during winter, from seeing and eating nothing but snow. So, by adoring and receiving Him Who is beauty, goodness, and purity Itself, in this august Sacrament, you will be insensibly purified from your sins, and become better and more pure every day.

This is the advice St. Francis of Sales gives to all those who have a horror for every kind of mortal sin, and a real desire of securing their salvation. It is true that the desire to communicate is ordinarily found in all who have a lively faith and who really love Jesus Christ; and, on the contrary, we too often experience that in proportion as we mix with the world, and as the love of Jesus Christ grows cold within us, we feel the greater difficulty in communicating. It is superfluous, therefore, to preach to the wicked, that they must abstain from Communion. They are too ready to do it of themselves. We never find that souls, corrupted by vice and immersed in it, hunger after this heavenly food, which forms the delight of pure souls and of all who love Jesus Christ.

III. THIRD MEANS.—*Visits to the Blessed Sacrament.*

The third means is often to visit the Blessed Sacrament. Friendship is kept up and increased among men by visits and frequent conversations. It is by this means, also, that we shall continually increase in an ardent love for Jesus Christ. As He dwells on our Altars in order that He may be constantly with us, what must be His sentiments regarding those whom He rarely sees in His presence. It seems as if nothing gained His Heart more completely than these frequent adorations and visits. It is at these times that He usually bestows His gifts in greater abundance, and it may be said, that of all the favours He then grants, the most ordinary is the grace of His love.

There are visits of civility, and there are visits also of pure friendship. To fail in the first would be a fault, but it is only during the latter that His special favours are usually granted. The greater feasts, the time of Mass and of Divine office, are in respect of Jesus Christ the same thing as visits of duty and civility to great persons. We should be noticed, or even punished, if we were not there with the crowd. But the visits that are made at certain hours of the day, at which Jesus Christ is not generally visited, but, on the contrary, forgotten by the greater number, are visits of friendship. It is at this time, more than any other, that Jesus Christ converses familiarly, so to speak, with His favourites, and He showers upon them the treasures of His graces and inflames them with His love. Whether it be that the indifference of those who then forget Him, renders the fidelity of those who visit Him more precious, all the Saints have experienced that there is no more infallible means of soon obtaining a great love of Jesus Christ, than frequently to visit Him in the Churches, particularly at certain hours of the day when He is so little honoured and so rarely visited. In the third part will be found the manner of making these visits, and the reason is explained why those who make them often derive so little profit from them. We will here only observe, that when we make them in such a manner as if we really believed that it is Jesus Christ Whom we are visiting, they are an infallible means of obtaining, in a short time, a perfect love for Jesus Christ.

IV. FOURTH MEANS.—*Fidelity in accomplishing with exactness some practices of this devotion.*

The fourth means is, fidelity in accomplishing with exactness some little practices which Jesus Christ has declared to be very pleasing to Him, and well suited to honour His Sacred Heart, and inflame us, in a short time, with an ardent love of Him. These practices consist in some visits to the Blessed Sacrament, certain prayers, and some Communions, more frequent and more devout; and all this from certain motives which will be explained in the first Chapter of the Third Part.

There are some persons who, from a false idea of virtue, treat as frivolous all practices of devotion that seem to them too easy, and have little esteem for whatever does not give them an opportunity of distinguishing 'themselves. Such persons will not feel much fervour, perhaps, in regard of these practices, because they contain nothing striking or very extraordinary. They will imagine, that what every one can do, cannot be so very effectual a means of becoming what in effect few are. But, without examining here the true cause of this illusion, might we not make them the same answer which was made to Naaman, whose ideas were somewhat similar to these? Even though something very difficult were proposed to you in order to obtain so great a grace, you ought not to refuse to do it. With how much greater reason, then, ought you to try the efficacy of the means proposed to you, since it costs you so little.

It is necessary, indeed, that there should be perseverance and exactness in perfectly accomplishing what is enjoined in these little practices. This fidelity is usually what is most grateful to God and most meritorious in any devotional exercises. It is always the least suspicious sign of sincere love. It would be much better to do less and to be more constant. Our good works are perfect in proportion as they are less accompanied by self-will. Now, those who continually change their practices of devotion, or the time of these practices, are certainly persons who act only by the movement of their own will. For what other motive can they have in making these changes?

In perseverance, then, properly consists that generous fidelity which is the most certain proof of a great love for Jesus Christ. If we consider seriously what we do for God, we shall see, that however great may be our labour, we do but very little. In another sense, however, it may be truly said, that it is no little matter to persevere steadily, without taking notice of the disposition we happen to be in, or of our feelings at the time, or of numberless other specious pretexts which present themselves every day, and which our natural inconsistency represents to us as lawful reasons for changing, or at least interrupting, our practices of devotion. To be always constant, whether we be sad or joyous, in tranquillity or fatigued, in peace or in a tumult, and to fulfil steadily for Jesus Christ certain obligations which the love and gratitude we wish to show Him impose on us, is to be truly faithful to Him, and to have a true love for Jesus Christ.

V. FIFTH MEANS.—*A tender devotion towards the Blessed Virgin.*

The fifth means for gaining quickly an ardent love for Jesus Christ is to have a tender devotion to the Blessed Virgin, who has so absolute a power over the Sacred Heart of her Son. It cannot be doubted but that the Blessed Virgin is of all creatures the one who has had the greatest love for Jesus Christ, has been most loved by Him, and has had also the most ardent desire that He should be perfectly loved. She is the Mother of perfect love: "*Mater pulchræ dilectionis.*" To her we must have recourse, if we would be inflamed with it. The Sacred Hearts of Jesus and Mary are too much alike, and too closely united, for it to be possible that we should have an entrance into one and not gain an entrance into the other; with this difference, however, that the Heart of Jesus admits only souls of the greatest purity, whereas the Heart of Mary purifies such as are not so by the graces which she obtains for them, and makes them fit to be received into the Heart of Jesus.

Though all the other means of acquiring an ardent love of Jesus Christ are easy and efficacious, this appears the easiest for many. Few have all the dispositions necessary for being inflamed with divine love. But there are few who cannot very easily obtain them by means of the Blessed Virgin. Sinners even ought not to despair. Mary is the hope of sinners; Mary is the refuge of all the miserable (St. Aug. serm. xviii. on the Saints; St. Ephraim, Praises of the B.V.); she is the bulwark of help for all. Jesus Christ easily grants to her what we are unworthy to receive—" Quia indignus eras cui donaret," says St. Bernard (Serm. iii., Vig. of Nativity), " datum est Mariæ ut per illam acciperes quidquid haberes." He has established her as the dispensatrix of His graces, and has resolved to grant none that should not pass through her hands: " Nihil nos Deus habere voluit, quod per manus Mariæ non transiret." Let us have a tender love for the Mother, and we shall soon be inflamed with an ardent love for the Son. It is a mark that we do not desire the love of the Son, when we do not feel a great tenderness for the Mother. Without this great tenderness for the Blessed Virgin, we can never hope to have an entrance into the Sacred Heart of Jesus Christ. It has been observed that there has never been any one, who felt only indifference for the Blessed Virgin, who had not at the same time an aversion for Jesus Christ. Indeed, it is from the aversion such persons have for Jesus Christ, that their indifference and aversion for the Blessed Virgin arises. "*Qui me odit*," said the Son of God, "*et Patrem meum odit; he that hateth Me, hateth My Father also.*" For the same reason it may be said, that there never was a heretic in the world that was not an enemy of the Blessed Virgin, because there has never been one that has not hated Jesus Christ. All the works composed by them tend no less to extinguish the love of the Mother than that of the Son. There has never been one of these secret enemies of Jesus Christ, occupied as they are in destroying the means most suited to make us love Him, who has inspired us with devotion towards the Blessed Virgin, or rather who has not sought, by every possible means, to extinguish in the hearts of the faithful so just and so solid a devotion.

This has been remarked by one of the most zealous and distinguished prelates of these times, the illustrious Archbishop of Malines, in his admirable Pastoral Letter, on which Pope Innocent XII. has pronounced so high an eulogium, in the Brief which he wrote to this Prelate. This Pastoral Letter is full of the spirit and zeal which animated St. Charles Borromeo and St. Francis of Sales. It will rank as a masterpiece of this style of writing, whether we consider the beautiful instructions it contains, the sound morality which pervades it, or the solidity of the doctrine which it inculcates. Let us hear in what terms this great Prelate expresses himself, regarding the false zeal of those who, so far from urging all the faithful to devotion towards the Blessed Virgin, seem even to do all in their power to discredit it.

"It scandalizes Catholics," he says, "in the highest degree, to perceive that discredit is covertly thrown upon the devotion which they have imbibed with their mother's milk, and which has been so frequently and so earnestly recommended to them by those who have had the care of their instruction. It scandalizes them to see that images are no longer valued; that pilgrimages of devotion are made a jest of, and that the insipid and unchristian jests of Erasmus are used for this purpose; that in private conversations, and even in anonymous libels, the Sodalities instituted in honour of the Blessed Virgin are decried, whilst all who are faithful to the pious and holy practices of their forefathers are taking up their defence, and desire that they should be again now, as in the time of their ancestors, the mark by which a Catholic is recognized and distinguished from a heretic."

And elsewhere, " We recommend earnestly to all," he says, " devotion towards the Blessed Virgin. We desire that you employ your efforts to increase this devotion and make it flourish more and more amongst the Faithful; that her pictures be visited with devotion, especially those at which miracles are wrought; that they be carried in procession, as is customary; that wax candles be lighted, Hymns and Litanies sung, and devotions performed before her statues; that congregations and confraternities erected in her honour be spoken of with respect, as also the privileges and immunities granted by the Pontiffs to them; that those who are not yet admitted be invited to join them; that they be instituted in places where they do not exist, and re-established where they have been abolished; that it be known, that to injure any one of these objects is to wound us most deeply; how much more to censure or destroy them.

" We inherit from our ancestors these tender sentiments of piety towards the Blessed Virgin. In spite of the rage of the heretics who surround us, we have happily preserved them. I desire with all my heart, that they should strike root more and more deeply in the hearts of the faithful. We feel urged to this by the advice and example of many holy personages, whom it is not necessary to particularize here. We may say, that all who have distinguished themselves in past ages by extraordinary sanctity, have given, in their lives, manifest marks of this devotion towards the Blessed Virgin.

" Nor need we in this matter give ear to the vain scruples of heretics, and other enemies of Mary's honour, who pretend that the respect shown to the Mother wounds the rights of the Son. The faithful are not so ill-instructed, as not to know what they owe to the Son, and that it is only in consideration of Him that honour is shown to the Mother. . . . . All agree, that it is for the love of the Son that we honour the Mother, or rather, that in the Mother we honour the Son, who, on His part, will visit with rigorous vengeance all that wounds the honour of His Mother. The Saints often tell us this, and the deplorable fall of some Christians clearly proves it to us. No sooner does a Christian relax in devotion towards the Mother, than devotion towards the Son insensibly decays, and becomes at last wholly extinct.

" The zeal of St. Charles Borromeo in extending the devotion to the Blessed Virgin, the decrees he has made in her honour, are seen in the various Councils held by his care and authority at Milan. For there is hardly one, in which this virtuous Prelate does not manifestly show by words, and solid and lasting monuments, his ardent affection towards the Queen of Heaven.

" The works of the holy Bishop of Geneva are full of the same sentiments; and his life is replete with actions that attest the same devotion. He glories, in one place, that he belongs, as did almost the whole city, to the Confraternity of the Holy Rosary. I say nothing of St. Anselm, of St. Bernard, of St. Norbert. Let Pastors take these Saints as their models, and propose them to their flocks as excellent examples for imitation. . . . . "

It is rare indeed to meet with persons wanting in tenderness for the Blessed Virgin, and in an inclination towards that love which we should have for Mary, and that singular veneration which we owe her. We may say, that devotion to the Blessed Virgin Mary is universal in our days. It is certain that devotion to the

Mother will never be disparaged, but by the enemies of her Son. As for us, who desire to love her Son most ardently, we will neglect nothing that will help us to love the Mother tenderly; and let us be convinced that it is only by means of the Mother that we can find easy access to Jesus Christ, and be received into His Sacred Heart.

For the same reason, we ought also to have a special devotion towards the Holy Family—St. Joseph, St. Anne, and St. Joachim. For, as they loved Jesus Christ more ardently and more tenderly than others, they may be of greater use to us, in obtaining for us this love of tenderness, and procuring for us an entrance into that Sacred Heart, over which they exercise so great an authority.

VI. SIXTH MEANS.—*A special devotion to St. Aloysius Gonzaga.*

The sixth means that we propose, and which Almighty God has already shown, by evident marks, to be most useful in obtaining a tender love for our Lord Jesus Christ, is devotion to St. Aloysius Gonzaga, of the Society of Jesus; more illustrious still for his innocence and the sublime perfection of his life, than for the conspicuous position which his rank in the world had given him.

It is certain, that in heaven the Saints interest themselves greatly, for all those who love and specially honour them on earth. The most ordinary grace which they obtain for them, is the virtue in which they themselves have excelled, and which was in some degree their characteristic. This is what our Saint used to say, as was found written after his death :—" As men on earth are naturally more inclined to oblige those who have the same inclinations with themselves, so, in Heaven, the Blessed, who have excelled in some particular virtue, are pleased to employ their credit with

God, in favour of those who have a particular attraction for the same virtue, and who labour in earnest to acquire it. . . . ."

Now, as the devotion to the Sacred Heart of Jesus, in the exercise of an interior life, and continual union with God, was the distinguishing characteristic of St. Aloysius Gonzaga, it cannot be doubted but that he interests himself in a particular manner for those who have this devotion greatly at heart. Many persons have happily experienced the powerful effects of his intercession in this point. It might be said, that no one can be truly devout to him, without feeling at once a real tenderness for Jesus Christ. Devotion to him inspires a high esteem and love for the interior life. There seem to be few Saints whom we can propose more universally than St. Aloysius, to all sorts of persons, as a model for attaining easily, in the exercise of an ordinary life, solid and exalted virtue. To judge of his actions, we find nothing, so far as the exterior is concerned, extraordinary in his life. He died young, and never held any high office. Nor did he distinguish himself by any wonderful actions, but, on the contrary, he was extremely careful to remain hidden. Nevertheless, the sublime degree of glory to which he is raised, can be nothing but the reward of great merit ; and this great merit can only be the fruit of extreme purity of heart, an interior life, living continually in the presence of God, a most tender and ardent love of Jesus Christ—in fine, of a consummate perfection, which he acquired in a few years, by the excessive love and tender devotion which he always had towards Jesus Christ in the most Blessed Sacrament. Nor was it without a special providence of God, that this faithful servant of Jesus Christ died as he had predicted and desired, on the day which is appointed for the Feast of the Sacred Heart, to which he had always been so devout. It was in this adorable Heart, so to speak, that he received, from his childhood, the grace of most sublime contemplation, and a continual gift of tears. So abundant were these tears, especially at Mass, immediately after the Consecration, that his garments were all wet with them. From the same source sprung the extreme tranquillity of heart, which he preserved unaltered amidst all the events and all the occupations of his life. Finally, from this Sacred Heart, says the historian of his life, his soul was filled with such ardour and such sweet consolation, that his countenance appeared all on fire, and his heart palpitated so excessively, that it seemed as if it would burst from its place. Here he united himself so intimately with God, that, when he was obliged for any reason to distract himself from this union, his heart felt a pain like that which is felt when a limb of the body is dislocated, as he himself attested. "I do not know how it is," he would sometimes say, "I am forbidden to apply my mind to God, lest this application should injure my head. But the effort I make not to apply, does me more harm than the application itself. For it has become a habit with me, and I find it no longer a labour, but sweetness and repose. I will, however, try to obey in the best manner I can." But, to form some idea of the sublime degree of glory which he enjoys in Heaven, and which we may consider to be the fruit of his interior life, and of his most ardent and tender love for the adorable Heart of Jesus Christ, it is enough to read what St. Mary Magdalen of Pazzi has said of it. Hear what is related by the author of the life of this Saint.

"In the year 1600, on the 4th of April, the Saint, being in one of her accustomed raptures, saw in Heaven the glory of St. Aloysius Gonzaga, of the Society of Jesus, and surprised at the extraordinary sight, she began to speak, pausing between her words from time to time. 'O how great is the glory of Aloysius, the son of Ignatius! I could never have believed it, if our Lord had not shown it to me. It seems to me that there can be no glory in Heaven like that of Aloysius. I say it again, Aloysius is a great Saint. We have many Saints in the Church, whom I do not believe to be as exalted. Would that I could go over the whole world, to say that Aloysius, son of Ignatius, is a great Saint; and would that I could show the glory he enjoys, that God Himself might be glorified thereby. He is raised to this high degree of glory, because he led an interior life. Who can express the price and value of an interior life? There is no comparison between the interior and the exterior. All the time Aloysius was upon earth, he had his eyes fixed on the Divine Word. Aloysius was a hidden martyr. For whoever knows Thee, oh my God, knows Thee to be so great and so amiable, that it is a great martyrdom to see that he does not love Thee, and that Thou art so far from being loved by creatures, that Thou art even offended by them. He was also a Martyr, because he knew well how to suffer. Oh how Aloysius loved upon earth! It is for this that he now enjoys God in Heaven with so great a plenitude of love. Whilst he was in this mortal life, he continually shot forth darts of love into the Heart of the Eternal Word. Now that he is in Heaven, these darts return into his own heart, and remain fixed there; for the acts of love and charity, which he then made, caused him extreme delight.'" Such are the Saint's own words.

It is easy to recognize in this description, the exact portrait of one, truly and perfectly devout to the Sacred Heart of Jesus Christ. Those who sincerely desire to become so, and to obtain a love of tenderness for Jesus Christ, and the gift of an interior life, and of living continually in the presence of God, should have a tender devotion to this great Saint. He will make them soon feel the sweet effects of his intercession with

Jesus and Mary, whom he loved with so much ardour and tenderness, and by Whom he was so tenderly loved.

On this account the Nuns of the Convent of the Angels at Florence, besides a daily devotion to this great Saint, celebrate his feast annually in their Convent, in the most solemn manner, to obtain by his intercession this interior recollection, continual union with God, most ardent and tender love of Jesus Christ, and perfect devotion to His Sacred Heart.

VII.—A Day of Retreat every Month.

The seventh and last means for acquiring and preserving this ardent love of Jesus Christ is so useful and necessary, that we may say that without it, all the others which have been proposed are but of little avail. However sincere may be our will to have an ardent love for Jesus Christ, we require to renew from time to time the reflections from which it took its rise. There is not a more suitable means for renewing, from time to time, these salutary reflections, and with them the fervour that is their ordinary fruit, than by making a day's Retreat every month. For this purpose it is not necessary that we should seek solitude elsewhere than in our own house. We may even make this retreat without interrupting our ordinary business, or omitting the smallest obligations of our state. All that is required is that we withdraw ourselves, for a day, from some kind of amusement, from some unnecessary visit, in order to examine whether we have relaxed in the practice of virtue, whether we fulfil with punctuality the least duties of our state, whether we have more love and gratitude towards Jesus Christ, whether we make any progress in virtue, and what fruit we draw from the use of the Sacraments.

The manner of making this Retreat will be found in the book we have referred to above. Meditations for each month on the most important truths of faith are given there at length, with the considerations that may be made each day. It seems to me there cannot be a more effectual means for continually advancing in virtue. One day in the month is all that is required. We are at liberty to choose whatever day is most convenient. We must indeed have but little love for Jesus Christ, if we refuse to consecrate to Him at least one day in each month.

END OF THE SECOND PART.

THIRD PART.—PRACTICE.

Chapter I.

What are the motives and sentiments with which we should practise this devotion.

As the sanctity and merit of our actions depends on the motive and spirit with which they are actuated, the practice of the devotion to the Sacred Heart of Jesus, however holy, would be of little use, unless it were animated with the spirit and the motive which gives it all its value. This motive, as we have said, is to repair, as far as possible, by our love, our adoration, and by every kind of homage the indignities and outrages which Jesus Christ has endured, and still daily endures, in the most blessed Sacrament. It is in this spirit, and in these sentiments, the devotion should be practised.

But as it may not always be convenient to read over what has been said on this subject, in various parts of this book, and as it is not always easy to remember what we have read, I have thought it well to recapitulate in the beginning of this part, the principal reflections which may help to inspire us with this spirit and these sentiments. We shall perhaps be obliged to repeat much that we have said before, but I have thought it well to make these repetitions in order to render the practice of the devotion more useful and convenient.

To enter, then, into the sentiments with which we should practise this devotion, we have only to consider seriously and attentively, in what manner Jesus Christ

treats us in the adorable Eucharist, and how He is
treated. Let us represent to ourselves the eagerness
with which He offers us this heavenly food, and the
disgust with which we receive it. If His love is unbounded, the ingratitude with which men receive this,
the greatest proof of His love, can go no further. Had
it been left to our choice to ask of Jesus Christ the
greatest proof He could give of His love for us, could
we ever have imagined to ourselves anything so wondrous? Had it even entered our minds, should we
ever have had the boldness to ask or hope for it?

And yet this wonder has been wrought. It is this
means which Jesus Christ has chosen for proving to us
the excess of His love. After having done all, and given
everything, to show us to what a degree He loves us,
He gives us His own Body and Blood. He gives Himself in the most blessed Sacrament of the Altar. If
He had possessed anything better or more precious, He
would have given it to us. No place keeps Him aloof;
no person, however wretched he may be, disgusts Him;
no time obliges Him to delay. And yet so marvellous
a condescension, so wonderful a love, which has astonished the universe, has not been able to secure Him
from the ingratitude and outrages of mankind. The
first Communion of all was dishonoured by the most
horrible sacrilege. This has been succeeded by all the
outrages and profanations that hell has been able to
invent. All respect for Jesus Christ upon our Altars
has been lost. He has there been treated as a mock
king, and a false divinity. Churches in which He had
deigned to remain continually for the love of man have
been plundered, demolished, and burnt. The Altars, on
which He daily immolates Himself for mankind, have
been destroyed. The sacred vessels, which had been so
often used in the awful sacrifice of the Mass, have been
broken, melted, and profaned. Nay, even His Sacred
Body, in the consecrated Host, has been dragged along

I

the ground and trampled under foot. And, what might horrify the very devils themselves, monsters, worse than demons, have pierced these sacred Hosts with repeated blows. The miraculous Blood, which has often been seen to flow from them, has served only to increase their fury and impiety. They have cut them in pieces, thrown them into the flames, and as if their sacrilegious hands and detestable hearts were not sufficiently impure, they have thrown them to the most unclean animals. In a word, they have put them to such execrable uses, that Thou alone, oh my God, couldst have endured it. The very thought fills the soul with horror. This is what the love of Jesus Christ has exposed Him to. This is the gratitude of men for so wondrous a gift. There is no one, however abject, who would not have been treated with less contempt. There is no criminal who would not have met with less insult, and for whom the most lively compassion would not have been felt, had he been so ill-treated. Is Jesus Christ then to be the only one who is to be outraged without awakening any compassion in us? Has He done us any wrong in loving us to this excess? If it be a crime, pardon me the expression, O my God! if it be a crime to have loved us too much, then is Jesus Christ guilty. But should this excess of love excite hatred in those who will not believe how much He loves us? Are we to take occasion from hence to forget Him, to show no respect in His presence, and to have no feeling for the injuries done Him? It is true that the greater part of these horrible sacrileges are the effect of the rage of heretics. But, oh my Saviour, how many Catholics are there who treat Thee no less ill? The abomination penetrates even into the sanctuary. It is difficult to say which is the most guilty of impiety and ingratitude, the heretic who profanes the temples in which he does not believe Jesus Christ to be really present, or the Catholic who, whilst he professes to believe it, presents himself before Jesus Christ with so little respect.

Some talk of news or of business even at the very foot of the Altar. Nay, we must confess it, oh my God, even abominable and impious conversations are held there. Many show a greater respect in the presence of well-bred persons than they do in the presence of Jesus Christ. What would not be tolerated in children at home, is allowed them in the Church. The apparel of our Altars is not always as clean and costly as the dress of many Catholics. Many Churches, owing to the negligence of those who have charge of them, are less cleanly than the commonest apartments of an ordinary dwelling-house. Some assist at Mass as if they were at the theatre. Many are more attentive and less restless during a play than they are at the celebration of the sacred mysteries. After touching the ground with one knee, and doing just enough to show that they are not disrespectful through inadvertence, or from want of faith, they sit, stand up, or talk. Such is the homage, the love and gratitude that Jesus Christ receives in return from the very many of the faithful!

Priests are raised by their sublime dignity above the rest of men. They are obliged by their condition and their ministry to approach more closely and more frequently to Jesus Christ, and they are loved in a special manner by Him. But can it be said that all Priests love Jesus Christ, and that, though elevated by their character above the very Angels themselves, they are as grateful as they should be? Does their life correspond with the sublime perfection of their state? Jesus Christ has distinguished them, in His mercy, from the rest of the faithful. But do they distinguish themselves from other Christians by their virtues, and especially by their lively faith? Alas, one would say, to see some Priests at the Altar, that the Body of Jesus Christ, which they hold in their hands, is some mere instrument which they are using to perform some trivial ceremonies. As they often feel nothing but indifference for Jesus Christ, the time which they employ in offering this august sacrifice is often very short. They pass from some profane occupation to the Altar, and often from the Altar to amusements and profane employments. Mass would seem to be some task which they learn to go through boldly, without thinking of it, and as it were from habit, by dint of going through it repeatedly. They hold the Body of Jesus Christ in their hands with as little feeling as they hold the Missal. This negligence, coldness, and insensibility show too plainly the little esteem they entertain for this adorable Body, or at least the incomprehensible blindness in which they live. If from our Lord's ministers we pass to the rest of the faithful, and cast a glance on the majority of Christians, we shall have no less reason to deplore our ingratitude and want of faith. There are, it is true, some who communicate frequently. But how few are the true servants of Jesus Christ who are to be found amongst them? Not to speak of the little fruit they gain from Communion (a sure sign of the bad disposition in which they communicate), it is impossible to think of the little devotion with which they receive Jesus Christ without a deep feeling of indignation. We may add also to the insults offered to Jesus Christ by those who have so little love for Him, the indifference and forgetfulness of those who make a profession of loving Him. There is no visit paid with more weariness and less eagerness than the Visits which are paid to Jesus Christ in the adorable Sacrament. It is enough that the Holy Ghost invites us to them by His inspirations to make us at once find numberless excuses for exempting ourselves from them. If we are obliged by our state to make them more frequently, do we not on this account accustom ourselves to perform them with less respect? We have only to observe the manner in which some enter the Church. They enter it as if it were a room. They present themselves before the Blessed Sacrament as if it were merely an image. Their want of modesty and respect, their eyes glancing in every direction, show that the visit to the Blessed Sacrament, with the greater number, is little else but affectation. They make it with little respect, because they make it with little faith. These two defects destroy all the fruit.

Thus it is, oh Lord, that the greatest of all Thy benefits is repaid! This is our gratitude! We should treat Jesus Christ better if He had loved us less! Had He retained in the Blessed Sacrament that air of majesty which renders Him terrible even to the devils, were He to chastise on the spot those who insult His Divine Majesty, He would, without doubt, be more respected and feared. But Jesus Christ cannot resolve upon this. He prefers to expose Himself to the insults of the wicked, and suffer everything, rather than keep a single one of His children at a distance, by pardoning nothing. He prefers, so to speak, the outrages which He endures from the first to the want of confidence which the terror of His chastisements would create in the last. This very excess of goodness, which should of itself gain for Him the love and respect of all, exposes Him daily to fresh insults, and is the reason why He meets with less love.

What can awaken our feelings if this does not? We feel for a stranger whom we see cruelly treated; we compassionate any poor wretch whom we see abused. Shall Jesus Christ be the only one to Whose sufferings we are insensible? Shall we look with indifference only on Jesus Christ, despised, outraged, ill-treated by all in the Blessed Sacrament? There is no outrage which He has not received, no injury which He has not suffered; there is not a spot in the world where due respect is paid Him. And all this because He has loved us too much. It is plain that He has loved us to excess. How is it that this very excess of love freezes the hearts of those for whom He has such love? Indeed, if we have any feeling of humanity left, can we reflect on the derision He meets with from so many wicked and ungrateful men, in which number, perhaps, we ourselves are; can we look on Jesus Christ, so neglected, so little loved, so unworthily treated, without feeling our hearts pierced with grief? Can we be contented with mere ordinary feelings of gratitude? Can we fail to do all we can to repair these injuries by our profound adoration, our love and homage? It is true the Church has instituted for this end one of the most solemn festivals, in which Jesus Christ is borne in triumph with great pomp, in order to make Him a reparation of honour for the many injuries He has received in the adorable Eucharist. But does not this very feast, through the disrespect and irreverence committed throughout the Octave in the presence of the Blessed Sacrament, become an occasion of new insults to Jesus Christ? It is on this account that our loving Saviour has chosen the Friday after the Octave as a second special feast, on which His Sacred Heart may be truly adored by His perfect friends. The first is the feast of His precious Body; the second the feast of His Sacred Heart. His love for us triumphs in the first; our love for Him should triumph in the second. In the first the Church solemnly exhibits to us the excess of the love of Jesus Christ for us; in the second we should protest, before Heaven and earth, how sincerely we love Jesus Christ.

With this view, all who have any feeling of love for Jesus Christ should celebrate solemnly, and with great care, the Feast of the Sacred Heart of Jesus. In it He desires to distinguish, as it were, His dearest friends, who love Him with a generous, grateful, and tender love, from those who love Him only coldly and in appearance. He desires that, full of grief for the unworthy treatment He has received in the Blessed Sacrament, and sorrowing at the sight of so much ingratitude, they should make Him a reparation of honour, an acknowledgment of the love He has shown us, and an attestation of their own, by making some return, and consecrating the whole of this day in honour of the Sacred Heart. These are the sentiments that should animate us in all the practices of this devotion. We should occupy ourselves with them more particularly during the visits we pay to the Blessed Sacrament, in time of Mass, and at Holy Communion. We have already shown, in another part of this work, what is the spirit in which these holy actions should be performed. But, as they are singularly adapted, of all exercises of piety, for honouring the Sacred Heart of Jesus Christ, and inflaming our hearts with His holy love, it has been thought well to speak of them a little more at length here, in the hope that hereby they may be practised with greater fervour. We will afterwards treat of them separately, distributed according to the different times of the year, together with meditations adapted to this devotion.

Chapter II.

Visits to the Blessed Sacrament.

I. *Motives that should induce us to visit the Blessed Sacrament.*

Before the coming of our Saviour, in that period of rigour when Almighty God would be called the avenging God, the strong God, the God of armies; when He only spoke, as it were, in a voice of thunder; when princes and sovereigns alone were permitted to enter the holy place specially consecrated to Him; when He exacted so respectful a worship, and punished so severely the slightest faults committed against the respect due to Him ; when kings and priests, overcome by holy fear, hardly dared to enter the Temple on beholding a simple cloud, which was only a somewhat more sensible sign of God's presence in that place ; when this prodigy obliged the people to prostrate themselves and cry out, full of admiration, and with the deepest feelings of gratitude : " How good is the God, Whom we adore ! we will sing His mercies for ever, because He has deigned to choose Himself a dwelling amongst us : " if at that time what we have since witnessed could have been more clearly foreseen, if they had been told that this God, so terrible, would humble Himself so far as to become man for the love of men, and that, after dying for these very men, He would continually work one of the greatest miracles, in order to be with them even to the end of ages, would they have believed it?

There is, however, something which would have appeared more incredible to them still. Would they ever have believed, that after Almighty God had humbled Himself in this manner, mankind would refuse to love Him, pay court to Him, and visit Him ? And yet this is what has happened. There are Christians, and those not a few, who consider it a trouble to pay this respect to Jesus Christ. And would not the disrespectful manner of the greater number of those who visit Him give us reason to ask the same question as our Saviour once asked : *The Son of Man, when He cometh, shall He find, think you, faith on earth ?* (Luke xviii. 8.)

If this faith is not extinct, is it not more extraordinary to believe the real presence of Jesus Christ on our Altars, and to have no other feeling for Him than indifference, and to be no more eager to pay Him our homage than those who do not believe in His presence ? Civility, friendship, gratitude, and interest are usually the motives that induce mankind to pay visits. We cannot with propriety exempt ourselves from honouring a person distinguished for his merit, his employment, or his rank. Great friends part with regret, and allow few occasions of seeing one another to escape. We make at least some visits of civility to persons from whom we have received some service, and we are assiduous in our attendance upon those from whom we expect some benefit, or we fear some chastisement.

Does not Jesus Christ hold a sufficiently distinguished place in the world to merit that court should be paid Him? Has Jesus Christ loved us much? Have we received any benefit from Him? Have we reason to expect that He will do us any service? Since He will be our Judge, and since our eternal felicity or misery depends upon Him, have we any interest in gaining His favour? It is extraordinary that on this subject all agree on what ought to be done, and yet no one takes the trouble to do what he ought.

If it had been left to our choice to ask our divine Saviour for some manifest proof of His love for us, would it ever have occurred to us to entreat Him, when He was about to ascend into Heaven, to remain on earth with us to the end of ages? If He Himself had made this offer, with what sentiments of admiration, respect, and gratitude should we not have accepted it? Jesus Christ has granted us this signal favour. The excess of His love has led Him to give us this manifest proof of His tenderness. But His excessive love has only served, we may say, to make us carry our ingratitude to the highest pitch. What would be said of any one who rarely visited, and merely saluted in passing, a person of the highest rank and worth, who had come solely for the purpose of rendering him some service, and was residing for a long time in some foreign country, merely out of regard for him?

What is the motive which induced Jesus Christ to remain with us, after the work of our Redemption was accomplished? After He had ascended to His Father, why would He return invisibly on earth? Why does He remain, day and night, in an obscure and humble guise upon our Altars, except that He cannot, as it were, separate Himself from mankind, and that His delight is to be with them? Be not afflicted, my children, He says to us, I will not leave you orphans. I am ascending to Heaven, but at the same time I remain on earth. You are weak, sick, and languishing. You will be often afflicted. You will fear the anger and the justice of My Father. But you will find in Me, in the Blessed Sacrament, a Father who will console you, a Physician who will heal you, a Guide who will conduct you, a Master who will solve all your doubts, a Heavenly Food which will give you new strength, and finally, your Redeemer and your Saviour. Will not this be enough to move mankind, who have so much feeling for their own interests, and are naturally so strongly inclined to gratitude? To any other person we should be less ungrateful, even though it were for smaller favours. But when it is to Jesus Christ that gratitude is to be shown, ingratitude ceases to be a crime.

We abandon and forget Jesus Christ upon our Altars. We can always spend many hours of the day in idleness and in vain amusements. But if we have to find some time in the afternoon to visit Jesus Christ in the Blessed Sacrament, our employments will not admit of it; we have no time. Is it then so very difficult to perform this duty, though it is, as all allow, so just and reasonable? Does it require so much time? No: a quarter, or half a quarter of an hour, is enough. Very often we have only to take a few steps. But our want of love for Jesus Christ makes this visit difficult and inconvenient. We at once find a hundred false reasons, a hundred obstacles, which in any other case would have no weight with us, but which hold us back when we have something to do for Jesus Christ. Instances are recorded of newly-converted Christians among the savages in Canada, in the Indies and Japan, who have travelled 200 leagues to some Church, in order there to adore Jesus Christ. Others, who could not undertake so long a journey, prostrated themselves more than a hundred times a day in the direction in which they knew there was a Church. They would thus fain satisfy, by their repeated adorations, their desire of assiduously paying their court to Jesus Christ. In the day of judgment what answer will so many negligent Christians be able to make, who have only to take a step, as it were, to adore Jesus Christ, and yet repeatedly pass by the spot where Jesus Christ resides, and allow whole days to elapse without visiting Him? What answer will so many religious persons be able to make who, having Jesus Christ in their own house, care so little about visiting Him? *Populus vero meus oblitus est mei* (Jerem. ii. 32). Those who profess to be wholly consecrated to My service, and whom I regard as My special people, even they have forgotten Me.

Medius vestrum stetit, quem vos nescitis (Joan. i. 26). We know Him not, nor do we desire to know Him, though day and night He is in the midst of us. He is our Lord and our God, Who is on our Altars expressly to hear our prayers, and to receive our homage. Are we sad, afflicted, or unhappy? Let us have recourse to Jesus Christ. Let us go and lay before Him, as our good Father, the misfortunes that have happened to us, or that threaten us. Do we find it difficult to make some resolution? would we see peace restored in the bosom of some family? is there some one whose conversion we have at heart? are we tepid, inconstant, imperfect in God's service? Let us run to Jesus Christ, let us ask Him for these graces with simplicity, with a humble and respectful familiarity, but above all with great confidence. Let us seek, let us knock, let us ask even with importunity. It is this importunity, this confidence that gains the Heart of Jesus Christ. It is all powerful. Jesus Christ often defers granting our request merely to oblige us to visit Him more frequently.

What a loss it is for Christians to neglect so easy and powerful a means of becoming happy and holy! What remorse will so many religious persons feel at the hour of death, who now feel this loss so little? They need not be surprised that they feel so little devotion, that they go on creeping day after day in the path of piety, that they do not receive consolation or interior sweetness, that they live in uneasiness and melancholy, and that at last they die in remorse and fear. Our neglect in not frequently visiting Jesus Christ in the Blessed Sacrament, our dissipation of mind, our want of modesty and respect when we make these visits, are the most ordinary source of the greater part of our misfortunes.

Those, on the contrary, who are faithful in visiting the Blessed Sacrament as often as they can, know by their own experience, that there is no more easy or certain means for obtaining all they ask for from Jesus Christ. They know that if they only visit Him with faithful assiduity and respectful confidence, especially at certain hours of the day when few visit Him, there is scarcely any grace that they do not receive, but most especially true devotion, and a tender love of Jesus Christ. *Venite ad me omnes qui laboratis, et onerati estis, et Ego reficiam vos. Come to Me all you that labour and are burdened, and I will refresh you* (St. Matt. xi. 28).

II. *Method of Visiting the Blessed Sacrament.*

If our visits to the Blessed Sacrament should be frequent, they should not, on that account, be less respectful. We should never enter the Church but with the greatest modesty. We should keep ourselves, whilst there, in profound respect, full of sentiments, of gratitude, confidence, and love. To make a place holy, it is enough that it is destined to honour Almighty God. From the moment of its solemn consecration to this purpose it becomes an object of reverence to the Angels, and of terror to the devils. It is only just that the majesty of God, with which it is then in a special manner filled, and the presence of Jesus Christ who dwells therein, should render it still more an object of holy awe to men, and in a special manner to Christians.

All the sanctity that the birth of Christ communicated to the stable of Bethlehem, His precious Blood to Calvary, and His Sacred Body to the Sepulchre, we find in our Churches. If, on our entering them, and approaching the Altar, we do not experience that holy fear which is felt in drawing near the holiest spots, and are not moved by those feelings which cause such sweet tears of piety to flow at the sight of the manger where Christ was born, or the place where He expired, it can proceed from nothing but a want of faith or a want of reflection.

We shall remedy this evil if, before entering the Church, we reflect awhile on the sanctity of the place and the majesty of Him Whom we are going to visit. If it were as easy to gain an entrance into the palaces of the great, and to approach their persons, as it is to enter our Churches, how many would think themselves happy, who now think nothing of the happiness they can enjoy so easily, in approaching the adorable Person of Jesus Christ at any hour.

Modesty, then, and profound respect, impressed on our demeanour as often as we enter a Church, are the visible signs of our faith. Love towards Jesus Christ must be, as it were, the soul of our prayers. We must never omit to honour and to adore, in a particular manner, the Sacred Heart of Jesus, whenever we visit the Blessed Sacrament. It is a devotion highly pleasing to Him, and it will be most profitable to those who practise it. It is generally better, when we are before Jesus Christ, to speak little and meditate much. An affectionate silence, which is, as it were, the language of the heart, pleases Jesus Christ much more than a great number of vocal prayers, said with haste, and commonly without attention. The excessive love of Jesus Christ for us, His goodness, His meekness, His liberality, and His patience in this adorable mystery, ought to excite in us the tenderest affections. We should be filled with respect, gratitude, confidence and love of Jesus Christ. We should go to visit Jesus Christ as the angels, the shepherds, and the kings visited Him at His birth; and, like them, adore Him; or like the Apostles, hear Him preach; or like Magdalen, prostrate at His feet, deplore our sins, or contemplate His adorable perfections; or finally, like sick persons, beg to be healed of our infirmities. One of the reasons why we derive so little profit from these visits is, that we do not go to Jesus Christ with the simplicity and confidence He requires. We pass the whole time in some practices of devotion in which the mind has more share than the heart, instead of simply laying open our wants, infirmities, and weaknesses to Jesus Christ; as the Psalmist says, *pouring out our hearts before Him*, in the language of the Prophet: *Effundite coram illo corda vestra* (Ps. lxi. 9); saying to Him with the sisters of Lazarus: *Ecce, quem amas infirmatur* (Joan. xi. 3). *Lord, behold he whom Thou lovest is sick*, he for whom Thou hast become man, for whom Thou hast given Thy Blood, to whom Thou givest Thyself every day in the adorable Eucharist, and for the love of whom Thou remainest continually on this Altar, he has long laboured under such and such an infirmity; he wants this or that help or grace. *Ecce quem amas infirmatur*, or with the leper: *Domine, si vis, potes me mundare: Lord, if Thou wilt, Thou canst make me clean* (St. Luke v. 12). Why shouldst Thou not will it? After all Thou hast done for me, and after all that Thou still dost in my favour, can I doubt that Thou willest it? And if Thou willest it, who shall have power to hinder it? At other times, let us imagine to ourselves that, like Magdalen, we are at the feet of Jesus Christ. If we do not feel devotion enough to shed as many tears as she did, still let us, like her, remain in silence. Or, if we speak, let it be to express, with St. Thomas, the sentiments of admiration, respect, and love which should reign in our hearts: *Dominus meus, et Deus meus: my Lord and my God* (St. John xx. 28); repeating often with the Centurion: *Credo, Domine, adjuva incredulitatem meam: I do believe, Lord; help my unbelief* (St. Mark ix. 23). We must also, like the Cananean woman, ask our Divine Lord, with earnestness and importunity, for all the graces we stand in need of. Jesus Christ loves us tenderly. He is on our Altars only to do us good. He can and He will do it. Say, then, to Him with confidence: *Jesus, Son of David, have mercy on me* (St. Luke xviii. 38). Though He seems to reject us, and does not answer, but refuses everything, let us still persevere with fidelity, let us ask more and more earnestly; and, as if we did not perceive the harsh manner in which He seems to treat us, let us cry out more and more, *Lord, help me*. It is true, we may add, that *it is not good to take the bread of the children, and to cast it to the dogs, but the whelps also eat of the crumbs that fall from the table of their masters.* Treat me at least in the same manner. If we oblige Him by our sins not to hear our prayers, let us say to Him, with simplicity and confidence: " Thou hast solemnly engaged Thyself, oh Lord, to grant me all that I shall ask in Thy name. In Thy name I ask grace to correct myself of that imperfection which has so long kept me back in the path of piety, to overcome that ruling passion which is the source of so many defects, to acquire that virtue which is so necessary for my salvation and perfection. In Thy name I beg for the conversion of this son, the health of a husband, the successful issue of this or that business, and the assistance which is necessary in such and such necessities. Thou knowest, oh Lord, that I labour under this defect, that I possess not that virtue, that I want courage in adversity, moderation in joy, strength in certain circumstances, and great graces in all. Thou knowest that I have not a sufficiently strong faith; my confidence sometimes wavers; I love Thee but feebly, and hardly have I the desire to love Thee. Give me, then, oh Lord, give me all these graces, and let them be efficacious. Remember that Thou hast promised to refuse me nothing that I ask in Thy name. Perhaps what I ask is not pleasing to Thee, and Thou refusest me because I do not know what I ask. But there is no danger of this, nor canst Thou reproach me thus when I ask for Thy perfect love. Inflame me, oh Lord, with this ardent love, and let it be generous, constant, and faithful; a love that is rather solid than sensible and sweet, a love that may make me live for Thee alone. Give me, oh Lord, this perfect, ardent, and tender love, and I am satisfied: *Amorem tui solum cum gratia tua mihi dones, et dives sum satis.*"

It is good to consider sometimes what must be the sentiments of Jesus Christ upon the Altar on seeing Himself forgotten and abandoned by almost all. We may imagine, at the same time, that He says to us what He said to His Apostles for a similar reason: *Numquid et vos vultis abire?* (John vi. 68): *Will you also go away?* At the same time, with the tenderest sentiments of love, grief, and gratitude, we must answer with St. Peter: *Domine ad quem ibimus? verba vitæ æternæ habes* (John vi. 69): *Lord, to whom shall we go? Thou hast the words of eternal life; we have believed and known that Thou art the Christ, the Son of God.* We may also, in order to excite ourselves to greater love, and to force Jesus Christ, as it were, to embrace us with a more tender and ardent charity, represent to ourselves that He asks us from the Altar, as He once asked St. Peter: *Simon Joannis, amas me?* (John xxi. 17): *Simon, son of John, lovest thou Me?* We must reply with the same Apostle: Yes, Lord, Thou knowest well that I love Thee; or rather, my loving Saviour, Thou knowest how much I desire to love Thee.

It would be well, if we could detach ourselves from all that is not God, and often say to Him, with the Prophet, "*Quid mihi est in cælo et a te quid volui super terram? Deus cordis mei et pars mea Deus in æternum?*" (Ps. lxxii. v. 25.) *What have I in Heaven? and besides Thee, what do I desire upon earth, but Thee, my God, the God of my heart, and my portion for ever!* I know, O Lord, that Thou art the Way, the Truth, and the Life. I am convinced that All who depart from Thee, shall perish eternally! *Quia ecce qui elongant se a te, peribunt.* (Ps. lxxii. v. 27.) As for me, my loving Saviour, I find my repose, my joy, and my supreme felicity, only in being united with Thee, and in never separating myself from Thee. *Mihi autem adhærere Deo bonum est et ponere in Deo meo spem meam.* (Ps. lxxii. v. 28.) In Thee, I place all my confidence. All my consolation would be to pass the rest of my days at the foot of Thy Altars. But as I cannot be there always in person, I will always be there in spirit. My treasure is upon the Altar; my heart shall be there too. My heart shall be eternally united to Thy sacred Heart. It shall be to me in future my shelter, and the place of my rest. *Hæc requies mea, hic habitabo.* (Ps. xiii. v. 14.)

Full of these sentiments of love and confidence, we may sometimes say to Him with great simplicity, and in a respectful, yet familiar manner, "Thou art in this place, oh Lord, only to do me good. Who is there then, that shall hinder it? If my imperfections are an obstacle, begin, if it please Thee, by freeing me from these imperfections. Cure these wounds, which make me displeasing in Thy sight. I have not loved Thee, it is true. I am deeply grieved that it has been so. But at least, it seems to me that I have a true desire of loving Thee, and if this desire were not sincere, I should not so often come before Thee, who seest to the bottom of the heart, to ask for Thy love. Until I am wholly inflamed with this love, I shall never cease asking for it with earnestness, and even with importunity. *Diligam te, Domine, fortitudo mea et refugium meum.*" (Ps. xvii. v. 1.)

We may also occupy ourselves usefully at this time, in making acts of faith, adoration, thanksgiving, hope, and love, each one according to his devotion. For example: "I believe, O Lord, that Thou art really present on this Altar, and it is my wish that the modesty and respect which I desire to show in Thy presence, should be a proof of the sincerity of my faith. I render Thee thanks for having loved me to such an excess. Humbly prostrate at Thy feet, I make Thee a reparation of honour, in atonement for all the insults and outrages Thou hast endured since the institution of this august Sacrament. I hope, oh Lord, and I am certain that Thy Providence will never fail me in my necessities, and will happily lead me to the accomplishment of thy designs, by the path which Thou wilt deign to show me. Open to me, oh Lord, Thy sacred Heart; for this is the place of my repose. I wish to dwell therein all the days of my life, and there, at the hour of my death, to breathe out my last sigh." This is but an example of such acts as we may make. We can extend them as much as we please.

It is well, however, to remember the advice given by St. Francis, of Sales, on this subject, (Introd. to a Dev. Life. p. iii., ch. 13.) "Prayers of this sort, which are indeed, properly speaking, only aspirations, are most useful. But it is my opinion." says this great Saint, "that we should not force ourselves to repeat always the same words." Pronounce often, either with the heart or lips, those which love suggests to you at the time. It will always furnish you with what you want. There are, it is true, certain verses of the Psalms, and some passages of holy Scripture, which are most powerful in moving the heart. We must make use of those in which we find most devotion, and spend most time in them.

III. *Practice for spending every day, a quarter, or half an hour in prayer, before the Blessed Sacrament, suited to all sorts of persons.*

This practice of devotion is easy. For, properly speaking, it consists only in loving Jesus Christ, and in making use of Jesus Christ Himself, in order to love Him. The method is as follows:—

1. After having adored our Lord in this mystery, with all the respect that His real Presence requires, unite yourself to Him, and to all His Divine operations in the holy Eucharist, where He ceases not to love and adore God His Father in the name of all men, and in the most perfect manner which we can imagine, in the condition of a victim. Meditate and endeavour to understand His recollection, His solitude, His hidden life, that wonderful deprivation of all things to which He is reduced, His obedience to the word of the Priest, whoever he be, His humility, and His other virtues, according to the example He gives us of them, in the Eucharistic state. Excite yourself to imitate them, and resolve to do it on such occasions as shall present themselves. But especially take time to consider the admirable dispositions of His Sacred Heart towards us, and all the sublime virtues of which He is the source, the immense love He has for his Father, His ardent charity for all men, and His eagerness for their salvation. Try to discover in that Divine Heart all the abysses it contains, of humiliation, abjection, poverty,

suffering. Consider what are the sentiments of His holy soul, at the sight of the ingratitude of men who have nothing but indifference for Him. Excite yourself to produce suitable acts, to make reparation as far as possible, for all these insults, by sentiments of gratitude, and chiefly by an ardent love of Jesus Christ.

2. Offer to the Eternal Father, Jesus Christ, His Son, as the only Victim worthy of Him, and by Whom alone we can render homage to His supreme dominion, thank Him for His benefits, satisfy His justice, and oblige His mercy to come to our assistance: Say to Him with the Prophet: *Respice in faciem Christi tui. Look on the face of Thy Christ.* (Ps. lxxxiii. v. 10.) It is true my God, that I deserve to be treated as a rebellious servant. But, behold, oh Eternal Father, Thy dear Son, Who is perfectly obedient, and Who offers Himself to Thee at this moment upon this Altar. Look upon the profound abasement to which He is reduced, for the pardon of my infidelities and disobedience. *Respice in faciem Christi tui.* On whatever side Thy justice may accuse me, I will immediately offer Thy beloved Son to disarm it. Did I see Thy anger, a hundred times on the point of bursting over me, a hundred times I would say the same words: *Respice in faciem Christi tui.* I deserve nothing, but I offer Thee a victim that merits all. I consent that Thou shouldst refuse me both the pardon of my sins and all other graces, if He Whom I offer Thee, has not fully satisfied Thee. But thou canst not refuse me anything that I ask in virtue of the merits of Jesus Christ, of His sufferings and death. The reward of these belongs to us; for He hast ransferred them to us. I ask Thee much oh Eternal Father, but I offer Thee the Body, the Blood, and the life of Thy Son immolated on this Altar, in payment of what I ask. What can I desire, that will not fall short of the value of what I offer to obtain it?

3. Offer yourself to God, by the hands of Jesus Christ; and offer to Him, your life, your employments, your inclinations, your passions, and in particular, some virtuous action, which you resolve to perform, or some mortification which you resolve to practise, in order to overcome yourself. And all this, for the same ends, for which our Lord immolates Himself in the blessed Sacrament.

4. Offer yourself to Jesus Christ, in order to unite yourself more closely to Him. Entreat Him to make you enter into His spirit and into His sentiments, and especially into His Sacred Heart, so as never to depart from It. Look upon Jesus Christ as your head, and consider yourself as one of His members, His associates, and His brethren, to whom He has surrendered all His merits, and to whom He has left as a legacy, the reward due to Him from His Father, for His labours, and His death. In this character you may dare to present yourself before God with confidence, to converse familiarly with Him, and to oblige Him in some sort to hear you favourably, to grant your petitions, and to bestow upon you His graces, on account of the alliance and union existing between you and His Eternal Son, and through the infinite Value and dignity of the Victim, Whom we offer to Him in the Blessed Sacrament. You may conclude by making a spiritual Communion, accompanied by a perfect consecration of all your affections and desires to His Sacred Heart.

This method of prayer is excellent, and there is more reason for making it familiar to us, in as much, as our happiness in this life, depends on our union with Jesus Christ in the Blessed Sacrament. It might be well to practise it once a day. Any time is suited to it, especially certain hours of the day, at which Jesus Christ is seldom visited.

There is another most useful method of prayer, in presence of the Blessed Sacrament. After having made an act of faith, and adored Jesus Christ, excite yourself to a tender love of Him, and entreat Him to inflame you daily, more and more, with His love. Then enter into yourself, and examine the state of your soul, your defects, your passions, your weakness, your infirmities, and the depth of your miseries, and lay them open with simplicity before Jesus Christ. Submit yourself entirely to His holy will, and bless Him equally, for the chastisements of His justice, and for the favours of His mercy; humble yourself before His sovereign majesty ; make a sincere confession to Him of your sins and infidelities, ask His pardon for them, detest all the evil you have committed, and resolve to amend for the future.

Enter then, as it were, into the adorable Heart of Jesus Christ. Consider the contempt He feels, for all that this world esteems : what idea He entertains of these vain honours, these apparent goods, and these insipid pleasures, mixed with so much bitterness. Reflect at the same time on the esteem He has for all, that the greater number of men look upon with disgust. How pleasing in His eyes is a poor and obscure life, full of humiliations and contempt. Which of the two, then, is deceived? Are we, who esteem and love so passionately all that Jesus Christ despises, or is Jesus Christ Himself, Who wholly despises, and expressly condemns, what we so eagerly seek after? These reflections, if seriously made, are most useful for freeing us from numberless false notions which deceive us, and for inspiring us with that true wisdom which we admire in the Saints. This kind of prayer is most useful. It is unconstrained, and gives room for the exercise of every affection. We may make it at any time, but especially after some unexpected misfortune, in order that we may submit ourselves to the chastisements of God's justice, or after the hurry and embarrassment of business, in order to regain our recollection. In fine, we have only to visit Jesus Christ often, to learn how to visit Him, and to taste the pleasure which is to be found in conversing with our Divine Lord. There is no one who is more amiable in the world, and no one who loves us more. His conversation has no tediousness. To say, that we know not what to do before the Blessed Sacrament, is to say, that we do not know how to believe, how to ask for the graces which we need, how to love. We are unhappy in this world, only because we do not know our happiness. We do not know Him, who is in the midst of us. Is it possible that we should know Him, and yet love Him so little. Can we love Him, and yet so seldom visit him?

IV. *A few words of advice on frequent visits to the Blessed Sacrament.*

In order to derive all the benefit we can, from frequent visits to the Blessed Sacrament, we shall do well to observe what follows:—

1. We should never enter the Church, but with great modesty. This should be a visible proof of our faith, and of the reverence we feel for the holiness of the place. For this, it is enough, to reflect on what we are doing. A humble and respectful posture, a modest countenance, accompanied by interior recollection, are very necessary dispositions for receiving signal favours from Jesus Christ.

2. Our vocal prayers, should be short; but tender and affectionate. The simplest and least studied are best suited to one who speaks from the heart.

3. Though all times are seasonable for rendering our

homage to Jesus Christ, there are certain hours of the day, and certain days in the year, in which our visits are most pleasing to Him. Such are, the morning for religious persons and ecclesiastics, who have the Blessed Sacrament in their own house, and the afternoon for all kinds of persons. It is difficult to express the advantages gained by those who are diligent in being the first to visit the Blessed Sacrament on rising. The eagerness we show in going at once to adore the Blessed Sacrament, and in being the first to offer Him our homage, pleases Him exceedingly. It is very clear, that, were a servant, a friend, or a child, to show the same eagerness in our regard, we should be deeply touched by it. We may judge then, what must be the effect produced in the Heart of our Divine Lord. This fervour and exactness oblige Him to grant us during the day, the special graces we need, in the exercise of our employments and on various occasions. Weak and imperfect souls, who have hardly any love for Jesus Christ, never manifest this eagerness for any length of time, though it is so reasonable and just. For it is as much the effect, as the cause, of a most ardent love of Jesus Christ. The afternoon is also a very suitable time for receiving great benefits from our loving Saviour, and for showing Him our love: especially at certain hours when He is almost forgotten, and is very rarely visited. It is neither the crowd that draws us thither at that time, nor custom that impels us. The love of Jesus Christ must be our chief motive. It is this that obliges Jesus Christ to be so liberal during these visits. It is during them that many great Saints have received those singular graces, which have conducted them in a short time to the highest perfection. Besides Feasts, which are especially consecrated to the service of God, there are certain days in the year, on which it is most useful to visit Jesus Christ, more assiduously than usual. Such are days devoted by the world to amusement. The carnival; times of public joy, and other similar occasions, with which the greater part of the world are wholly taken up, may be turned to great account by such as are generous and faithful enough to consecrate them particularly to Jesus Christ. One single mark, such as this, of love and fidelity, has proved the first source of the sublime perfection, attained by some of the greatest Saints.

We must not depart from before the Blessed Sacrament before saying to Jesus Christ, in the words of Jacob: *Non dimittam te, nisi benedixeris mihi* (Gen. xxxii. 26): My Saviour, I will not leave Thee until Thou hast given me Thy blessing.

We should entertain so great a respect for everything consecrated to Jesus Christ, especially for the place where He dwells, that nothing should ever make us relax on this point. We should never, under any pretext, fail to maintain that respect and silence which are so carefully observed in the houses of the great. Let us never forget, each time we visit Jesus Christ, to honour His Sacred Heart by some special act of homage. Let us offer Him our hearts, that they may be so completely united to His, as of two hearts to form but one.

Finally, all in general may be told that the great means of becoming recollected, spiritual, and solidly virtuous, is frequently to visit Jesus Christ in the Blessed Sacrament. If we would make these visits with profit, we must make them like persons who really believe that they are visiting Jesus Christ. We must act towards Him with great respect, simplicity, and confidence, speak little, listen to Him attentively, and love Him much.

Chapter III.

Practice for celebrating and hearing Mass.

I. *Reflection on the Sacrifice of the Mass.*

As there is no act of worship on earth that renders greater honour to God than the holy sacrifice of the Mass, we ought to look upon it as the most important action of our lives. Everything is great and wonderful in this mystery. The power of God therein is infinite; His love excessive; His patience extreme. There is nothing about it that does not call for our admiration. We believe that God can work all these miracles if He wills, and there is no reason to doubt that He has willed it. But what is more incomprehensible and surprising is, to see a Priest at the Altar without gravity, devotion, or modesty; to see Christians assisting at these tremendous mysteries only to profane them by their disrespect, the sinful state of their hearts, the dissipation of their minds, and the wandering of their senses.

We can conceive that a man may be ungrateful enough to despise the benefits which he receives from another man, but it is incomprehensible that a man, who has, every day, the happiness of conversing familiarly with Jesus Christ, of holding Him in his hands, of distributing Him to the people, should set hardly any value on so sublime a dignity, and feel only coldness and indifference for Jesus Christ; that, possessing faith, he should go to the Altar burdened with considerable imperfections; that he should remain there without any sentiment of devotion or love; and that he should depart from the Altar as little touched by the excellence and sublime sanctity of this mystery as when he went up to it.

A Priest at the Altar is the mediator between God and men. He treats with Almighty God in the name of the whole Church. He offers to Him a sacrifice proportioned to the benefits which we have received from Him, and which we desire to obtain : a sacrifice capable of cancelling all the sins of men : a sacrifice, in a word, that cannot but be pleasing to God. And yet, are there not to be found Priests, who are not at all moved by so holy and so sublime a ministry? Are there not some who are only known as Priests when they are seen at the Altar, and who even, at the Altar, dishonour the sanctity of their ministry by their want of devotion? Is not the great haste with which this awful sacrifice is offered a visible mark of a want of faith? Whole hours are spent agreeably in conversation, but it is hard to spend half an hour with Jesus Christ. Is it possible that we feel weariness only when we are with Him?

If the account we shall have to give will be proportioned to the dignity of our employments and the benefits we have received; if, to be saved, our virtue must correspond with the holiness of our state and of our ministry, has not a Priest, who possesses only a low degree of virtue, and who, after offering this adorable sacrifice several thousand times, is not more devout, but is perhaps even more imperfect than before he was a Priest, reason to fear the formidable judgments of God? Has he, whom the Body and Blood of Jesus Christ could not move, when he held It in his hands, any ground for believing that there is anything in the world capable of making him less insensible?

The Priesthood is, without doubt, one of the highest dignities and greatest favours that God has ever granted to a mere creature. It is clear, then, that this exalted ministry requires perfect men. Though the virtue of the solitaries that lived in the time of St. J. Chrysostom had attained a great height of perfection, and the greater number possessed the gift of working miracles, yet their virtue, says the Saint, is as far inferior to that which is fitting and necessary for the state of Priests, as the rank of a private person is below the majesty of a king: Tantum discrimen quantum sit inter privatum et Regem. (Chrys. de Sacerd.)

Great graces, indeed, are required in order to attain to this degree of virtue. But has not a Priest the means of being all powerful? Is not the holy sacrifice of the Mass an infallible means of obtaining all sorts of graces? "Yes, my God," cries out a great servant of God (Fr. la Colombière, Ret. Chrét.), penetrated with these sentiments: "when I pray, when I fast, when I give alms, I do it with diffidence. Perhaps, I say to myself, I dishonour God more by my bad intentions, and by the circumstances of my actions, than I honour Him by the action itself. This penance, so far from blotting out my sins, possibly may itself require penance. But when I say Mass or hear it, when I offer the adorable Sacrifice in quality of minister or member of the Church, then, oh my God, full of confidence and courage, I dare to challenge Heaven itself to do anything more pleasing to Thee. Then, without being terrified either by the number or the enormity of my sins, I dare to ask of Thee the pardon of them, not doubting but that Thou will grant it me in the most perfect manner I can desire. However vast may be my desires, however great my hopes, I have no difficulty in asking for what is required to accomplish them. I ask of Thee graces, and great graces, and all sorts of graces for myself, for my friends, and for my bitterest enemies; and so far from being ashamed of my requests, or of being diffident of obtaining so many things at the same time, I even think that I ask too little in comparison with what I offer. I even feel as if I offered a slight to this living Sacrifice by asking infinitely less than It is worth. I fear nothing so much as not to expect, with a firm and constant hope, not only all I have asked for, but even something greater, if possible, than all I can ask."

Would to God that we understood the value of the treasure we possess! Happy, indeed, are Christians, did they but know how to profit by its value! What a source of every kind of good should we not find in this adorable Sacrifice! What graces, what favours, what temporal and spiritual riches for the body and the soul, for time and eternity! But, we must confess it, we do not even think of making use of our treasures. We do not condescend to put our hand into the treasury Jesus Christ has left us.

What a remedy have we in our power against all sorts of evils! We have a tree of life that can impart to us not only health, but even immortality, and yet we are oppressed with infirmities! Had you been on Calvary, what would have been refused you? When you are at Mass, you may receive the same benefits as you might have received on Calvary. Jesus Christ, in the Mass, places Himself in our hands as a victim of infinite value, to obtain from God all that we can desire, however precious the gift that we ask for. Jesus Christ, in the Sacrifice of the Mass, is not only our intercessor with His Father, to obtain from Him, through His merits, all that is necessary for us, and all that we wish for, He offers His Blood and His life as the price of what we ask. What can you desire that is not below the price you offer? How comes it then, that all complain, some of their temporal miseries, others of their imperfections and failings? How is it that our passions tyrannise over us; that bad habits keep us, as it were, in chains; that one is troubled with so many fruitless desires; that another so frequently yields to temptation; that impatience and anger daily infuriate some persons, and grief and melancholy oppress others? How is it that a wife can neither soften her husband, nor maintain peace in her family? that a father sees with grief his children following the path of wickedness? How is it that the greater number, even of those who make a profession of piety, pass nearly all their lives in gross imperfections, and especially in excessive tepidity in God's service? We desire to correct ourselves, and reform others, and yet we do nothing. It is as though we saw a miser in want of everything, though with gold and silver in abundance. Have you asked for this, as you ought, at Mass? How many times have you heard it for this intention? Will you ever persuade me that Almighty God, for so great a price, has refused you so trifling a request? that He has esteemed so lightly the Blood and the life of His Son, as not to think them equivalent to that grace, that virtue, that spiritual or temporal blessing you desire for yourself or for another, if it were for your good to grant it you? that you have asked with sincerity for a great love of Jesus Christ, and that Jesus Christ has refused it to you? No: I will never believe it, and I am sure that you do not yourself believe it. What, then, is the reason? It is that we neglect to assist at Mass, and to represent to Almighty God, at that precious and acceptable time of salvation, all our miseries, and to ask Him the graces which are necessary for us. Lastly, it is because we do not offer this adorable Sacrifice like persons who believe, and who seriously reflect on what they believe.

II. *Practice for the celebration of the Sacrifice of the Mass.*

If the Priest thoroughly understands the excellence of his state, and the sublime sanctity of his ministry, he would never approach the Altar but with a holy awe, nor depart from it without infinite gratitude. Almighty God is more honoured by a single Mass than He can be by all the actions of angels and men, however fervent and heroic they may be. We ought, therefore, to look upon this as the greatest and most important action of our lives, and to perform it with all possible perfection. All the offices with which Almighty God has honoured the Angels are inferior in excellence and dignity to this. To say Mass is something greater than to govern the universe, to raise the dead, and to work the greatest miracles. Judge, then, if a preparation or a thanksgiving of a quarter of an hour can suffice for so great an action.

Let us prescribe to ourselves whatever rule we please in this respect. The whole life of a Priest ought to be spent in preparation and in thanksgiving. No shorter time is sufficient. A Priest ought to do nothing but with the thought that he has to say Mass, or that he has said it. All his words and actions ought to be so holy, as to be a preparation for the celebration of the divine mysteries, and continual proofs of his gratitude and love. There is no one on earth who approaches Jesus Christ more closely than the Priest. There is no one, therefore, who ought to resemble Him more closely in sanctity of life. All other practices are insufficient. Purity and holiness of life must be his principal preparation.

We shall do well, on rising, to recite the prayers appointed by the Church, as a preparation for Mass. Our thanksgiving should end only with the day. The time immediately preceding or following the sacrifice should be employed in increasing our recollection, in renewing our intentions, in endeavouring to render ourselves less unworthy of it; by deep reflections on what we are about to do, or have already done, with acts of faith, contrition, humility, thanksgiving, and love.

The Priest, in going to the Altar, must no longer look upon himself as a man, but as Jesus Christ. It is Jesus Christ who is going to speak by his mouth, and immolate Himself by his hands. He should, therefore, perform no exterior action of which he cannot say, "this is an action of Jesus Christ." He must observe even the smallest ceremonies with the greatest exactness, if anything can be called small, that is done in the celebration of the greatest and most august of all sacrifices. He must observe these sacred ceremonies with a certain air of grandeur and majesty, and with so much modesty that his countenance and his very appearance may inspire all with devotion and respect. He should offer this adorable Sacrifice in so serious, devout, and respectful a manner, that God may be honoured, Jesus Christ recognized in the person of His minister, and all who are present edified.

As Jesus Christ immolates and sacrifices Himself by the hands of his minister, the minister ought also to offer and immolate himself with Jesus Christ. He is chosen and, as it were, deputed by the whole Church, to offer adoration to God, to thank Him for his benefits, to appease His anger, and implore His mercy. He ought to discharge his commission with diligence, especially after the consecration. Then he ought, like Moses, to bind, as it were, the hands of God's justice. Then he ought to acknowledge, by means of this precious victim, the infinite greatness of the Sovereign Being, and annihilate himself above all before Him, as does the Son of God on the Altar. Then he ought to represent all the wants of his people, convinced that he shall obtain all he asks; since he offers a sacrifice of infinite value, which cannot but be pleasing to Almighty God.

We need not wonder that the Apostles and Disciples, who conversed so familiarly with Jesus Christ, received such great graces; we should rather wonder, that a Priest at the Altar is not all powerful, that he loves Jesus Christ only imperfectly, that he is wanting in devotion, when he offers this adorable Sacrifice. He is with Jesus Christ, when he pleases, and as long as he pleases, but unhappily he does not wish to be long with Him. We sometimes lament, that when we are at the Altar, we feel no tenderness, or sensible devotion. But do we live in great interior recollection? Do we lead a life sufficiently pure? How can we experience this sensible devotion, when we are in continual motion during the time of the holy Sacrifice, entirely taken up with the external action, and so eager to quit the Altar, that we do not give time to Jesus Christ, or allow Him, as it were, to make us feel the sweet effects of His presence, much less to make His voice heard by us?

A little more faith; a few serious reflections on our ministry will easily teach us, how we ought to say Mass. We must endeavour to say Mass as Jesus Christ would say it. This reflection on the Person of Jesus Christ embodies in itself the holiest practices of devotion. This thought, which we should recall to mind from time to time at the Altar, "I here represent Jesus Christ, I speak in the name of Jesus Christ, I hold in my hands Jesus Christ," is well fitted to inspire us with that air of sanctity, that serious and majestic manner, that divine appearance which this action calls for, and which all who are present at it expect from us.

The devotion to the Sacred Heart of Jesus is a powerful means of helping us to say Mass with more devotion. Whether it be that this object is more calculated to move us, or that Jesus Christ has attached to this devotion, special and abundant graces, it is certain, from the experience of those who practise it, that, as soon as persons begin to be earnest in devotion to the Sacred Heart, great devotion at the Altar is the immediate result. The mere thought of the Sacred Heart of Jesus, inspires sentiments, with which we were before entirely unacquainted. Faith grows stronger, and our love for Jesus Christ sensibly increases.

We must only be mindful, first, to say Mass with

attention and without hurry. Eagerness to quit the Altar, is a clear sign that we do not willingly remain with Jesus Christ. We are only required to spend a few moments longer at the Altar, and shall we, for so little, deprive ourselves, during our whole life, of the benefit of the greatest, the holiest, and the most important of all our actions. 2dly. To make, every time we say Mass, a sort of reparation of honour to Jesus Christ, with a view to atone, by the homage we render Him in this august Sacrament, for the insults and outrages, which He has endured, and still endures in the most Blessed Sacrament. 3rdly. To thank Him for all the benefits, and all the graces, which He has bestowed on the Blessed Virgin. This gratitude is very pleasing to Him. 4thly. To ask Him with all simplicity and entire confidence for many things, and especially for His perfect love. " Lord, make me holy. The glory will be Thine. Thou wilt find elsewhere subjects more worthy of Thy graces, than I am, but I dare to say, that Thou wilt not find any one, who will endeavour to be more grateful. *Inveni quem diligit anima mea, tenui eum, nec dimittam.* Permit me, oh Lord to say to Thee, that however great may be the benefits Thou hast granted me, Thou hast not yet given me enough, if thou hast not given me Thy love. Give me, my divine Saviour, a heart like Thine. Give me Thy Heart." Truly, a Priest, who does not feel the effects of a sacrifice, which has power to cancel the sins of the whole world, has great reason to fear. My God! what graces dost Thou not shower on a well-disposed soul! Who can explain the sweetness that Thou makest us experience at the Altar. "I have received such great graces, and have felt so sensibly, the effects of this Bread of Angels," says a person who was truly devout to the sacred Heart of Jesus, " That I cannot think of them, without being at the same time, touched with sensible gratitude. I have conceived in consequence, a strong confidence, that I will persevere in virtue, and in the desire I have of belonging entirely to God, notwithstanding the immense difficulties, which I represent to myself in the course of my life. I will say Mass every day. This is my hope. This is the only foundation of my support. Jesus Christ can do very little, if He cannot sustain me, from one day to another. He will not fail to reproach me with my want of courage, if I begin to despond. He will give me every day fresh counsel and fresh strength. He will instruct, console, and encourage me, and grant me, through the sacrifice of Himself, all the graces that I ask. If I do not see that He is present, I feel it. It seems to me, that I am like those blind men, who threw themselves at His feet, and had no doubt that they touched Him, though they did not see Him." This is the manner, in which we ought to say Mass; such are the sentiments we ought to have in the presence of Jesus Christ.

III. *Practice for assisting at the Sacrifice of the Mass.*

Those, who hear Mass, should be convinced, that there is no action of their lives, which requires more respect, attention, and devotion, than this. The Mass is, truly, the representation of the Sacrifice of the Cross, and at the same time, the true sacrifice of the same victim, Who was immolated on Calvary. In the Mass, Jesus Christ still offers Himself to His Father as a holocaust for the expiation of our sins, and applies to us, the price of the Blood which He shed for us on the Cross. We ought, on this account, to assist at Mass, in the same sentiments, as those we should have had, had we been present at the death of our Lord on Calvary. Or rather, we should endeavour to enter into the sentiments of His Blessed Mother, and His beloved disciple at that time.

Modesty, interior recollection, silence, a humble

posture, and a profound respect, are necessary dispositions; but they would be useless, unless animated by a lively faith. We must believe, and we must often reflect on what we believe. We are in a place, sanctified by the presence of Jesus Christ, and filled with the majesty of God, to Whom we are come to offer our homage, and to ask from Him the graces we require. We assist at a sacrifice, in which Jesus Christ is the Victim. This sacrifice is offered for us. Is it possible that we should be convinced of this, and not feel respect and confidence? We should carefully avoid whatever might distract us, from attending to all the actions of the Priest. Of all methods of hearing Mass, this is the most conformable to the spirit of the Church. Vocal prayers are very useful, when they are said with devotion. But they should not occupy us, all the time of Mass. We should not be always intent on speaking. We should sometimes cease, and listen, to hear what our Lord says to us. We must imitate the poor, who, after stretching out their hands, and making known their wants, remain in silence, waiting till an alms be given them. This silence during the adorable Sacrifice is not idleness, it is the mark of a deep attention to the presence of God, and of a humble confidence in His mercy. A few serious reflections on what is done at the Altar, a few acts of faith in the truth of this mystery, will produce in us the holiest sentiments.

But of all methods of hearing Mass, none is more useful than that which is taught us by devotion to the Sacred Heart of Jesus. It consists chiefly in interior acts. As soon as the Priest has consecrated, animated with lively faith, we must adore Jesus Christ, and adore Him in the sentiments of a person, who is present only to render Him homage, and make Him a sort of reparation of honour, for all the insults and outrages, to which His love has exposed Him, in this august

Sacrament. We must then adore His Sacred Heart, and thank our Divine Saviour, for the love which inflames His Sacred Heart, and for all the admirable dispositions of His Heart towards us. We must then enter into His Divine Heart, to admire all the treasures of virtue and of grace which It contains. We shall there admire the most profound humility, that it is possible to imagine: an heroic patience, undismayed by any misfortune: an excessive meekness towards all: the infinite grief He felt for our sins, which He vouchsafed to take upon Himself. We shall behold an unbounded love for the glory of God, His Father, and for all mankind, a solicitude, a zeal, an excessive eagerness for their salvation, and for mine in particular. We must represent to ourselves, what are the sentiments of Jesus Christ on that Altar, at the sight of so much contempt and so many outrages. Filled with the deepest sentiments of love and gratitude, we must say to Him all that grief and love can suggest to a generous and grateful heart. By these interior acts, we shall dispose ourselves for a spiritual Communion. This consists, chiefly, in an ardent desire of really communicating, in order to repair, by the respectful and loving manner in which we desire to receive Jesus Christ, for the coldness, the insensibility, and little preparation, with which we have hitherto received Him.

It is extraordinary that there are to be found Christians, and those not a few, who grow weary and do not know what to do at Mass. Can a sick man be tired of seeing the efforts made to cure him? or can a person, loaded with debts, find it difficult to know what to do, in presence of a powerful monarch who has offered him all his treasures? You do not know what to do at Mass? How is this? says Fr. la Colombière, in his Reflections on this subject; have you never received any favour from God? Alas, we are surrounded, loaded, overwhelmed with His benefits, and we have never thanked Him as we ought. At Mass, at least, give a thought to these various benefits; so many sins overlooked, so loving a Providence continually exercised in your regard, so sweet and so constant an effort to draw you to Him, to gain your heart, to make you holy. The graces that you receive in one single day would suffice to occupy you during the whole of Mass. Is not all this deserving of your remembrance? After repassing through your mind all these benefits, say with holy confidence to the Eternal Father: "Lord, these are the benefits I have received from Thee. But Thou seest this Host, this divine Body, this precious Blood, this adorable Sacrifice? This is what I offer Thee for so many benefits. I cannot doubt but that they are well repaid by so magnificent an offering. But what can I render Thee, oh Lord, for having given me the means of acknowledging so liberally the benefits of Thy Father, the means of expiating all my sins? I have only one heart to offer Thee. Wilt Thou deign to accept this heart, agitated by so many passions, and defiled with so many sins? It is at least broken with grief, and in this state I offer it to Thee. Thou openest to me Thine own; shall I dare, my loving Saviour, to refuse Thee mine? O God of majesty! who am I, that Thou shouldst deign to accept the sacrifice of my heart? It shall then be all Thine. Creatures shall have no part in it. Do Thou, then, my loving Jesus, be my Father, my friend, my Lord, my All. Since Thou art pleased to be content with my heart, how can it desire anything but Thine? I wish, in future, to live only for Thee. Receive then, oh loving Saviour of the world, the sacrifice made to Thee by the most ungrateful of mankind, to repair the injury which, up to this time, I have not ceased to do Thee by offending Thee."

You do not know what to do at Mass? Have you never offended God? Do you not offend Him every day, and every hour of the day? Run over, during Mass, all the faults you have committed since the Mass of the preceding day, and ask His pardon for them. But do you want nothing? You complain every day of your parents, your friends, your children: ask then Almighty God to make such a one more reasonable, another more modest, another less exasperated; to change the heart of another, to grant yourself more meekness, more patience, more courage and more zeal for your salvation, and above all, His perfect love. To obtain all these graces, offer to Him Jesus Christ as a sacrifice. He can never refuse your requests. For what you offer is worth infinitely more than all that you can ask for.

It is extraordinary that our Lord can fill His house only by using violence, and forcing us, as it were, to enter. But it is still more extraordinary that we should enter the house of God so often, and assist every day at the most august of all sacrifices, and yet draw no fruit from it. We do not even understand the ineffable advantages which we can derive from it. This ignorance and negligence is one of the things we have most reason to deplore among Christians. What a misfortune, that we possess in the midst of us an immense and inexhaustible treasure, and that, from not being aware of it, we live in indigence! But if we know this treasure, and yet derive no benefit from it, are we not still more to be pitied?

Chapter IV.

Practical reflections on Communion.

As the Blessed Eucharist is the greatest and the most august of our sacraments, the frequenting it is the most important action of our life, and consequently requires the greatest care and application in preparing for it. Were we to communicate only once in our life, our whole life, however long it might be, would not be too long to prepare ourselves worthily for receiving so holy and so awful a mystery. This should not, however, keep us from it. It should only urge us to approach it with the requisite dispositions. We are wrong, then, when we say: "I will not communicate, because I feel I am unworthy." We should say, on the contrary: "I will endeavour, as far as possible, by the innocence and regularity of my life, to make myself worthy to communicate." To approach worthily, is to believe ourselves unworthy; whilst, at the same time, we do what we can to make ourselves less unworthy. A single good Communion is enough to make a Saint. Not much more is necessary than a good will, and a few reflections, in order to make a good Communion.

Those who communicate often without becoming more devout, more mortified, more recollected, without loving Jesus Christ more and more, are in a more dangerous state than they think. What would have been said, if those who often conversed with Jesus Christ, and usually ate at His table, had not become daily more virtuous? What further hope would there have been for those sick persons who were presented to Jesus Christ, if Jesus Christ had not cured them? Famine and dearth are not the severest chastisements with which God punishes His people. The most terrible, says the Prophet, is when He threatens so to chastise us, that we die of hunger in the midst of an abundant harvest. Many bunches of grapes shall be pressed, and they shall not yield a drop of wine: *Auferam robur panis* (Isaiah iii. 1). This is the most fearful of all punishments; the bread you eat shall have no more nourishment for you. You shall eat much, and yet die of languor and weakness. You shall die of hunger. Whatever may be our danger from sickness, there is always some hope as long as we can have

CHAPTER IV.

recourse to the last remedies. But when the most violent have been several times tried without effect, what must we think of the sick person? If we were ill, and had repeatedly tried the most powerful remedies without effect, we should be filled with alarm, and consider our death inevitable. We have repeatedly received the adorable Body and the precious Blood of Jesus Christ without profit. Have we reason to be satisfied? There are many fatal causes from which this misfortune may proceed. Each one should examine himself on this point.

The general dispositions which we ought to bring to Communion are: profound humility and a sincere acknowledgment of our poverty; a certain spiritual hunger, which indicates, at the same time, the need we have of this food, and our good dispositions to profit by it; a great purity of heart, an ardent love of Jesus Christ, or at least an ardent desire of loving Him, and of accomplishing the design which He had in giving Himself to us in the Eucharist—namely, to unite us intimately to Him by a perfect conformity of heart and mind. Those who, at Communion, have no sentiment of devotion, no fervour, no tenderness, are certainly without some of these dispositions.

It is an ordinary defect in those who communicate often not to make much preparation for communicating well. All books contain very useful practices of devotion for Communion. Each one can choose what suits him best. Devotion to the Sacred Heart of Jesus is suited to all. Experience teaches that there is, perhaps, no practice which makes us communicate with more devotion. All these practices should be accompanied, by serious and deep reflections, on the admirable qualities of the divine food which we are about to receive, by generous mortification, by the gifts of the Holy Ghost, which are the rewards of perfect mortification; and lastly, by the imitation of the virtues we admire and love in Jesus Christ. Let us imagine that the Communion, for which we are preparing, is to be the last in our lives. Let us prepare, every time, as though, on quitting the holy table, we had to pass from this life to eternity. If we desire that the sacrament of the Eucharist should produce in us sentiments of the love of God, let us think of the immense love which God has shown us in instituting this mystery, and of His design to oblige us thereby to love Him perfectly. The reproof of Jesus Christ to Martha for too great solicitude, should teach some souls, who are disquieted and wholly taken up with reciting many vocal prayers, that tranquillity of heart, interior recollection and attention in listening, from time to time, to Jesus Christ in silence, like Magdalen, is the best preparation we can make. So that we should employ the greater part of the precious time that precedes, accompanies and immediately follows Communion, in making many interior acts, of which the love of Jesus Christ should be the principle, and the increase of this love the chief effect. Let us say some prayers before Communion, but let us spend at least a quarter of an hour in making profound reflections on the action we are about to perform. It is very difficult for a person to be convinced that he is going to receive Jesus Christ, and yet to have no desire of it, not to think of it, and to be but little impressed with it. The presence of a prince in disguise does not in any degree diminish the respect due to Him on the part of those who really believe him to be the prince. Any signal benefit, any mark of friendship he may show us under this condition, obliges us to love him all the more, especially if he has assumed this disguise in order to render us some important service. Let us apply this to Jesus Christ. Oh Jerusalem, if thou didst but know who He is that comes to visit thee, and the benefits thou canst derive from this visit! Consider particularly that you are about to receive the adorable Body of Jesus Christ, with the sacred wounds which He allowed His disciples to touch ; and with this adorable Body you are going to receive His Sacred Heart. Into this Sacred Heart, Which is open to us, we must enter. In this Sacred Heart we must learn to pray, to thank God, to praise Him, to annihilate ourselves in His presence, but above all, to love Him. What wonders does not Jesus Christ work during these precious moments in a pure soul, in a soul that really loves Him. The mere thought of this divine Heart fills us, at that time, with extraordinary devotion. If Jesus Christ, in coming to us, gives us sensible marks of His presence, as is generally the case with those who have a tender devotion to His Sacred Heart, let us profit by these precious moments, let us preserve great interior recollection, let us listen to our Lord, let us allow grace to work. If we do not hinder its operation by voluntary distractions, and a kind of dissipation by which the devil seeks to make us lose all the fruit of Communion, it will work wonders in us.

The occupation of a fervent soul at this time, should be principally, to abandon herself entirely to the love of her Divine Saviour, and to enjoy the sweetness of His presence. A tender and sincere love is, at the same time, the best disposition for Communion, and the chief fruit we should draw from it. A soul that loves much is generally silent in the presence of Jesus Christ, and shows her love for him, by fervent interior acts. Magdalen lost in admiration at our Saviour's feet, is the model of a soul that has communicated. If she speaks, her words must only be expressions of her love, her admiration, and her joy.

We may say from time to time, " *Inveni quem diligit anima mea, tenui eum, nec dimittam.* I have found Him Whom my soul loveth. I have held Him, and I will never separate myself from Him." At other times, " *Deus meus et omnia* ; My God and my All. *Dilectus meus mihi, et ego illi;* My beloved to me, and I to Him. *Quid mihi est in cœlo, et a te quid volui super terram, Deus cordis mei, et pars mea Deus in æternum.* What have I in Heaven? and besides Thee, what do I desire upon Earth? The God of my heart, and the God that is my portion for ever. *Pone me ut signaculum super cor tuum.* Put me as a seal upon thy heart, as a seal upon thy arm." We must endeavour at that time, to enter into the sentiments of Jesus Christ, and consider what displeases Him in us, what are His designs upon us, what He wills we should do, and what can hinder us in future from doing what He desires. Let us remain in spirit at His feet, and renewing from time to time, our faith in the presence of Jesus Christ, let us adore Him with profound respect, mingled with fear, seeing that this God of Majesty, before Whom the Seraphim tremble, humbles Himself as far as to dwell in the heart of a mortal man and a sinner: that for this purpose. He destroys the laws of nature, and works such stupendous miracles. Then passing from sentiments of admiration to those of gratitude, let us, with a sense of our absolute incapability of testifying it sufficiently to our Lord, invite all creatures to bless Him with us. Let us offer to Him the love which all the Blessed feel for Him, and the fervour with which so many holy souls communicate. Let us offer Him, His own Heart, with the immense love that inflames it. Let us then unfold to Him, with great confidence and sincerity, our weaknesses, our miseries, and our wants. *Ecce quem amas infirmatur*, we may say with Martha: "Alas, Lord! he whom Thou lovest so tenderly, is sick. Can I doubt of Thy love, after all Thou hast done for me, and all that Thou now dost? If thou lovest me, canst Thou see my infirmities and not heal them? But, above all, canst Thou see that I love Thee so little, without inflaming my heart with the sacred fire of Thy love? Even though Thou shouldst refuse me all the rest, couldst Thou deny me Thy perfect love? I know that I have put great obstacles to Thy designs in my behalf. But do Thou begin, Thyself, I beg of Thee, by removing those obstacles."

Let us never fail, at each Communion that we make, to offer some pleasing sacrifice to Jesus Christ. Let us promise Him to apply ourselves to correct some defect, which we know to be greatly displeasing to Him. Let us bear in mind, that we shall never feel the sensible effects of Communion, if we are not careful to spend the rest of the day, in great interior recollection. Coldness, sloth, and dissipation of mind, immediately after Communion, can never be habitual in those who communicate often, without being, at the same time, fatal signs of the unhappy state of a soul, which is insensible to the greatest of all benefits, and has therefore the more reason to fear, in proportion as she has less apprehension of the unhappy state of tepidity, in which she lives, and of the false security with which she seeks to tranquillize herself.

St. Bonaventure (Process vii., Relig. c. 12,) distinguishes eight different motives, which may lead the faithful to receive holy Communion. Some communicate, says this holy Doctor, because, being sensible of their infirmities, they are desirous of being visited by the physician, Who alone has power to cure them. Others, because, having sinned greatly, they have nothing to offer, more acceptable to the Divine justice, than this sacred Host, this Immaculate Lamb, Who takes away the sins of the world. Others, oppressed with grief, or attacked by violent temptations, because, there is no one to whom they can have recourse, but to a strong and powerful God, Who is always ready to assist and defend them. Others, because they desire to obtain some grace from the Eternal Father, and hope to obtain it, through the merits of His Son, our only Mediator. Some have no other intention in this holy action, but to offer our Lord the chalice of salvation, out of gratitude for the benefits they have received from His hand. Many desire to honour God and His Saints, by making this oblation to God, in honour of his Saints. Some, urged by charity for their brethren, living or dead, make use of the Blood of Jesus Christ, to obtain, for the living, the pardon of their sins, and for the dead, relief in their sufferings. Lastly, others, inflamed with a sincere desire of loving our Blessed Saviour, receive Him in the Adorable Eucharist, in order that they may be wholly inflamed with His love. This motive, we may say, is the most perfect, and the most conformable to the designs of Jesus Christ, in giving Himself to us.

Our divine Saviour comes to us, in order to unite us closely to Him. He opens His Heart to us, He gives it to us: shall we dare to refuse Him ours? Let us enter into this loving Heart, and as It comes to us, let It in future take the place of our own, that we may no longer have any sentiments but His. But let us enter well into these sentiments. Let us consider what Jesus Christ loves, what He esteems, and what He despises. We cannot doubt that He judges wisely of things, and that we deceive ourselves, when we judge differently from Him. What idea, then, has He of those honours, those riches, those pleasures, which I as passionately seek after? On the contrary, are not those crosses, which I abhor, the object of His complacency? They are the only objects of His esteem.

By such reflections as these, it will be easy for us to ascertain whether the Heart of Jesus Christ be united to ours, whether we have truly the spirit of Jesus Christ. We will explain the matter more fully.

CHAPTER V.

What are the marks of the perfect love of Jesus Christ, and of true devotion to His Sacred Heart.

MARKS of a true love for Jesus Christ are the qualities, opposite to the defects, we have enumerated above, in the second Chapter of the second Part. Jesus Christ is the object, and at the same time, the source of solid virtue. He is also the most perfect model. Whatever is not conformed to His example, does not deserve the name of virtue. There is little doubt, but that the imperfections noticed in devout persons have done great injury to solid piety. Some, who pass for devout, are observed to be full of self-love, puffed up with self-esteem, and ready to resent the smallest slights. Some, appear continually melancholy, obstinate, anxious, and sometimes, even furious with passion. Others there are whom, at the same time that they are in want of nothing, the fear of injuring their health in the slightest degree renders idle, negligent, useless, excessively indulgent to themselves, and always severe with others. Hence it is, that many are in the habit of looking at virtue only, through the imperfections of those, who pass for spiritual persons. They think, that no one can be devout, without being melancholy, secluded, obstinate, troublesome, a lover of himself, and exceedingly disagreeable. The high esteem in which true piety was once held, is lost in consequence of the low idea which is formed of it. The most licentious have persuaded themselves that it was no great misfortune to be deprived of virtue, when they see it united with so many defects in the greater number, who make profession of it. Although the imperfections of some afford no real excuse for the vices of others, they tend, without doubt, to disgust many. Dissatisfied with a life so little in accordance with the idea, which had been presented to them of devotion, they imagined, either, that the virtue of those who really love Jesus Christ is not true, or that it is impossible to practise true virtue. We do not undertake here to refute so false an opinion. The Saints overthrow it sufficiently by the sanctity of their lives, and we will content ourselves with showing, in a few words, who are the solidly virtuous, by giving the sure marks of true devotion, and describing the character of a person who loves Jesus Christ perfectly.

I. *Character of one who has a true love for Jesus Christ.*

The description given us by St. Paul is the most just and natural. The true love of Jesus Christ, says this Apostle, without which, even though we had given our property to feed the poor, and our bodies to be burnt, we should have done nothing, is patient, is kind, is not envious, is not rash nor inconsiderate, is not puffed up with pride, is not disdainful; seeks not its own interests, is not provoked to anger, thinks no evil; bears all things, believes all things, hopes all things, ensures all things. This is the true description of solid virtue and devotion. If one only of these qualities is wanting, devotion is imperfect; there is an imperfect love of Jesus Christ. Hence, a person of solid virtue, one who truly loves Jesus Christ, is one without self-love, without disguise, without ambition; one who is, at all times, severe to himself, pardoning himself nothing, and thoroughly kind to others, in whose favour he excuses everything; affable, without affectation; condescending, without baseness; obliging, without interest; strictly exact, though without being scrupulous; constantly united to God, without constraint; never idle, yet never appearing too busily engaged; never too much occupied, and yet less distracted in business than others, because he keeps his heart free, occupying it only with its great affair, the affair of its salvation.

Full of a low opinion of himself, he has nothing but esteem for others; for he beholds in them only the virtues they possess, and in himself only his own defects. Supernatural maxims his only guide, he thinks that those who despise him do him no injury, because he does not consider the honour which they refuse him to be his due. Lastly, he is never in ill-humour, because he has always what he desires. As he never desires what he has not, he is always content, always peaceful, always equal. Prosperity does not puff him up, and misfortunes, however severe, do not cast him down, because he knows that from the same Hand come the goods and evils of life. As the will of God is his only rule of life, he always does what God wills, and wills always what God does.

On this account, actions which make most noise have no attraction for him. Convinced that what we do has no merit, except so far as it is conformable to what God wills, he does not trouble himself to do much, provided he does perfectly what is pleasing to His sovereign Lord. For this reason, full of diffidence in his own natural disposition, his inclinations and his self-love, he prefers the smallest duties of his state to the greatest actions of his own choice and taste. Animated by this spirit of Jesus Christ, he is as perfectly resigned in the privation of those talents which it has not pleased God to give him, of the virtues which God does not call him to practise, and of the good which He does not require him to do, as he is faithful in receiving the graces God offers him, in practising the virtues, and in doing the good works, of which He gives him the opportunity, and grants him the desire. Lastly, he is one who distinguishes himself from others by his meekness, his humility, his ardent love for Jesus Christ, his tender affection for the Blessed Virgin, and by a certain appearance of modesty and odour of sanctity which never fails to be recognized and admired. He is one whom the use of the Sacraments continually makes more holy, and who is constantly more and more inflamed with that thirst after justice of which Jesus Christ speaks. Full of faith, he never assists at our sacred mysteries without the deepest sentiments of gratitude, of love, and profound respect. He seeks God without interruption and without dissimulation. He knows not what it is to be sparing with a God, Who gives us all, Who gives Himself wholly to us, without reserve, in order to oblige us to refuse Him nothing. In fine, he is one who is perfectly mortified at all times, at every period of life, and in all conditions, because he is convinced that in all things Jesus Christ crucified is his model. For this reason, full of His spirit, he aims at nothing but directing, on every occasion, both in prayer and in action, all his intentions and all his thoughts to the simple view of God, Who is the sole object that occupies him. He centres in God all the motions of his heart by a simple and loving resignation to His holy will. This is the character of true and solid virtue which Jesus Christ Himself has given us, which all the Saints have so well copied in their lives, and which alone has constituted the sanctity and the merit of all the Saints. This is the faithful portrait of one who has a true love for Jesus Christ. From this we see at once how false it is that true virtue is disagreeable and forbidding; that persons of solid piety are unaccommodating, melancholy, impatient, troublesome, full of self-love, jealousy, and ambition. It will appear yet more clearly what an injury is done to true piety, and what prejudice is created in the minds of the faithful, by those who, with a reputation for devotion, nourish in themselves such serious imperfections, and throw discredit by their defects upon the virtue which is attributed to them, and thus make their own example serve as a kind of pretext to the licentious. Let it not be said, that this perfect love of Jesus Christ, that true piety as here described, has no existence but in idea; or that if it really exists in the world, a life regulated by such maxims must be necessarily very singular, and that any one who lives in this manner must be very unhappy. The life and the spirit of all the Saints is itself the model from which this description has been taken. There is not one who, by leading a life in accordance with this idea, has not enjoyed a peace and joy beyond all conception. If many among such as seem most circumspect cannot be recognized from this description, it is because many of those who profess piety have not courage to do all that is necessary to attain this height of perfection. They make some efforts. They even make some progress in the path of piety. But they generally stop half way, and many who seem to have hardly a step to make, deprive themselves of all the advantages of a life of perfection, from not having courage to take this step.

But most persons, says St. Francis of Sales, form to themselves a false idea of devotion. You find few who do not represent it to themselves in accordance with their humour, their natural disposition, and their passions. A person subject to melancholy makes solid virtue consist in leading a secluded life, and cannot imagine that any one can be always cheerful, and at the same time truly devout. Others, looking only at the exterior, in the spiritual life, make it consist in exterior penances, in hairshirts, fasting, watching, and similar macerations of the body. Many imagine they have attained consummate virtue when they have acquired the habit of reciting long vocal prayers, of hearing many Masses, of assisting at the whole divine office, of remaining a long time in the Church, or of frequently communicating. Some, even among those who serve God in religion, think that to be perfect (La Colomb. R. sp. ch. 1) it suffices to be assiduous in the choir, to love retirement and silence, to be faithful in observing religious discipline. Thus, some place perfection in one exercise, and some in another. But it is certain that they all deceive themselves. For, as exterior works are only either dispositions for becoming perfectly holy, or the fruits of perfect sanctity, it cannot be said that Christian perfection or the perfect love of God consists solely in works of this kind. They may be excellent fruits of consummate virtue in truly holy persons. But they may be very injurious to those who become so attached to them, as to neglect to watch over the motions of their hearts, to occupy themselves with true interior mortification, and to conform their will, in all things, to that of God.

The true love of God—in other words, true devotion, and the spiritual life—properly consists, as we have seen, in loving God, and hating ourselves; in submitting ourselves, not only to Him, but to every creature for the love of Him; in entirely renouncing our own will to follow His; in mortifying pride and self-love; and, above all, in doing all this solely for the glory of His name, without any other design but to please Him; for the sole reason that He desires and merits to be loved and served by His creatures. This is what is contained in the law of love, which the Holy Spirit has engraved in the hearts of the just. It is in this manner that we are to practise that abnegation of ourselves so much recommended by our Blessed Saviour in the Gospel. It is this that makes His yoke so sweet, and His burden so light.

Not every one that saith to me, Lord, Lord, says the Son of God, *shall enter into the kingdom of heaven, but he that doth the will of my Father Who is in heaven. Many,* continues our divine Master, *will say to me in that day, Lord, Lord, have not we prophesied in Thy Name? and cast out devils in Thy Name? and done many miracles in Thy Name?* And He will say to them in a loud voice : " *I never knew you; depart from me.*"

This is a good but severe lesson for those who labour much, and even with success, for the salvation of souls, should they, after guiding others to sublime perfection, be so unhappy as to go on creeping all their lives, and to die in the great imperfections in which they have lived.

It would be well if we were thoroughly convinced that the love of Jesus Christ, true devotion, Christian virtue, and solid piety properly consist in sincere humility, universal and constant mortification, and perfect conformity of our will to the will of God. If any one of these three virtues be wanting, all the rest is mere deceit and affectation. There is no devotion. There can be no virtue.

This is the opinion of the Apostle, and of all the masters of the spiritual life. Or rather, it is the opinion of all true Christians, for it is the sentiment of Christ Himself. It must consequently be the sentiment of all who have the true spirit of Jesus Christ. In our designs and undertakings, says a great servant of God, it is better to propose to ourselves, to do the will of God, than to procure the glory of God. For, by doing God's will, we infallibly procure His glory also. But, in proposing to ourselves the glory of God, as the motive of our actions, we are sometimes deceived, and do our own will under the specious pretext of the glory of God. This delusion is not uncommon in those who employ themselves in good works and in ministering to the salvation of souls. True perfection, which is open to no deception, is to fulfil in all things the holy will of God. But there are very few souls sufficiently enlightened to know the excellence of this perfection, as there are also few who experience the happiness which results from it.

God has loved us too much, says a faithful friend of Jesus Christ, to allow of our being niggardly towards Him. The mere thought of not being wholly His should horrify us. Shall I not belong wholly to God, after the mercy He daily shows me? Shall I refuse Him anything, seeing that I have received all from Him? My heart will not allow it. When I think of the little we can do for God, even though we devote ourselves wholly to His service, I blush at the thought of refusing Him anything. We are not safe in taking a middle course. We very soon fall lower and lower. None but those who give themselves to God without reserve can hope to die with consolation. They alone can promise themselves a life of tranquillity and joy. We see how completely the life and the sentiments of the true servants of God agree with the character we have drawn of the true servant of God, and what sweetness they experience. Those who, from want of true devotion, have never tasted these heavenly consolations, imagine that it is the same with those who are truly devout, and who have a true love for Jesus Christ. But they deceive themselves.

We may judge also how far removed from the true love of Jesus Christ, and from real piety, are certain persons who adopt its practices exteriorly, and never cease talking about it; persons who are devout through whim, impulse, or caprice; whom an affliction or a retreat may keep for two or three days in recollection, without, however, making them more holy or less imperfect; persons who refuse nothing to their senses, who perform the holiest exercises in a purely natural manner, who are continually distracted, whose heart is always open to foreign objects, exposed to the assaults of the enemy, agitated by a thousand passions, always troubled, and rarely ever without some disturbance; persons whose sensitiveness is so excessive, that the slightest thing offends them; full of disguise and subterfuge, never acting but through self-love, never attaining their end but by manœuvring and deceit, and varying in humour every hour because they only follow the different emotions of their passions.

We may easily see that such persons have not the spirit of Jesus Christ ; that their virtue is only outside ; and that as long as they persevere in this unhappy state, their devotion to the Sacred Heart of Jesus will be too imperfect to merit for them an entrance into that divine Heart, or at least to dwell there long.

II. *Effects of the perfect love of Jesus Christ.*

From what has been already said, it will easily be understood, that the ordinary effects of the perfect love of Jesus Christ, may be reduced to this ; that it forms in us a resemblance to this divine model, as far as is possible in this life, by a perfect imitation of His admirable virtues ; so that our exterior and interior life becomes a true copy of His ; and, as He is the living image of God the Father, so we also become His living images, by copying in ourselves, the features of His life, His mysteries, and His virtues. We easily imitate what we love much. Our perfect imitation of Jesus Christ shows itself in an unalterable meekness, in a perfect liberty of spirit, in an entire dependence on Jesus Christ in all our actions, and in a great love of the Cross.

Such are the ordinary effects of the true love of our Divine Saviour ; and in proportion as our love is more ardent and tender, we possess these virtues more perfectly. Meekness is so peculiarly the virtue of Jesus Christ, that the Prophets rarely allude to any other, when giving the description of Him. Amongst all the Saints of the Old Testament, those who have been the most perfect figures of Jesus Christ, as Moses and David, have excelled in this virtue. *Erat enim Moyses vir mitissimus super omnes qui morabantur in terra.* For Moses was a man exceeding meek above all men that dwelt upon earth. (Num. xij. 3.) *Memento Domine David, et omnis mansuetudinis ejus.* O Lord, remember David and all his meekness. (P. cxxxi.) It is said of the first that he was the meekest of all men then living on the earth: and the second seems to have preferred meekness to all other virtues. Does not Jesus Christ Himself plainly teach us, by His example and His words, that meekness, properly speaking, forms His character, and that it is not possible to be like Him, without having his meekness? Perfect love always seeks resemblance. Now this unalterable meekness is the virtue which more particularly impresses upon us the external and visible features of resemblance to our Blessed Lord, and it is also the ordinary effect of His love.

This lovely virtue contains, it is true, many others. For it is impossible to be always good humoured, to receive all things with a smiling countenance, to practise an unalterable meekness on all occasions, if we have not also sincere humility, continual mortification, perfect charity, an undisturbed tranquillity of soul, superior to all annoyances. For, if one of these virtues be wanting, meekness also will fail. That reserve, that austere and disagreeable exterior, that stern expression which is seen sometimes in persons who pass for spiritual, is usually the effect of a natural disposition, not yet mortified. It was never the characteristic of a disciple of Jesus Christ. For our Divine Saviour desires that meekness, and perfect humility of heart, should be the distinguishing qualities of His disciples. We daily find by experience, that we are never more meek towards others, than when we feel most tender love for Jesus Christ. It was by meekness, that the Apostles gained the most obdurate nations. Apostolical men will never gain anything for the Church, if they do not possess this amiable virtue.

Liberty of spirit makes our interior conformable to that of Jesus Christ, by a perfect forgetfulness of ourselves, and perfect resignation to what He ordains, so that we behold, in all things, only the will of God, and are always disposed to fulfil it, without uneasiness, and without anxiety. It is a sure sign, that we have not much love for Jesus Christ, if we are not in this disposition, of perfect resignation to His will. If we feel so much pleasure in doing what is agreeable' to those we profess to love, is it not evident, that we cannot truly love Jesus Christ, without being inclined to do all that He desires? When a person loves Him, he does only what is pleasing to Him, and nothing gives him pleasure, but what He wills.

When we have once entirely given up our hearts to the love of Jesus Christ, this love no longer admits of either our own sentiments, or our own will; it takes from us all our affections, and places us in a holy indifference, in which all things are the same to us. We desire nothing, and yet will every thing: we care not in what the will of God employs us, whether in great or little things, pleasant or disagreeable. Every kind of event is the fulfilment of our desires, because, since we will whatever God allows to happen, nothing can happen that does not please us. Those who are attached to their employments, to the place of their abode, to their conveniences, or to any thing else, cannot serve our Lord with liberty of spirit, because they are slaves of their own will. This causes them to gain little merit, and disturbs the peace of their souls. They withdraw themselves from the guidance of the Holy Spirit and the ways of grace. They find the yoke of the Lord bitter and heavy, and expose themselves to many illusions and dangers. Fervent souls should therefore, abandon any occupation whatever for the love of Jesus Christ, when He requires it. Nothing should seem of consequence to them, nothing should influence them, but the love of Jesus. All other things should be indifferent to them. We must only be careful, that this indifference does not degenerate into negligence and sloth.

All our application and all our delight should be to do what God wills, when He wills it, and in the manner He wills it. Without this, there can be no virtue; all is illusion and self-love. This perfect conformity to the will of God, and perfect submission to the appointments of Divine Providence, which lead us to wish for nothing but what God wills that we should do, whether He makes use of us, for distinguished employments, or leaves us to lead a life of obscurity, are not only the shortest and most secure path, but properly speaking, the only one, by which to acquire perfect purity of heart, a great love of Jesus Christ, and at the same time, great merit. A man who places his reliance on God, is immoveable, and cannot be shaken. Whatever adverse circumstance may happen, he is content, because he has no other will than that of God. What a happy state of peace and tranquillity! But we must fight courageously, if we would attain it.

The third effect of this love, is an entire dependence on Jesus Christ in all our actions. This consists in a constant remembrance of Jesus Christ, by which we keep Him in view, and continually represent Him to ourselves, as the model of our actions. To this model, we strive to conform ourselves. We do only what He wills. We try to do it in the manner in which He Himself did it, whilst He was amongst us visibly on earth. This sight and example of Jesus Christ regulate the life of those who love Him, and give to them that modesty of manner and odour of sanctity, which equally attract and edify all, and inspire veneration for their persons, and love for their virtue.

It cannot be conceived what advantage may be drawn from this exercise of the love of Jesus Christ, and from looking on Him as the perfect model of our actions. By this means, our heart becomes insensibly detached from creatures; self-love dies away and becomes extinct: defects are corrected, the soul is filled with the spirit of Jesus Christ, and great progress is made in perfection.

Esteem and love of the cross are also the ordinary effects of the perfect love of Jesus Christ. A person who loves our living Saviour affectionately, has no difficulty in entering into His sentiments. He easily conforms himself to His inclinations and His desires; he respects whatever He esteems; he finds attractions in all that He loves: he feels nothing but disgust for what displeases Him. It may be said, that this conformity of desires and sentiments is a necessary effect of true love. Hence also springs that wonderful love of the cross, in all those who ardently love Jesus Christ. We find a difficulty in the exercises of piety; our Lord's yoke seems heavy, the very name of cross and humiliation alarms us; and yet there are numbers of persons of all ages, of various characters and ranks, who find so much delight in crosses, that they would be inconsolable were they, for a moment, without suffering. How are we to account for such difference of sentiments? It is because we have but little love for Jesus Christ, whilst they love Him much. To be without suffering in this life, seemed to St. Teresa more bitter than death. St. Mary Magdalen, of Pazzi, only felt death hard, because it deprived her of the pleasure she enjoyed in the sufferings of this life. Both were ardent lovers of Jesus Christ.

The view of Jesus Christ, said a great servant of God, makes the cross so sweet, that it seems to me impossible to be happy without it. I feel disposed to remain all my life without any consolation, even spiritual. The love of Jesus Christ is everything to me. The cross has its charms, and whoever loves Jesus Christ perfectly, finds ineffable delight in crosses. We have not the same sentiments, because we have not the same love.

"Many persons fly from the cross," says the author

of the Interior Christian, " under the idea of glorifying God in a more exalted manner, by important actions for the good of their neighbour. But they do not see that this is merely an effect of their self-love, not of the love of Jesus Christ. We must serve Him in His way, and not in our own. His love ought to inspire us with sentiments conformable to His. Jesus Christ loved the cross to excess. We cannot fail to love the cross, if we really love Jesus Christ. This love of Jesus Christ daily produces a greater desire of loving Him in those who love Him, and the more perfect this love is, the more ardent will be this desire.

The last effect of this love is a high esteem and a great veneration for everything connected with Jesus Christ. We feel an insatiable hunger after Holy Communion. The mere representation of Jesus Christ inspires devotion when we love Him. We pronounce His divine words with profound respect, and the very name of Jesus causes in us an increase of His love. In the world, even the lowest servants of persons of rank are honoured. Their arms are treated with respect. Whatever bears their name or their livery is safe from insult. The poor bear a special relationship to Jesus Christ. They, in a special manner, wear His livery. Jesus Christ acknowledges what is done for them as done for Himself. Charity, then, towards the poor is the ordinary effect of the true love of Jesus Christ. This love inspires us not only with compassion for the poor, but also with affection and a certain respect, which has sometimes led the greatest monarchs to serve them with their own hands. We feel a certain pleasure in giving alms to them ; we do not know how to refuse a poor person, being convinced that we reject Jesus Christ in their persons, and we feel that this charity is more or less ardent, in proportion as we have a more or less ardent love for Jesus Christ. We may ascertain by these signs whether we love Jesus Christ perfectly. The more ardent our love, the more evident will be these signs. Nor can we have less equivocal proofs of our love than these effects.

As we do not undertake to relate here all that the love of Jesus Christ operates in pure souls, we will say nothing of all these wonders, which are rare, only because pure souls are rarely found; it is enough to say, that as soon as a soul is inflamed with this divine love, she loses all relish and affection for creatures. Her desires can no longer find their object in earthly things. They are directed only in search of Jesus Christ, the centre of their repose. The soul then sends forth deep sighs from time to time; a secret languor slowly consumes the body. The impression of divine love increases to such a degree, that she can do nothing but seek her God continually. She is occupied with Him at all times, and in all places, whether she be at rest or working, whether she sleep or watch, pray or recreate herself. She continually thinks of the Object of her love, and has no wish but to love and please Him. But, to attain to this, we must continually purify ourselves more and more, renounce every other love, and eradicate from our minds all ideas, which have no reference to Jesus Christ.

The devotion to the Sacred Heart, according to the method we offer in this book, is a sure and certain means of attaining this sublime state of perfection, and of acquiring that exalted virtue we have described. All the practices of this devotion tend to give us an ardent and affectionate love of Jesus Christ, and this sublime perfection consists in the perfect love of Him.

Adorable Heart of my Divine Saviour, seat of all virtues, treasury of all graces, refuge of all holy souls; Sacred Heart, Who art the object of the complacency of the Eternal Father, Heart worthy to reign over all hearts, to possess the hearts of men and angels; Adorable Heart of my beloved Jesus, Who lovest us with so marvellous a tenderness, and Who art, nevertheless, so little loved by those whom Thou lovest so tenderly: why cannot I, oh my loving Jesus, go to every place upon the earth, and make known to all, the ineffable sweetness and the extraordinary graces, Thou bestowest so abundantly on all those who honour Thee, and love Thee with their whole hearts! Accept at least the sacrifice I make to Thee of mine, and the ardent desire I feel that Thou shouldst be blessed and praised by angels and men, eternally loved, eternally honoured and glorified.

CHAPTER VI.

Practice of devotion to the Sacred Heart of Jesus for the day of the Feast.

ALTHOUGH Almighty God should be the end and motive of all our actions, and all the days of our life belong to Him, by so many titles He has, however, ordained that certain days of the year should be specially consecrated to Him. Thus He appointed certain solemn festivals in the Old Testament, and for the same reason the Church has also her particular festivals, and distinguishes certain days of the year with greater solemnities. Though we are always obliged to love Jesus Christ, we have great reason to believe, that our dear Lord has wished a certain day to be fixed, on which this love should display itself in a more particular manner. As there was a day specially appointed for honouring His precious Body in the Adorable Sacrament, and as other days were consecrated in honour of His Sacred Wounds, so He has willed that there should be one fixed for honouring His Sacred Heart. The feast of the precious Body of Jesus Christ is celebrated by exposition of the most blessed Sacrament, by solemn processions, and other magnificent functions. The feast of His Sacred

Heart should be solemnized, wherever it is established, with evident marks of the most sincere and most ardent love of Jesus Christ in the Blessed Sacrament.

Though we have elsewhere mentioned that Jesus Christ has Himself chosen the day for this Feast, it will not be out of place to repeat it here.

The person, whom we have named, being one day during the Octave of Corpus Christi in the presence of the Blessed Sacrament, replenished with more than ordinary graces, and touched with a desire of making some return, and rendering love for love, the Son of God appeared to her and said, that she could not do anything more pleasing to Him than what He had so often asked of her. "Then," she said, "my beloved Saviour, showing me His Divine Heart, said: 'Behold this Heart, which has loved men so much, that it has spared nothing, even so far as to consume itself, in order to show them Its love; and in return, I receive from the greater number only ingratitude, irreverence, and sacrileges. But what is more afflicting to Me is, that I receive this treatment from hearts which are consecrated to Me. Therefore I ask of Thee, that the first Friday after the Octave of the Blessed Sacrament be dedicated as a special festival in honour of My Heart; that a reparation of honour be made with an act of atonement, and that Holy Communion be received on that day, to repair the insults It has received when It has been exposed on the Altars, and I promise thee that my Heart shall dilate Itself to pour out abundantly the influences of Its divine love on those who shall render It this honour.'"

We see from these words what this practice is, what profit we should derive from it, and what is its fruit. In order to receive without fail the great graces which God promises us through the practice of this devotion, and especially an ardent love of Him, which is the greatest of all His graces, we should do as follows:—

The Feast (when it is established) begins on the last day of the Octave of Corpus Christi. We may spend part of this day in reading some chapters of this book, especially the first, second, and third of the first part, that we may understand well the motive that should influence us on this feast, and what should be our dispositions, and with what sentiments we should perform all the exercises of this devotion. We should spend all the time we can, before the Blessed Sacrament, with profound respect. Each of us may recite there the Rosary or other prayers, as his devotion suggests. Towards evening we should spend an hour, or half an hour, in reading attentively and with reflection the first chapter of the third part. This lecture or consideration will serve as a meditation, and will help us much in preparing for the feast of the following day. We should be particularly careful to spend, as far as we can, the rest of the day in silence; for interior recollection is a necessary disposition for this devotion. We should do well to spend, if we can, about a quarter of an hour, before retiring to rest, in reflecting on the motive of the feast we are going to celebrate, and on the sentiments awakened within us during the consideration we have made. We may reflect how reasonable it is to have an ardent love of Jesus Christ, and to repair, as far as we are able, the insults which He receives, in the most loving of all mysteries, from those who will not love Him. We must avow to Jesus Christ our desire to pass the remainder of the night, were it possible, at the foot of the Altar, beseeching our angel guardian to supply our place, and preparing ourselves to testify, on the following day, the sincerity of our desire, by our diligence in going to the Church. We must endeavour to keep alive these good sentiments, and if we awake in the night, we must immediately adore Jesus Christ in the Adorable Eucharist, and renew the desire we have to go and visit Him.

We must, if we can, consecrate the whole of the following day to honouring the Sacred Heart of Jesus in the most Blessed Sacrament, and should keep ourselves free from all unnecessary business, and from anything that can easily be deferred to another time. We must carefully avoid all useless occupations. The least moment of such a day is infinitely precious. As soon as we have risen, we must prostrate ourselves and adore Jesus Christ, accompanying this act of adoration with all the sentiments which a heart, deeply touched and inflamed with love, is capable of feeling. We must offer to Him all that we shall do in honour of His Sacred Heart, and with a view to acknowledge His love and His benefits. Those who are so happy as to have Jesus Christ in their own house, must make more haste than ever to be the first to visit Him. Others must try to do so as soon as possible. Confession should be accompanied, if possible, by a more perfect contrition than usual, at the thought of so much ingratitude, and of our own acts of irreverence, of which we should do well to accuse ourselves, if not in particular, at least in general. We must omit nothing in order to make a good preparation for holy Communion. As on this day Communion is received to repair the defects in all previous Communions, it is unnecessary to say with what devotion we should communicate. Our profound respect in the presence of Jesus Christ must be a proof of our ardent desire to repair all past irreverence. The ardent love, the tender devotion, and the lively faith with which we communicate must be a mark of our sincere desire to repair, as far as we can, the coldness, the incredulity, and the irreverence with which so many have communicated. Moved with sensible grief at seeing Jesus Christ so little loved, and even outraged in the adorable Eucharist, we must receive Him as an angry God, Whom we wish to appease by this action; as an offended Saviour, with Whom we wish to be reconciled; as a Spouse, disgusted by our indifference, Whom we desire to love perfectly for the future. Full of tender and affectionate sentiments, we must approach the holy table with unusual modesty and profound humility. As we should be chiefly influenced in this action by an ardent love of Jesus Christ, this love will inspire each one with the sentiments, the affections, and the acts that he should produce at this precious time. Immediately after Communion, comparing the excessive love of Jesus Christ with our extreme ingratitude, humbly prostrate at His feet, humbled in mind, and with a heart pierced with grief at the sight of so many insults, we must make, with particular devotion, the act of reparation. In this our heart must have more share than our lips, or rather our lips must only interpret the sentiments of our heart. We then make the act of consecration to the Sacred Heart of Jesus, and the offering which will be found in the eighth chapter of this last part. We must endeavour to spend the remainder of the day in great interior recollection, passing, if possible, the whole morning, or at least a great part of it, before the Blessed Sacrament, and the entire day in the practice of good works, and especially in a continual exercise of love towards Jesus Christ by frequent acts, each one according to his devotion. Towards evening we must make the appointed meditation for this day. If, however, our state, our employments or duties should prevent us from making it, it would be well at least to read it attentively, and to remain some time in silence, giving scope to the sentiments of devotion we have conceived. We may pray at each hour of the day, and then make some spiritual reading out of this book. Nothing should be neglected which may prove to Jesus Christ how much we love Him, and how greatly we desire to see Him ardently loved. As religious persons have the advantage of possessing Jesus Christ in their own houses, they ought on that day to be assiduous in paying Him their homage, passing all the time at their disposal, before the Blessed Sacrament. Secular persons should also spend more time than usual, and both must endeavour to visit Him at least five times on this day, with special devotion.

The first visit should be made to thank Jesus Christ for the infinite love He has shown us in instituting this mystery.

The second, in thanksgiving for all the times we have received Him in the adorable Eucharist and for all the special blessings that we have received through It.

The third, to make him a kind of reparation for all the outrages He has received from infidels and heretics.

The fourth, to repair, as far as possible, by profound respect, and every kind of homage, the irreverences, the acts of impiety, and the sacrileges, which Catholics themselves have committed against Him.

The fifth, must be expressly to adore Jesus Christ in spirit in all the Churches, of the town or country, where He dwells in the most Blessed Sacrament, where He is abandoned by almost all, and where He is kept with so little reverence, so rarely visited, and so universally forgotten.

As the love of Jesus Christ is the chief motive of all these practices of devotion, many persons, in order to please Jesus Christ the more, add many other good works, which love suggests to them, and which all tend to the same end. Some visit on that day, all, or at least some of the Churches in which the Blessed Sacrament is kept, and endeavour, by their devotion and modesty to repair the profanations and contempt which Jesus Christ has suffered. Others induce some poor persons to go to confession and communion on this day, and after giving them a good meal, dismiss them with an alms. Many accompany these practices of devotion with some austerities. All in general should try to do what they can with lively faith, fervour, and particular devotion, and with most ardent love of Jesus Christ.

CHAPTER VII.

Practice of devotion to the Sacred Heart of Jesus for every month, every week, every day, and for certain hours every day.

It is not necessary to appoint certain days and certain hours for particular exercises of devotion when there is an ardent love of Jesus Christ. For whoever loves much, says St. Augustin, never fails to give proofs of it. It is however useful to point out certain periods for testifying this love more particularly. This is what we propose to do in the present Chapter.

I. *Practice of devotion to the Sacred Heart of Jesus for the first Friday in every month.*

The first Friday of every month is particularly appointed for honouring the Sacred Heart of Jesus. The practices of devotion for it, are very much the same, as those which we have pointed out for the day of the feast, and we should undertake them with the same motive. We should prepare for it the day before, by reading the first Chapter of the third part of this book, and passing some time, on the Thursday evening, before the Blessed Sacrament. The following day, immediately on rising, we should offer to Jesus Christ, and consecrate in honour of His Sacred Heart, all the actions of the day. We should endeavour to go as soon as possible to the Church, where we shall find it easy, if we really love Jesus Christ, to conceive a great sorrow for all the insults He has received in the adorable Eucharist. It will not be difficult to obtain this true love of Jesus Christ, if we reflect ever so little on the motives we have for loving Him. We may accuse ourselves in confession of all the defects we have been guilty of in the presence of our divine Saviour in this adorable mystery, and of the negligence with which we have received and visited Him. We should communicate in the same dispositions and for the same intention as on the day of the feast, and we should make the act of reparation, and the act of consecration, with all possible devotion, and in the sentiments of one, who ardently loves Jesus Christ, and grieves deeply to see Him so little loved. We must endeavour to keep alive these sentiments during the day. In the evening for an hour or half an hour, we can make the meditation we have assigned for the first Friday in every month. We must remember to make on this day the five visits, the motives of which we have explained in the preceding Chapter. We may add to the good works we are accustomed to perform every day, some alms, or penance, to make atonement, on our part, as far as we can, for the insults and outrages which Jesus Christ has endured, and still endures every day in the Blessed Sacrament. We should often think, during the day, on the sentiments He must have, at the sight of our ingratitude, and on the admirable dispositions His Sacred Heart still retains in our behalf. Each one will see how necessary, for all this, are silence, retirement, and interior recollection. We should visit the adorable Sacrament more frequently and with more respect and devotion than usual, and should continually excite ourselves during the day to love Jesus Christ with a love of tenderness. This we can do, without neglecting our occupations, or our necessary employments; entreating our beloved Saviour to open to us His Sacred Heart and to grant us the grace to dwell there the rest of our days.

Besides these exercises of piety, charity towards our neighbour, which is an ordinary effect of the true love of Jesus Christ, obliges all who have a devotion to His

Sacred Heart, to pray particularly every month for all, whom the same love unites, in a more strict and special manner, in this Sacred Heart. All Priests who practise this devotion, should say Mass every month for all who have a devotion to the Sacred Heart of Jesus Christ, offering this divine Sacrifice for all the necessities of these chosen souls, begging our Lord to increase their number, and to inflame the hearts of all who truly love Him, with a more and more ardent love. Those who are not Priests should offer up holy Communion once a month for the same object. Besides the merit of this act of charity, it has also this advantage, that all who practise the devotion to the Sacred Heart of Jesus may be certain, that a very great number of very virtuous persons, and of those who love Jesus Christ most ardently, pray particularly for them every month. This charity should also include those, who, having practised this devotion during life, are suffering after death in Purgatory, for whose relief we must offer the adorable sacrifice, or our Communion.

As this devotion has no other object, but to procure an ardent and perfect love of Jesus Christ, and to repair, as far as possible, all the insults that have been offered Him, and are still daily offered Him in the adorable Eucharist, it is quite clear that it is not so confined to certain days, that it cannot be practised at other times also. Jesus Christ is at all times deserving of our love. He is always despised and ill-treated by men in this adorable mystery. It is most just, then, that at all times, reparation should be made Him, so that whoever is prevented from performing this devotion on the first Friday of the month, can do so on another day of the month. In every month, the first day of Communion may be consecrated to so religious a practice, by endeavouring to do on that day what could not be done on the first Friday of the month.

II. *Practice of devotion to the Sacred Heart of Jesus for every week.*

The Friday in each week is also an appropriate day for honouring, specially the Sacred Heart of Jesus. Our beloved Saviour gave us on this day too evident marks of His love, for us not to make Him some return of love. Jesus Christ has shown us plainly, how pleasing it is to Him, that the whole of this day should be consecrated in honour of His Sacred Heart. We should therefore offer and consecrate to Him all that we are going to do during the day, wishing to do a great deal, but especially to perform well all we have to do, in order to honour more particularly His Sacred Heart. The desire of repairing the contempt and the insults, that Jesus Christ has received in the Adorable Sacrament, and to give Him marks of our love and gratitude, should be the motive of every practice of this devotion. Priests should offer up Mass on this day, for this intention. Those who are not Priests, and can communicate, would do well to do so. They should at least assist at Mass with more respect and devotion than usual, with the intention of repairing, as far as possible, by their love and homage, the insults and outrages to which love exposes Jesus Christ in this adorable mystery. They should offer up this divine sacrifice for this end, and may communicate spiritually. If any thing prevents them from assisting at Mass, they must endeavour to supply for it by some other exercise of devotion. But no one should omit the following points. The first is, to excite and keep up during the day, a great sorrow at seeing Jesus Christ so forgotten, so little loved, and unworthily treated by men in that state especially, where this loving Saviour more manifestly shows to men, the excess of his liberality and His love. The second is, to visit on this day the adorable Sacrament with more respect and devotion than usual, and with the intention, of making reparation by our love, for the ingratitude of men, towards Jesus Christ in the Blessed Sacrament. If, however, our occupations and obligations prevent us from making these frequent visits, we may at least adore Him in spirit from the place where we are, and supply by interior acts for the want of these exterior marks of devotion. We may enter, from time to time, as it were, into the adorable Heart of Jesus, considering what are the sentiments of our loving Saviour towards us, and the earnest desire He has to fill us with His graces, and inflame us with His love.

These reflections which may be made at any time, and in any place, cannot fail to inspire us with affectionate sentiments, suited to the intention we propose to ourselves in this devotion. It will suffice for this, if we are careful to enter into ourselves from time to time, if we keep silence a little more, and endeavour to be less dissipated, and more recollected. This practice is suited to all kinds of persons. It is extremely useful; nor is it easy to express what great favours and graces, even sensible ones, it procures for those who are careful and faithful in frequently making use of it. The third point we should bear in mind on this day, is, to perform some good work, or little act of mortification, exterior or interior, with the same motive, and for the same intention.

We may read such parts of this book as are best suited to excite in us an ardent love of Jesus Christ, and we must try to find half, or a quarter of an hour, to make the meditation assigned for the first Friday in each month.

III. *Practice of devotion to the Sacred Heart of Jesus for every day.*

Besides these exercises of devotion to the Sacred Heart of Jesus, for every year, every month, and every week; we must also have certain hours every day, at which to think more particularly of Jesus Christ and to honour His Sacred Heart, by giving Him more particular proofs of our gratitude and our love. The morning, as soon as we rise, the time of Mass, certain hours of the afternoon, and the period before retiring to rest, are the most suitable times for this purpose. In the morning, immediately on rising, we may prostrate ourselves, after the example of many Saints, in the direction of the nearest Church, where we know that the Blessed Sacrament reposes, and while in this position, make an act of faith, adore Jesus Christ in this august Sacrament, and love Him with tenderness, for this love is as easy as it is reasonable. After thanking Him for instituting this mystery of love, and declaring the grief we feel at seeing Him so outraged, and the desire we have of visiting Him as soon as possible, and of loving Him continually, we may recite some prayer, protesting that we wish to have no desire or sentiment during the whole day, but what is conformable to the desire and sentiments of the Sacred Heart of Jesus Christ.

The time of Mass is certainly one of the best for honouring and loving the adorable Heart of Jesus Christ. We do not give any particular practice for this precious time. The love of Jesus Christ, which ought to occupy us all at this time, does not fail to inspire each one with what is most appropriate. We have only to consider with faith, what Mass really is, and to assist at it with deep respect and singular modesty, in other words, like one who really believes. A little before the Priest's Communion, we may make the act of consecration. We must communicate spiritually, that is, we must have a great love of Jesus Christ, and a great desire to receive Him. The rest of the Mass should be employed, in thanking Jesus Christ for having loved us to such a degree, as to institute this mystery, in asking pardon for the ingratitude of men, who value this mystery so little, and lastly, in endeavouring to supply for their irreverence and insensibility by our adorations, and our ardent love. Priests, who have the happiness of offering up this divine Sacrifice, will feel more devotion every day; their faith will become daily more perfect. Jesus Christ will fill them with greater graces, and they will daily love Him more, if they remember to offer up daily this divine Sacrifice, with the intention of repairing, as far as possible, by means of this adorable Victim, the insults which Jesus Christ receives in this adorable Mystery; and if when Jesus Christ is present before them, they are careful to adore His Sacred Heart. All who visit the Blessed Sacrament, or assist at Mass, should do the same, and it will be difficult not to feel devotion, and behave with respect in the presence of Jesus Christ, when we go before Him with no other end, than to make Him this reparation of honour, and to atone by this very action, for the irreverences and insults which He has received.

The afternoon is also a very fitting time for honouring the Sacred Heart of Jesus Christ and for proving our love to Him. As this is the time when Jesus Christ is visited by comparatively few persons, those who go to visit Him at this time, are sure to be well received. It is not difficult to find a quarter, or half a quarter, of an hour in the afternoon, to go and adore Jesus Christ in the Blessed Sacrament.

It cannot be custom that induces us to go at that time, nor is it the crowd that draws us. It is therefore evident that these visits are the effect of pure love, and consequently they are abundant sources of grace, for Jesus Christ never allows Himself to be surpassed in liberality. The love of Jesus will assuredly occupy us during these visits. This love is usually more sensensibly felt, when we give these sensible marks of a true, faithful, and constant love.

At night, before retiring to rest, we should adore the

Sacred Heart of Jesus, regarding It as a place of refuge and of retirement, in which we wish to take our rest.

We should also thank Jesus Christ for having instituted the Blessed Sacrament. Though it is the greatest of all benefits, there are few who thank Him for it. We should make many acts of contrition and love, towards a God so loving, and Who loves us infinitely. It was a practice of St. Aloysius, to recite every night immediately before retiring to rest, three Hail Mary's, to place himself specially under the protection, and as it were, in the Heart of the Blessed Virgin. He would afterwards make a profound reverence in the direction of the Church to adore the Blessed Sacrament, entreating the Sacred Heart of Jesus who watches continually over all the Church, and in particular over those who love Him tenderly, to preserve him, by His mercy, from all the artifices of the enemy; declaring, that in that Sacred Heart he desired to take his repose, saying with the Author of the Imitation of Jesus Christ: *In pace, in idipsum, hoc est in te uno summo bono, dormiam et requiescam.*

Such, then, is a method of practising the devotion to the Sacred Heart of Jesus Christ. But we must remember that, as, with the true love of Jesus Christ, respect and veneration for the most Blessed Sacrament form the distinguishing characteristics of this devotion and of all these practices, so all who perform them, should distinguish themselves by their assiduity, their profound respect, and their modesty, in presence of the Blessed Sacrament. Thus, an ardent love of Jesus Christ, and a special devotion towards the Adorable Eucharist, should be their peculiar characteristic.

This love should be the spring of all our desires, the end of all our thoughts. In a word, the true love of Jesus Christ, should be the principal object and motive of all these practices. And most certainly, if we persevere with fidelity in these holy practices, we shall soon find this perfect love sensibly increase within us.

This devotion is so dear to Jesus Christ, that it seems as if He could refuse nothing to those who practise it. This is what our Divine Saviour promised to the person whom He employed, to inspire the faithful with it. It is what experience has happily confirmed, and continues daily to prove.

We must also take notice: 1st, never to fail to adore in a tender and affectionate manner the Heart of Jesus Christ, every time we go before the Blessed Sacrament of the altar; 2nd, to visit It as frequently and as respectfully as we can, and to inspire all kinds of persons with this devotion. For it is the property of the perfect love of Jesus Christ, to inspire the desire, not only of loving Him daily more and more, but also of seeing Him every day more known, and more respectfully adored, more frequently visited, and more ardently loved.

Chapter VIII.

Exercises of this Devotion.

Under the name of exercises of this devotion, are understood the act of Reparation, the Act of Consecration, and the other vocal prayers, which are offered to Jesus Christ on certain days of the year, more specially dedicated to the honour of His Sacred Heart; as also the Meditations which may be made on these days.

It is well to remark here, that though these exercises are assigned to certain days in the year, they are not so limited to these days, as not to be also most useful at any other time, provided they are performed with devotion.

Act of Reparation to the Sacred Heart of Jesus Christ, to be made before the Blessed Sacrament on the Friday after the Octave of Corpus Christi, and which it may be well to renew on the first Friday in each month, after Communion.

Most adorable and most amiable Jesus! Ever full of love for us, ever touched with compassion for our miseries, ever actuated by the desire of making us partakers of Thy treasures, and of giving Thyself wholly to us: Jesus, my Saviour and my God, Who, through an excess of the most ardent and most wonderful love, hast placed Thyself in the condition of a victim, in the Adorable Eucharist, where Thou offerest Thyself for us in sacrifice so many times every day, what must be Thy sentiments in this state, at finding no return for all this, in the hearts of the greater part of men, but hardness, forgetfulness, ingratitude and contempt! Was it not enough, Oh my God, to have taken the most painful means of saving us, when Thou couldst have shown us Thy excessive love at much less cost? Was it not enough to abandon Thyself once to that cruel agony, and deadly sorrow, caused in Thee by the horrible sight of our sins, with which Thou wast loaded? Why wilt Thou still expose Thyself daily to all the insults of which the unspeakable malice of men and devils is capable? Ah! my God and my most loving Redeemer, what are the sentiments of Thy Sacred Heart at the sight of all this ingratitude, and of all these sins? How great was the bitterness with which so many sacrileges, and so many outrages, afflicted and tormented Thy Heart?

Moved by extreme sorrow for all these insults, behold me prostrate and annihilated before Thee, to make Thee an act of reparation in the sight of Heaven and earth, for all the irreverences and the outrages which Thou hast received on our Altars, since the institution of this adorable Sacrament. With a heart humbled and broken with grief, I ask of Thee a thousand and a thousand times pardon for all these indignities. Why cannot I, oh my God, wash with my blood every spot where Thy Sacred Heart has been so horribly outraged, and the greatest proof of Thy love received with such incredible contempt. Why cannot I, by some new kind of homage, humiliation and annihilation, repair so many sacrileges and profanations? Why cannot I, for one moment, be master of the hearts of all men, that I might repair, in some manner, by the sacrifice of all of them to Thee, the forgetfulness and insensibility of all those who refuse to know Thee, or who, though knowing Thee, have loved Thee so little?

But oh, my beloved Saviour, what covers me still more with confusion, and should fill me with greater grief is, that I also have been of the number of these ungrateful souls. My God, Who seest the depths of my heart, Thou knowest my sorrow for my ingratitude, and my distress at seeing Thee thus unworthily treated. Thou knowest how I am disposed to do and suffer all, in order to repair them. Behold me then, oh Lord, my heart penetrated with the deepest grief, humbled and prostrate, ready to receive from Thy hand, whatever it shall please Thee to require of me in reparation for so many outrages. I shall bless and kiss a hundred times the hand that shall inflict upon me so just a punishment. Why am I not a victim capable of repairing so many injuries? Why cannot I bathe and wash with my tears and blood every spot, where Thy Sacred Body has been thrown to the ground, and trampled under foot? Too happy should I be, if I could, by every possible torment, repair such outrages, such contempt, and such acts of impiety! If I do not merit this grace, accept at least the true desire I have of it. Receive, oh Eternal

Father, this act of reparation which I make Thee in union with that which was made to Thee by this Sacred Heart on Calvary, and with that which Mary also made at the foot of the cross of her Son. Pardon the many negligences and irreverences I have committed, and give me grace to carry out the resolution I now make, of neglecting nothing, in order that I may ardently love and honour, in every way possible, my Sovereign, my Saviour, and my Judge, Whom I believe to be really present in the Adorable Eucharist. I intend to show in future, by my respect in His presence, my assiduity in visiting Him, that I believe Him to be really present. And as I profess to honour in a special manner His Sacred Heart, I desire to spend the rest of my life in this same Heart. Grant me the grace which I beg of Thee, that I may breathe out my last sigh in this Divine Heart, at the hour of my death. Amen.

Act of Consecration to the Sacred Heart of Jesus.

[It should be borne in mind that by the words consecration and donation, which are sometimes used in this act, it is not intended to make a vow, but merely a resolution.]

Adorable Heart of my beloved Jesus, seat of all the virtues, inexhaustible fountain of all graces, what couldst Thou see in me worthy of Thy affection, that Thou shouldst love me to such an excess, whilst, defiled with so many sins, my heart felt nothing for Thee but hardness and indifference? The wonderful proofs of the tenderness of Thy love for me, even when I did not love Thee, make me hope that Thou wilt accept the proofs by which I desire to declare to Thee, that I do love Thee. Accept, then, oh my adorable Saviour, the desire I feel of consecrating myself entirely to the honour and the glory of Thy Sacred Heart. Accept the donation I make to Thee of all that I am. I consecrate to Thee my person, my life, my actions, my labours and sufferings, desiring nothing in future, but to be a victim consecrated to Thy glory. May I be now set on fire, and some day, if it please Thee, be wholly consumed by the sacred flames of Thy love. I offer Thee, then, oh my Lord and my God, my heart with all the sentiments of which it is capable. I desire that they may be always perfectly conformed to the sentiments of Thy Sacred Heart. Behold me, then, oh Lord, entirely in accordance with Thy Heart, behold me altogether Thine. Oh my God! how great are Thy mercies towards me! God of Majesty! Who am I that Thou shouldst deign to accept the sacrifice of my heart? This heart shall be in future wholly Thine. Creatures shall have no share in it, to Thy prejudice. Be Thou in future, my beloved Jesus, my Father, my friend, my master, and my all. I wish to live only for Thee. Receive then, oh loving Saviour of mankind, the sacrifice that the most ungrateful of all mankind makes to Thy Sacred Heart, to repair the injury which hitherto it has never ceased to inflict upon It by corresponding so ill with Its love. It is but little, indeed, that I give to It; but at least I give all I can, and all that I know It desires. I consecrate to It my heart. I give it, and will take it back no more.

Teach me, oh my loving Saviour, the perfect forgetfulness of myself, since this is the only path that can give me entrance into Thy Sacred Heart. As I shall do nothing in future but for Thee, grant that all that I do may be worthy of Thee. Teach me what I must do to attain to the purity of Thy love. Do Thou give me this love, a most ardent and generous love. Give me that profound humility, without which no one can please Thee, and accomplish in me all Thy holy desires both in time and eternity. Amen.

Offering to the Sacred Heart of Jesus Christ.

Fr. la Colombière, of whom we have already spoken, having found, by his own experience, how useful the devotion to the Sacred Heart of Jesus is, for speedily enkindling in the heart a great love of Jesus Christ, and for attaining a high perfection in a short time, composed this offering, and renewed it several times a month with great devotion. This offering, he says, is made to honour the Sacred Heart of Jesus Christ, the seat of all the virtues, the source of all blessings, and the refuge of holy souls.

The principal virtues which we design to honour in Him are, first, a most ardent love of God His Father, joined to a profound respect, and the greatest humility that ever existed. In the second place, an infinite patience in sufferings, an excessive grief and contrition for the sins which He had taken upon Himself, the confidence of a most affectionate son, joined to the confusion of a great sinner. In the third place, a most lively compassion for our miseries, and an immense love for us, notwithstanding these miseries; and notwithstanding these affections, each of which He possessed in the highest degree possible; an unalterable equanimity, arising from so perfect a conformity to the will of God, that it could not be disturbed by any event, however contrary it might appear to His zeal, His humility, His love itself, or to any other of His other dispositions. This Heart is still, as far as it can be so, in the same sentiments. It is, above all, constantly burning with an ardent love for men, though in return for all this, He meets, in the hearts of these very men, with nothing but hardness, forgetfulness, contempt and ingratitude. He loves, and He is not loved. We do not even know His love, because we will not condescend to receive the gifts by which, He desires to manifest it,

o

nor listen to the sweet and tender declarations He would make of it to our hearts.

In reparation for so many outrages, and for such cruel ingratitude, O most adorable and most amiable Heart of my Jesus, and to avoid, as far as it is in my power, falling into a similar misfortune, I offer Thee my heart, with all the affections of which it is capable. I give myself entirely to Thee. From this hour I protest sincerely that I desire to forget myself, and all that in any way relates to me, in order to remove any obstacle that might prevent my entrance into this Divine Heart, which Thou hast the goodness to open to me, and into which I desire to enter, to live and die therein together with Thy most faithful servants. Filled with Thy love, and burning with its flames, I offer to Thy Heart all the merit, all the satisfaction of all the Masses, all the prayers, of all the acts of mortification, all the religious exercises, all the actions of zeal, humility and obedience, and of all the other virtues that I may practise to the last moment of my life. Not only do I offer all these, in honour of the Sacred Heart of Jesus, and of Its admirable dispositions, but I also earnestly beg Him to accept the entire donation I make Him of them, to dispose of them in the manner most pleasing to Him, and in favour of whomsoever He pleases. And, as I have already given over, to the holy souls in Purgatory anything there may be in my actions, capable of satisfying the divine justice, I desire also that it be distributed to them according to the good will of the Heart of Jesus.

This will not prevent my fulfilling any obligations I am under of saying Masses, and of praying for certain intentions prescribed by obedience, nor from saying through charity Masses for the poor, for my brethren and friends, who might request them of me. But, as I then make use of a treasure that does not belong to me, I intend, as is just, that the obedience, charity, and other virtues I may practise on these occasions, may all belong to the Heart of Jesus, from which I have learned how to practise them. They, therefore, rightly belong to Him without reserve.

Sacred Heart of Jesus, teach me the perfect forgetfulness of myself: teach me what I must do to attain to the purity of Thy love, of which Thou hast given me the desire. I feel within me a great desire of pleasing Thee, and a great impatience to carry out this desire in practice. But what can I do without a clear light and a most powerful help? And this I can only look for from Thee. Accomplish in me Thy will, oh Lord. I oppose it, I know well. Yet it seems to me that I wish not to oppose it. It must be Thy work to do all, Divine Heart of my Jesus. Thou alone wilt have the glory of my sanctification if I become a Saint. This appears to me clearer than the day. It is for this alone that I wish to desire perfection. Amen.

Act of love to the Sacred Heart of Jesus Christ, which may be made in visiting the Blessed Sacrament, after reflecting on the immense love which Jesus manifests towards us in this mystery, and on the forgetfulness and ingratitude which men show towards Jesus Christ.

Permit me to turn to Thee, oh Divine and Adorable Heart of Jesus my Saviour, abyss of love and mercy, and to ask Thee, full of astonishment at the sight of Thy goodness and of my own ingratitude, why, oh my God, hast Thou invented a new method of immolating Thyself for me in the Divine Eucharist? Dost Thou think it little, oh Lord, to have once endured for me the scourges, pains, insults, and death of the Cross? Now that Thou art glorious and immortal, must I still see Thee continually exposed to insults in Thy Sacrament of love, wherein Thou art so often despised, insulted, and trodden under foot even by those who ought to love Thee most ardently. Can I see myself in the number of those ungrateful wretches without dying of grief and shame? Oh my God, pierce my heart with Thy love, and put an end to my ingratitude. Remember that Thy adorable Heart, bearing the weight of my sins on Mount Olivet and on the Cross, was afflicted and grieved at the sight of my miseries. Do not permit that Thy sadness and Thy sorrows, Thy Blood, Thy tears and Thy sweat should be unprofitable to me. Touch my heart efficaciously, oh my divine Saviour. Though I am ungrateful and unworthy of Thy love, Thou dost not cease to love me. Thou didst love me when I loved Thee not, when I did not even wish that Thou shouldst love me. But now that I wish it, grant me what I ask of Thee. I give Thee my heart, place me within Thine. Grant that this moment may be that of my conversion, that I may begin to love Thee, never again to cease doing so; that I may be wholly dedicated to Thy love as Thy slave; that I may die to myself to have no longer any life but for Thee, and in Thee. Amen.

Act of Adoration to the Sacred Heart of Jesus Christ, which may be made at any time, but principally in the morning at the time of prayer, and at night before retiring to rest.

Jesus Christ, my Lord and my God, Whom I believe to be really and truly present in the Blessed Sacrament of the Altar, receive this act of most profound adoration, to supply for the desire I feel, of adoring Thee continually, and in thanksgiving for the sentiments of love which Thy Divine Heart therein entertains for me. I offer Thee all the acts of adoration, resignation, patience, and love which Thy Sacred Heart made during Thy mortal life on earth, and still makes, and will make eternally in Heaven, in order that I may adore Thee, love Thee and praise Thee, as far as is possible to me, by means of this Sacred Heart, during the whole time of my life. Open to me Thy Sacred Heart: It shall be in future the place of my refuge and repose.

Act of Contrition.

Oh my Saviour and my God, Whose Heart, pierced with love and grief, did feel such sorrow for the sins of the whole world, why cannot I feel the same grief which I have caused Thee by mine? Supply, I beg of Thee, by the contrition Thou didst feel, for what is wanting to me. Imprint in my heart a horror and fear of the slightest offences. Change and remodel this unhappy heart after Thy own, which is infinitely pure, infinitely holy, and always inflamed with the love of Thy Heavenly Father. I protest that I wish to love nothing in future but what He loves, and to detest everything that displeases Him. Amen.

Offering that may be made during the time of Mass.

As the Mass is the sacrifice of love, in which the Heart of Jesus Christ offers Itself for us, and continually immolates Itself to His Father, it is principally in assisting at this mystery, that we should love and adore this Sacred Heart, and especially after the Consecration, considering what thoughts Jesus Christ can entertain of us, and those that He has for us—namely, the disposition of His Heart, His designs, and His desires. Filled with a sincere feeling of gratitude and affection, we may make the following act :—

Eternal Father, permit me to offer Thee the Sacred Heart of Jesus Christ, Thy beloved Son, as He offers Himself to Thee in sacrifice. Receive, if it be pleasing to Thee, for me, all the desires, all the sentiments, all the affections, all the emotions, all the acts of this Sacred Heart. They are all mine, because He offers Himself for me: they are mine because I desire to have in future none but His: receive them in satisfaction for all my sins, and in thanksgiving for all Thy benefits. Receive them to grant me through their merit all the graces which are necessary for me, and especially final perseverance. Receive them, lastly, as so many acts of love, adoration, and praise which I offer to Thy Divine Majesty; for through Him alone Thou art worthily loved, honoured, and glorified. *Quoniam per ipsum, et cum ipso et in ipso est tibi Deo Patri omnipotenti in unitate Spiritus Sancti, omnis honor et gloria.*

Prayer which St. Gertrude recited every day in honour of the Sacred Heart of Jesus Christ.

I salute Thee, oh Sacred Heart of Jesus, living, vivifying fountain of eternal life, infinite treasure of the Divinity, burning furnace of Divine love. Thou art the place of my repose and my refuge. Oh my beloved Saviour, inflame my heart with the ardent love which inflames Thine; pour into my heart the great graces, of which Thine is the source, and grant that my heart may be really united to Thine, that Thy will may be mine, and that mine may be eternally conformed to Thine; for I desire that, in future, Thy holy will may be the rule of all my desires, and of all my actions. Amen.

Act of Love.

I have nothing, oh my loving Saviour and my God; I have nothing that can please Thee, I can do nothing, I am nothing; but I have a heart, and that suffices. My health, my honour, and my life may be taken from me, but no one can ever take from me my heart. I have a heart, and with this heart I can love Thee, oh my adorable Jesus, and with this heart I desire to love Thee. O my God, I wish to love Thee, and always to love Thee, and for no other reason than to love Thee always.

END OF THE THIRD PART.

MEDITATIONS FOR THE FEAST

OF THE

SACRED HEART OF JESUS,

For each Friday of the month, and for certain days of the year, more especially consecrated to the honour of the Sacred Heart of our Lord Jesus Christ.

THE two Meditations that follow have been given at length, to facilitate their use by all sorts of persons, and by those also, who say they do not know how to meditate. I ask these last, only to read them with attention, reflecting on what they have read, and I hope that they will find that this reading has not been altogether useless, since, when accompanied with the affectionate sentiments towards Jesus Christ, with which grace will not fail to inspire our hearts, it will be a true prayer. Those to whom the habit of prayer is familiar, can content themselves with looking over the subject of each point.

MEDITATION FOR THE FIRST FRIDAY AFTER THE OCTAVE OF THE BLESSED SACRAMENT.

On the incomprehensible love shown us by Jesus Christ in the most Blessed Sacrament of the Altar.

THE subject of this Meditation is the incomprehensible love shown us by Jesus Christ in the Adorable Sacrament of the Altar, where He is so little known to men, and still less loved, even by those to whom He is known.

The end that we should propose to ourselves in this Meditation, and which should be its fruit, is to have a most lively feeling of the extreme ingratitude of men, the greater part of whom are insensible to the evident marks of this ardent love, in order to repair, by a return of love, by our adorations, and by every kind of homage, all the insults that the adorable Heart of Jesus Christ has received, until now, in the most Blessed Sacrament.

The subject of the three points may be taken from three motives, or three desires of Jesus Christ, in the institution of this mystery.

1. The excessive desire that Jesus Christ has had to be always with us.

2. The desire He has to make us partakers of all His benefits.

3. The desire He has to be closely united to us, though men are insensible to the proofs of so ardent a love.

1. Prelude. We may represent to ourselves the upper-chamber in which the Son of God, seated in the midst of His Disciples, instituted this adorable mystery, the contempt to which He exposed Himself, even at that time, in communicating, the traitor Judas, not being able to deter Him for a single moment, from the institution of this mystery of love.

2. Prelude. Convinced, by an act of faith, of the truth of this adorable mystery, and disposed, by an act of contrition, to receive the lights and graces, which God is ready to grant on this occasion, let us ask of the Holy Ghost, in the name of Jesus Christ Himself, and through the intercession of the Blessed Virgin, and of our Angel Guardian, the grace to conceive a great sorrow for so much contempt and ingratitude, penetrating deeply into the loving sentiments of the Heart of Jesus Christ in the Blessed Sacrament.

FIRST POINT.—*The ardent desire Jesus Christ feels to be with us.*

Consider that the Sacred Heart of Jesus Christ was no sooner formed within the womb of the Blessed Virgin, than it was inflamed with an immense love for all men; but, as it is the property of love, to desire to be continually with those, for whom this love is felt, a life of thirty-three years appeared to Him too short, to satisfy His excessive desire of being continually with us. It was necessary to work the greatest of miracles, to content the greatest of all desires. This Heart could not place limits to the excess of Its love. Be not afflicted, oh my Apostles, said our loving Jesus, if I am obliged to leave you to ascend to Heaven; my Heart desires with more ardour to be with you, than you desire to be with Me, and as long as there are men upon earth I shall be with them: *Ecce ego vobiscum sum usque ad consummationem sæculi.* All the motives that led the Son of God to clothe Himself with our flesh have ceased. The work of Redemption is fulfilled. Nothing but His excessive desire of being continually with us, obliges Him to work this constant miracle, and this compendium of all His wonders; His immense love making it, as it were, impossible to Him to be separated from us. Jesus has ascended to His Father: why does He every day return invisibly on earth, if not because He cannot separate Himself from men, and His delights are to be with us? Who would ever have thought that Jesus Christ could have loved us to this excess? From the greatest height of glory, He desires to come and dwell in our hearts, as if something were wanting to His felicity, when He is at a distance from us. A desire must be very violent, when it cannot be satisfied in Heaven, where all desires are fulfilled. Jesus Christ must love men passionately, since not restrained, by the great glory He has enjoyed since His

Ascension, He every day places Himself, in a humble and obscure state on our Altars, to satisfy the excess of His love and of His tenderness; proving to us the truth of what He had said by His Prophet, that His delights are to be with us: *Deliciæ meæ esse cum filiis hominum.*

Reflections.

1. These are the tender sentiments, with which the love that inflames His Sacred Heart, inspires Jesus Christ; but what must be His sentiments, seeing the forgetfulness and indifference of those, whom He loves, to such an excess, and who love Him so little?

2. Jesus Christ has no need of men, and yet He loves them to such a degree, that He counts it as nothing, to be shut up within a Host, until the end of ages, for the sake of the pleasure He has in being with us. Men, on the contrary, cannot do without Jesus Christ, and yet they love Him so little, that they think nothing of this prodigy, so little do they value the felicity of conversing with Him.

3. What were the sentiments of Jesus Christ, when He saw Himself abandoned by a whole people, whom He had loaded with benefits, and even by His most zealous disciples? What must be the sentiments of this blessed Saviour in the Adorable Sacrament of the Altar, where, for the greater part of the day, He is forsaken by all, and where perhaps so many religious persons, who possess Him in their own house, visit Him so rarely?

4. Jesus Christ dwells corporally amongst us, and there is no concourse in the places where He resides! All the places of amusement, all the public squares are full of people. There is always a crowd in the palaces of the great; time is always found for visiting them, though they are scarcely ever in so amiable a mood as to be pleased with the services rendered them; *Ego*

autem relictus sum solus; while Jesus Christ is left alone in the Churches, though He never refuses any one, and receives with exceeding mildness and joy all who approach Him. *Factus sum,* He says, complaining by the mouth of His prophet, *sicut passer solitarius in tecto.* I am left alone in My Churches, and no one can find half a quarter of an hour, to honour Me in the Blessed Sacrament of the Altar.

5. Visits among men are so ordinary and so frequent; it is only this loving Jesus Who is not visited.

6. If sweetness in conversation, or interest attracts us, what conversation is there sweeter or more useful than that which we have with the most amiable and most powerful person in the world, and Who loves us more than any other? *Non enim habet amaritudinem conversatio illius, nec tædium convictus illius, sed lætitiam et gaudium* (Sap. v. 13). His conversation has neither sadness nor weariness; those chosen souls give testimony of it, who are always immersed in sweetness in His presence, and who would willingly pass whole days and nights at the foot of His Altars.

7. Beloved Jesus, what must be the sentiments of Thy Heart, seeing the insensibility and the ingratitude of man? Thou offerest Thyself for them many times every day in sacrifice on our Altars, and one half hour spent in this solemn offering seems to them too long; they are compelled to relieve their weariness and the annoyance they feel by continual distractions of mind.

8. Ungrateful men! You do not know Him Who continually dwells in the midst of you: *Medius vestrum stetit, quem vos nescitis* (John i. 26). If we do not know Jesus Christ, we are lost without remedy, for eternal life consists in knowing Him. But what hope can there be, if when we know Him, we do not love Him?

9. Can we say that we love Him? Should we be satisfied, if He loved us no more than we love Him?

Should we not desire to be better loved by men than we ourselves love Jesus Christ? Would it be sufficient if our friends showed us no more affection than we evince towards this loving Saviour? Should we desire that persons, whom we think we have obliged, should feel for us the same gratitude we show Him? And should we allow our children and our servants, to be as little respectful in our presence, as we are, in the presence of Jesus Christ in His Churches, at the foot of His Altars? My God, the Angels surround these Altars in crowds, to adore and love this Adorable Jesus, though He is not in the Blessed Sacrament for them. Men, for whom alone He has wrought this miracle, do not condescend to visit Him. *Oblivioni datus sum tamquam mortuus a corde* (Ps. xxx. 23).

Lord! Who, to satisfy Thy excessive desire of being with me, hast invented this miracle, what sentiments hast Thou of the forgetfulness I have hitherto shown towards Thee? Is this my correspondence with Thy love? There is no man whom, if he had the least goodwill towards Me, I should not have visited more willingly and more frequently. There is no creature that I should not have loved more. I have forgotten Thee, oh Lord, and hitherto I have not loved Thee; what can I expect, ungrateful and unfaithful as I am? That Thou shouldst think of me? And when hast Thou ever ceased to do it? Have I not reason to expect that my wanderings, my insensibility, my forgetfulness, and my ingratitude, might oblige Thee to think of me no more. Ah, my beloved Saviour, remember this. I have given Thee so many reasons for forgetting me, for despising me, and for only remembering me, in order to cast me into hell. Thou hast not done it. God of goodness, I thank Thee, and in future I desire to serve Thee better. I humbly ask pardon of Thee for my ingratitude towards Thee. I hope that, by Thy grace, I shall repair in future, by my assiduity in visiting Thee, in this adorable mystery, the loss I have sustained by my indifference; and that if Thy Temple is not my usual habitation, I shall at least have a secure refuge in Thy Adorable Heart, which I choose at this moment for my habitation, and which I desire no more to quit: *Hic habitabo, quontam elegi eam* (Ps. cxxxi. 14).

SECOND POINT.—*The excessive desire of Jesus Christ to make us partakers of His blessings.*

Consider, that as Jesus Christ is the source of all goods, He wished to dwell among us, only to be ready at all times, to make us partakers of His treasures. And this loving Saviour has not only desired to make us, in this adorable Sacrament, partakers of all the blessings of which He is the source, but He has willed, in giving Himself, to give us the very fountain of all blessings. *Ostendam tibi omne bonum, quid enim bonum ejus nisi frumentum electorum?* (St. Bern.) I will bestow on you all sorts of benefits, but where else can you find all sorts of blessings upon earth, except in the most blessed Sacrament? The princes of the earth display their liberality, only at certain times, and to certain persons. Jesus Christ, in the Blessed Sacrament, gives all, at all times, and to all persons. *Venite ad me omnes qui laboratis et onerati estis.* It might be said, that we must be poor and afflicted, to have a right to draw near to this fountain of every good, and of all graces: that it suffices to be unhappy to be well received. *Venite ad me omnes qui laboratis.* This God of goodness, foreseeing our weakness and our infirmities, gives Himself to us, for food to repair our strength, and to be a sovereign remedy against all our evils. *Et ego reficiam vos.* Why do you weep, says this loving Saviour continually to us, and why are you grieved at the loss of your health, of your children, or of your property? *Cur fles? quare non comedis, et quamobrem afficitur cor tuum? Numquid non ego melior tibi sum, quam decem filii?* (1 Reg. v. 8.) Do you not find in Me all these goods, and even more? It did not satisfy the love our divine Saviour bears us, only to open to us His Divine Heart, and to pour on us His blessings and graces. He desires to be also our strength and our shield, against all the efforts of our mortal enemies. *Parasti in conspectu meo, mensam, adversus eos qui tribulant me.* (Ps. xii. 25.) Lastly, what more could Jesus Christ give us? What present could He make us, that He has not made, in giving Himself to us? *Quomodo non etiam cum illo, omnia mobis donavit.* (Rom. viii. 32).

Reflections.

1. This divine Saviour comes to us full of goodness, of love, and of the most ardent love, and we go to Him daily, with coldness and indifference. He comes to us, loaded with graces and treasures to enrich us, and how long shall we go to Him, with our hands empty of good works, and with our hearts so filled with the love of creatures, that they cannot have any share in the great liberality of this divine Saviour?

2. There is no blessing which Jesus Christ has not given us, in giving Himself in the blessed Eucharist; and there is no irreverence, no outrage, that has not been offered to Jesus Christ in this august Sacrament.

3. *Sacratissimum Corpus meum in cibum, et pretiosum Sanguinem in potum tibi reliqui, et factus sum opprobrium hominum, et abjectio plebis.* (Blos. Marg. ch. xix., num. 4). He is despised only because He has done us too much good, because He has loved us too much.

4. The house and the person, of the vilest and most wicked of men, would have been treated with more respect, than His Temples and His Sacred Body have received.

5. Love has obliged Jesus Christ to conceal Himself, to come down upon our Altars, but to what does He

expose Himself, by coming thus disguised? How much contempt, how many insults is He obliged to endure daily, from bad Christians, and from infidels. How many licentious men, how many heretics treat Him on our Altars, as if He were a mock divinity, renewing all the outrages that He suffered in His Passion, on account of the royalty to which He laid claim.

6. The Jews exercised less cruelty towards His Person, than is exercised daily, towards His sacred Body. The consecrated Hosts have been trodden under foot, they have been pierced with a thousand blows, they have been broken in pieces and burnt; without speaking of the execrable uses, to which they have been put, and which we cannot think of without horror.

7. The choice which Jesus Christ had made of the insults and outrages He received in Jerusalem, took away their bitterness; but who would dare to think that this Heart, which has only placed Itself in this condition to be more loved and honoured by men, could regard with indulgence the extraordinary contempt that is shown Him?

8. We feel compassion for a man that is despised and ill-treated. Jesus Christ is the only one to whose outrages we are insensible; it even seems as if every one took pleasure in ill-treating Him.

9. We make a child keep silence, if it cries or makes a noise, in the house of a person of quality, whom we are visiting, and we accustom it, by a sinful indulgence, to be ill-behaved in the Church, as soon as it can walk. We stand in Church, we laugh, we talk without restraint, even during the holy Sacrifice. We are more modest in a place of amusement: we are more attentive at a play, than at the celebration of these adorable mysteries. Young men carry their insolence to the foot of the Altar, and even glory in it: while

the Turks do not dare to raise their eyes in their mosques, in which to laugh or talk would be a crime punishable with death.

10. How many houses in these times, are most richly furnished! How many persons would be ashamed to wear the shabby ornaments, on which the Body of Jesus Christ reposes!

11. What answer could we make to heretics, if in reproving us for our immodesty in Church, they boasted of being more religious than we? If you believe that Jesus Christ is on that Altar in that Host, you who understand so well the rules of propriety and of civility, you who are so guarded, I do not say in the palaces and antechambers of the great, but in the houses of your friends, if you believe, how comes it that you lose so completely all respect for your God? We have nothing but contempt for your sacraments, might a heretic say to us, but do you not yourselves teach us to despise them?

12. It cannot be denied that the Gentiles treated with respect, even the most profane ceremonies. Christians have the most holy of all mysteries and they do not cease to profane them! Which merit the severer judgment? those who have been religious even to superstition, or those who have been impious even to sacrilege? And have we not reason to fear, that these infidels will one day be our accusers?

13. All agree that this is the most enormous of all acts of ingratitude: we feel horror when we think of it, and yet we are witnesses of all this impiety; sometimes perhaps we have authority over those who are guilty of it, and we allow it, and are insensible to this forgetfulness, this indifference, these outrages, these profanations, these sacrileges?

14. Jesus Christ, always full of compassion for our miseries, is continually despised, outraged, and pro-

faned by all sorts of persons, and who troubles himself about it, or has any feeling of it?

Oh hardness! oh insensibility of the hearts of men! Oh most adorable and most amiable Heart of my beloved Jesus! Heart worthy of the respect and adorations of men and angels: Heart truly worthy to possess all hearts, to reign over all hearts; what must be Thy sentiments at the sight of so many outrages? But, what ought to be the sentiments of my heart, seeing Thee so ill-treated? Thou seest Lord, what feeling I have of all these indignities. Humbly prostrate here before Thee, I make a reparation to Thine honour, and I humbly ask pardon for them. Why cannot I in some measure, repair so many outrages that have been committed, or at least, prevent others from being offered Thee. But, my beloved Saviour, all my desires are useless, if I were to shed all my blood I could not hinder either one or the other, but at least I have a heart capable of loving Thee, capable of offering Thee homage: and this, my Saviour, is what consoles me. I have a heart, and this heart shall love Thee, and shall love nothing in future but Thee. I offer Thee, with this heart, all the desires and emotions of which it is capable. I offer Thee, oh my Saviour, all that I can do, aided by Thy grace; all that can please Thee, all that can honour Thee. I invite and humbly beseech all the angels, all the Blessed, and also Thy own Blessed Mother to supply for my weakness and my desires. I beg them to honour Thee, praise Thee, adore Thee, and love Thee for me, and for all men. Permit me, in order to honour Thee worthily, to offer Thee Thyself: for I may say that Thou art mine, and that in future all Thy desires shall be mine. I will praise Thee, oh beloved Jesus, and I will publish everywhere, that thou alone oughtest to be loved, served, praised, and honoured eternally.

THIRD POINT.—*The excessive desire of Jesus Christ to be united with us.*

Consider that the union of hearts is the uttermost effect of love: and yet this has been the intention of Jesus Christ, in instituting this august Sacrament, in which all His actions are those of a passionate lover of men; for in this Sacrament love makes Him, as it were, go out of Himself, to live no more but in the beloved object. *Mysterium unitatis nostræ in hac mensa consecravit*, says St. Augustin. This Sacrament is a mystery of union. It is true that by the Incarnation, Almighty God has united Himself perfectly to our nature: but this hypostatic union was not the end of His Incarnation, as the sacramental union was the end of the institution of the Blessed Sacrament. He united Himself to our nature, to have a body capable of the sufferings He desired to endure for us: but He gives Himself to us in the Eucharist, only to unite Himself intimately to us. He invites us to this banquet by His promises. *Venite ad me omnes, et ego reficiam vos.* He induces us to go by His threats. *Nisi manducaveritis carnem Filii hominis, non habebitis vitam in vobis.* He commands that we should be made to enter as it were by force: *Compelle intrare.* Lastly, He does every thing to inflame us with a great desire of going to Him, that there may be nothing to oppose that which possesses Him of coming to us, and being closely united with us. Was there ever a stronger proof of a most ardent love? How is it Lord? Hast Thou forgotten the bad treatment Thou didst receive among us? or hast Thou not foreseen that, to which the excess of Thy love for us exposes Thee? The heart of a chaste and fervent person, is an agreeable dwelling for Thee, but how many such wilt Thou find? Canst thou endure the coldness of the number of slothful Christians that receive Thee? their contempt, their want of faith, and above all, the frightful corruption of their hearts? These are great obstacles, especially for a Heart that cannot endure anything defiled: but the strength of His love overcomes everything. Conceive, if possible, the hatred God bears to sin : it is infinite : and yet, in a certain manner, it is less than the desire He has of coming to us, for He prefers to give Himself up, so to speak, to the sacrilegious embraces of the most infamous sinners, rather than renounce the delight He feels, in being closely united with those who love Him. See to what an excess our Saviour loves us in this adorable mystery. That a God should deign to be Himself our reward. *Ego ero merces tua.* (Gen. xv. 1.) What a wonder! But that Jesus Christ should be Himself our food: *Caro mea vere est cibus, et Sanguis meus vere est potus.* (Joan vi. 57.) This is a miracle of love that surpasses our comprehension : it is a liberality in which, so to speak, Jesus Christ has exhausted Himself. These are the effects of the tenderness and of the immense love of our Blessed Saviour.

Reflections.

1. We believe this miracle : and we are insensible to this excess of love.

2. It is surprising that our Lord can love men to this extent: but it is most extraordinary that men should not love this Divine Saviour, and that no motive, no benefit, no excess of love, can inspire us with the least feeling of gratitude!

3. Ungrateful man! Insensible man! What do you see in Him, that keeps you at a distance? Has He not done enough to merit our love? Alas! He has done more than we should have dared to wish for, more than we can believe, more in a certain way than was becoming His Infinite Majesty, and shall we still remain in doubt, whether we will correspond with so

great generosity, or whether we shall continue to despise it?

4. A mark of affection, a service rendered, gains the hearts of men: Jesus Christ alone, who, after exhausting Himself in this mystery of love, after giving Himself to men, does not gain their hearts.

5. All agree that Jesus Christ loves us infinitely, that He is infinitely worthy of love, that He has, besides, done all that can be imagined to make Himself loved by men. Yet very few love Jesus Christ in reality.

6. Whence is it that He desires so eagerly to come to us, and that we must be constrained to go to Him? Because He loves us passionately, and we do not love Him at all.

7. Whence is it, that we depart from Communion quite frozen, though we have been nourished with the Sacred Heart of Jesus Christ, which is all fire, all love? Because we approach with a heart full of creatures, with a closed heart, impenetrable to the darts of His love. Because His Heart indeed enters into ours, but ours does not enter into His, because we have a sort of dislike to enter therein.

8. We prefer to give up Communion rather than our vices. We should be obliged to be more circumspect, to love Jesus Christ more, to lead a more regular life, if we received oftener this Bread of Angels. The love of Jesus Christ is inconvenient to us: we prefer to abstain longer from this Bread of Life, and even to condemn frequent Communion, because our heart feels an excessive disgust for the Body and even for the Heart of Jesus Christ.

9. I desire with ardour, with eagerness, might Jesus Christ now say to us, to unite Myself closely to you, *Desiderio desideravi: et quomodo coarctor!* And how is it, that nothing is neglected to render these desires inefficacious which so well merit universal gratitude? *et quomodo coarctor!*

10. Jesus Christ desires to come to us frequently, well knowing that this is the only means, of rendering us daily less unworthy of it: and there are Christians, who under the pretext that they are not worthy, render themselves daily more unworthy, by withdrawing from Jesus Christ.

11. If this were a true sentiment of humility, they would most certainly possess the virtue that render us most worthy: but it is only disgust for the Body of Jesus Christ that keeps them at a distance, and even makes them blame those who approach more frequently.

12. The apparent humility of St. Peter, which led him to refuse to allow Jesus Christ to wash his feet, was so strongly condemned, that he would have been irremediably lost, if he had not changed his conduct: *Nisi lavero tibi pedes, non habebis partem mecum in æternum.* (Joan xiii.) How many, through a pretended respect, through false modesty, keep away from life, and are lost without remedy, by abstaining from holy Communion.

13. The Gentiles and the barbarous nations of the East cried out, on only hearing of this mystery: What a good God is the God of the Christians! What a benefactor! He is most worthy of love! but, what would they have thought, had they been told that this loving God was scarcely loved at all by Christians, that this exquisite food had no attraction for them, and that on the contrary, they had a disgust for it, and that they made use of the humble and obscure state to which the excess of His love has reduced Him, to commit the greatest sacrileges and the most execrable profanations.

14. What must be the sentiments of the Sacred Heart of Jesus, the source of all purity, when He is, as it were, buried in a heart full of filth, in a heart which breathes nothing but hatred, revenge, and imprecations against the Saviour Whom it receives? But

what ought to be ours, knowing with what malice this innocent Lamb is treated, Who opens not His mouth amidst so many insults and outrages, Who allows Himself to be led to the Altar, Who allows Himself to be sacrificed for our salvation?

15. Will such excessive goodness, so great meekness, never have power to touch us? It softened the heart of His judge; it changed into respect and love the insolence and rage of His executioners; it has softened the hardness of the hearts, of the most barbarous people: shall there be no hearts but ours, that it cannot move?

16. Every one shudders with horror at the mere recital of the treason of Judas, or of the rage of the Jews; we are daily witnesses, and perhaps accomplices, in the sacrileges and outrages, that are offered to our loving Jesus, in this adorable mystery, and we are not touched by them.

17. *In conspectu tuo sunt omnes qui tribulant me:* Thou hast before Thine eyes those who so ill-treat Me in this sacrament of love, says He to us by the mouth of His Prophet; thou art a witness of their irreverence: *Improperium expectavit cor meum:* My Heart exposed to so many indignities, bears them with patience; *et sustinui qui simul contristaretur,* I thought there would be some one at least to take part in My griefs; *et non fuit,* I have waited until now, and no one presents himself; *qui consolaretur:* I expected that some one would try to repair by his love, his adorations, and his homage, the indignities with which My Heart is afflicted, and the contempt that is shown for My love, *et non inveni,* and I have not found any one.

No, no, Lord: it shall never be true that Thou art thus abandoned; I will put an end to these just complaints. Oh my loving Saviour, is this the way in which we correspond with Thy love? Why hast Thou loved us so much? But rather, why do we love Thee so little ? why do we not love Thee at all ? I have not been satisfied with insensibility to the love and tender sentiments of Thy Heart; with insensibility to the outrages that have been committed against Thee. I have been myself of the number of those who have thus insulted Thee. My loving Saviour, Whose Heart is always burning with love for me, always open to receive me, always ready to show me mercy, pardon me my former forgetfulness of Thee, pardon me my tepidity, my want of faith, my irreverence, and receive the act of reparation that I here make Thee, prostrate before Thee. Thou thinkest of me continually in this august Sacrament, Thou lovest me continually, Thou hast only sentiments of tenderness for me ; and shall I forget Thee, O Lord ? and shall I feel only indifference for Thee ? and shall I not love Thee, O my God ? Take me out of life, if I am to continue to love Thee so little. Let my heart be annihilated, if it is to be in future insensible to the greatest of all benefits: that is, towards Thee, O my God, Who, in giving Thyself to us, hast given us the most precious present, and the most signal favour Thou couldst bestow.

Audi Israel quid nunc requirit Dominus, aut quid petit a te: hear, oh Christian, what the Lord asks of thee ; *nisi ut diligas eum in toto corde tuo:* He asks thee to love Him ; He only asks thy heart. What! can it be that I oblige Thee to beg for my heart, after Thou hast given me Thine? that I should make Thee ask for this heart, and even refuse it, though I daily give it lavishly to creatures ? Ah my loving Jesus, if I offer it now, wilt Thou deign to accept it ? *Cor contritum et humiliatum, Deus non despicies.* This heart is contrite, it is humble ; it cannot fail to please Thee, O Lord. Receive then this heart, which I offer with all the movements of which it is capable, to honour Thee and love Thee, all the rest of my life. The greater number of the years of my life are past and gone, and are lost, because I did not love Thee, but the happiest are left, because I will love Thee in future : *Diligam Te sacratissimum Cor Salvatoris mei Jesu, pro me vulneratum :* I will love Thee, oh adorable Heart of my beloved Jesus ; I will love Thee, oh Sacred Heart, wounded in the Eucharist by the love of me. *Diligam Te.* I will honour Thee during the rest of my life ; Thou shalt be my repose, my constant abode, and my place of refuge : *Hæc requies mea, hic habitabo.* Let no one seek me elsewhere ; I will in future be found no more but in the Heart of my loving Jesus : *Hic fidenter habito, hic me jucunde reficior, hic quiesco suaviter, hic pascor delectabiliter.* This Sacred Heart is the place of my abode ; this Heart shall be my food. In It I will rest from all my labours, burning with the same fire of love with which It burns, with It and in it I will love Him.

The Meditation may be concluded with the following Prayer :—

Anima Christi sanctifica me.
  Cor Christi accende me.
  Sanguis Christi inebria me.
  Corpus Christi salva me.
  Aqua lateris Christi lava me.
  Passio Christi comforta me.
  O bone Jesu exaudi me.
  Intra tua vulnera absconde me.
  Ne permittas me separari a te.
  Ab hoste maligno defende me ;
  In hora mortis meæ voca me,
  Et jube me venire ad te :
  Ut cum Sanctis tuis laudem te
  In sæcula sæculorum. Amen.

Meditation for the First Friday in each Month.

On the sentiments of the Heart of Jesus Christ at the sight of the ingratitude of men, and of the outrages, to which His excessive love for these very men, has exposed Him.

We may represent to ourselves the pitiable state to which the Son of God was reduced in the garden of Olives, when He allowed His imagination to bring before Him, with the greatest liveliness possible, and with all the circumstances that added to His affliction, the greatness of His torments and the indignity of the insults He would have to endure, unto the end of ages, from three kinds of persons: from the Jews who would not acknowledge Him; from heretics who, though they would acknowledge Him, would not believe in His benefits; and from the faithful themselves, who, believing in Him, would repay Him only with ingratitude. At this sight He began to fear, as the Gospel tells us, to be sad and sorrowful, and at last He fell into a sort of agony, receiving no consolation from any one, not even from His faithful disciples, to whom He complained of it, when He said to them: " My soul is sorrowful unto death, and you forsake me, when you see me reduced to so miserable a state." Let us imagine that Jesus Christ is making this complaint to us.

First Point.—*The sentiments of the Heart of Jesus Christ at the sight of the torments He would have to endure, from the cruelty of the Jews.*

Consider what were the sentiments of Jesus Christ, when He represented to Himself distinctly on one hand, the singular favours He had bestowed on this people, and on the other, the cruelties and the outrages, that He would have to endure from this very nation, after so many benefits. All the graces that had preceded His coming, had been granted only in consideration of the merits of Jesus Christ. For that nation chiefly, the Son of God had become man. From it, in preference to any other, He had selected His relations and His friends, He had therein worked His miracles, and preached His doctrine, and for so many benefits He receives no return but harshness, persecution, and insults. Shelter is refused Him when He is about to be born into the world: almost as soon as He is born, He is obliged to seek refuge among strangers. How unworthily was He treated during His whole life? but what did He not suffer at His death? He was taken like a thief, dragged like a culprit along those very streets through which, a few days before, He had been led in triumph as the Messiah. He was struck on the face, as an insolent man, in the house of Caiphas; He was spit upon as a blasphemer; He was treated with contempt and as a mock king; He was made for a whole night the butt of insolent soldiers, who load Him with insults; He was treated by Herod as an idiot and a fool; He was condemned to be scourged like a miserable slave—a criminal was preferred before Him, as if He were the more wicked; lastly, He was condemned to the most ignominious of deaths, and nailed to a cross, on which He expires in the sight of a great number of persons, the greater part of whom had been witnesses of His miracles, and in whose favour He had worked them, without one person being found in all this number of people to take His part, or even to compassionate Him. They pass even from insensibility to contempt, and from contempt to horror and execration. But they are perhaps deceived. No, they are not deceived. They know very well how blameless His life has been, how holy and exemplary, miraculous, and filled with benefits and prodigies; and for this they persecute Him.

All this presented itself clearly and distinctly to Jesus Christ. He knew well the dignity of His person, the greatness of His benefits, the disinterestedness of His love, the baseness, the rage, and the malice of those who treated Him so cruelly.

A noble soul, when it is powerfully possessed by love, and hopes by suffering to make known its passion, is capable of offering itself spontaneously to torments; but the more generosity and tenderness it has, the more pain it feels in bearing injustice and ingratitude; especially when it sees itself sacrificed to the envy of its enemies, and betrayed by those, from whom it had reason to expect help in its misfortunes, and when it sees that all that it suffers, is not capable of inspiring them with the smallest sentiment of compassion.

No one ever represented to himself events, with all their circumstances, more strongly or more distinctly than Jesus Christ. No one had ever a more generous heart, and consequently one more sensible to ingratitude. Oh God! with what a torrent of bitterness was this Sacred Heart then inundated, in representing to Himself what He had done for this people, and what this people would do against Him. Let us judge, who feel so deeply the least contempt, especially when it comes from those who are under some obligation to us, what must have been the feelings of Jesus Christ at such a spectacle.

The grief by which His Heart was oppressed, must have been very cruel, since it was the only torment of His Passion, of which Jesus Christ made any complaint: My soul is sorrowful unto death, He said to His disciples, and you forsake Me, when you see Me reduced to so pitiable a state: *Attendite et videte, si est dolor, sicut dolor meus!* Consider and see if there is a sorrow equal to mine. Oh ingratitude! oh cruelty! and in so terrible an oppression, in such mortal sadness, no consolation. *Generatio prava, atque perversa, hæccine reddis Domino popule stulte et insipiens?* (Deut. xxxii.) Ungrateful men! Insensible Christians! Is this your gratitude for your Saviour, and for your God?

No, no, Lord; it shall never be true that Thou art so universally abandoned; it shall never be true that Thou canst not find any one to participate in Thy sorrow. I ask of Thee, oh Lord, that Thou wouldst pour, from Thy Heart into mine, one drop of that torrent of bitterness with which Thine was inundated, at the sight of so much ingratitude and so many insults, that, if I am not happy enough, to be able to blot out my sins, by the shedding of all my blood, I may be at least afflicted enough, to wash them away continually by my tears.

SECOND POINT.—*The sentiments of the Heart of Jesus Christ at the sight of the outrages, which He should have to endure from the malice of heretics.*

Consider that the second object of the fear, and of the terrible sadness, in which the Heart of the Son of God was plunged, was the number of the outrages and injuries, that He would have to endure, from the malice of heretics, to the end of ages, and which His imagination represented to Him, with all the circumstances that added to His affliction, without diminishing them or concealing any of them from Him. Nothing is more painful to a generous heart than ingratitude, especially when accompanied by great contempt. But the most enormous of all ingratitude is that, by which man not only does not correspond with the benefits he has received, but even denies that he has ever received such benefits, in order to be at liberty to ill-use his benefactor, without being considered ungrateful. Jesus Christ knew distinctly, at that time, that there would be great numbers of Christians, who would renew, in His Sacred Body in the

Adorable Eucharist, all the outrages of which the malice of demons could be capable. That, to be at liberty to exercise upon Him all their fury and rage, they would carry their malice so far, as to deny in the Adorable Eucharist, the real presence of the Body of Jesus Christ.

Who would have believed that men could be capable of such excessive malice, and who can imagine anything more afflicting, than to see, that the most wonderful mark of the greatest love, is made use of only to heap injuries on Him, Who has so much loved us? His imagination represented clearly to Jesus Christ, all that has happened in these latter ages. He saw His temples profaned, His Altars demolished, His Priests murdered, and His Adorable Body thrown to the ground, trampled under foot, and made the object of the scoffs and insolence of the greatest sinners, the horror and the execration of impious men.

What must have been the sentiments of this tender and generous Heart? Was it necessary, oh Lord, to work so great a miracle, to furnish men with a means of treating Thee so unworthily? Was it necessary, through an excess of love, to remain with them unto the end of ages, to be until the end of ages, the object of their contempt and of their rage? Is not such a picture, enough to wither a heart with grief and sadness? Art Thou then, O King of glory, He Whom I see in so many places covered with insult and ignominy? Art Thou the God of Majesty before Whom the Seraphim bow down with respect, Whom I see so insolently treated by the wretched worms of the earth? Art Thou an object of horror and execration to Thy creatures, to Thy slaves, to Thy own children, and all this because Thou hast loved them too much?

Who could ever have imagined, that there would be in man, an excess of malice, equivalent to the excess of Thy goodness, an excess of ingratitude, corresponding so to speak with the excess of love with which Thou hast loved us?

But, my beloved Saviour, should not I be guilty of worse ingratitude if, in considering Thy sentiments at the sight of such cruel ingratitude, I were myself insensible to Thy grief?

Here is the place, oh Lord, where I see Thee, as Thy Prophet has described Thee: the last of men, the man of sorrows (Isa. liii. 3). Heretics have treated Thee as the last and most contemptible of men, and have fulfilled the Prophecy which said, that Thou shouldst be satiated with insults: *saturabitur opprobriis* (Thren. iii. 30). But oh my God, will these heretics, these inhuman children, these impious men never be satisfied with treating Thee so insolently, with offering Thee such outrages? And shall I never be touched by seeing Thee so ill-treated? This sad picture, this sight made Thee even sweat blood. I beg of Thee that it may move me to tears, and that if my heart cannot feel that grief which oppressed Thine, the confusion I feel at being so insensible to Thy sufferings may supply in some degree for my insensibility.

THIRD POINT.—*The sentiments of the Heart of Jesus Christ at the sight of the ingratitude of the greater number of the faithful.*

Consider that it was no less an object of affliction and sadness for Jesus Christ, to see the ingratitude of the greater number of the faithful themselves, who would show only coldness, indifference, and forgetfulness towards this most loving Saviour. He saw the little esteem, not to say contempt, that would be felt for the greatest proof of the most ardent love. He saw that whatever He might do to be loved by the faithful, and to be continually with them by instituting the adorable Eucharist, neither this excess of love, nor His benefits, nor even His presence would have power to oblige them to love Him, nor to prevent them from forgetting Him. He represented to Himself those Churches wherein He dwells for the greater part of the time, without adorers. He foresaw the want of respect and reverence with which persons would behave in His presence. He saw clearly, how many would be found, who, losing entire hours in vain conversation, or useless visits, or spending the greater part of the day in idleness, would never find time, or rather would never be in the humour, to spend a quarter of an hour at the foot of His Altars. Lastly, how many who would not be induced to visit Him at all, and who would scarcely go, once in eight days, to adore Him with coldness. He knew how many others would visit Him without devotion, and how much irreverence and formality there would be in these visits; and lastly how few would visit Him with eagerness. This loving Saviour knew distinctly, that the greater number would trouble themselves no more about Him, than if He were not upon earth, or as if when on earth, He were not the same as in Heaven.

When He foresaw that Jews, Gentiles, and heretics would feel nothing for Him but hardness and contempt, this bad treatment caused Him extreme pain; but, after all, these are His declared enemies: and what do we expect from an enemy? But, what pained Him most was, that those who acknowledge His benefits, that the little flock which professes fidelity towards Him, that His own children should be insensible to His benefits, and should not be touched at the sight of the grief caused Him by these insults, nay should also despise Him by their irreverences and sacrileges. If Gentiles, Turks, and men who are professedly wicked, had vomited forth abuse against Me, I would have borne it without complaining, might the loving Saviour say: *Si inimicus maledixisset mihi, sustinuissem utique.* (Ps. liv. 3). But that Christians, Catholics, of whom I have been not only the Redeemer, but am still the daily food; that my own children should feel nothing for me but indifference, that they should even treat me with contempt! *Tu vero homo unanimis qui simul mecum dulces capiebas cibos!* (Ibid.)

At this sight, at this thought, what were the sentiments of the Heart of Jesus Christ? that is of the most tender and generous Heart that ever existed; of a Heart that loves the hearts of men passionately, and Who meets in the hearts of these very men with nothing but coldness, hardness, and contempt. *Super omnes inimicos meos*, He says by the mouth of His Prophet (Ps. xxx. 12), *factus sum opprobrium:* I have been made the sport and the laughing-stock of My enemies. At least amidst the insults that I have received, I should have met with a great number of servants and devoted friends, but it is quite the contrary: *Qui videbant me foras fugerunt a me.* (Ibid.) Scarcely did I disguise Myself under the feeble forms of bread, to which the excess of My love has reduced Me for the sake of the pleasure of being continually with men, than they removed further from Me, they forsook Me, they forgot Me as One Who had no place in their heart: *Oblivioni datus sum tanquam mortuus a corde.*

But did our loving Saviour, in representing all this to Himself, exaggerate the cause of His grief and sadness? Did this frightful picture deceive Him, which placed before Him so many insults, and outrages, and so extraordinary an insensibility in the hearts of so many Christians? Is it then true that Jesus Christ has been treated thus? Is it true that His people have been insensible to this ill-treatment? Alas! It is enough for me to reflect on my own sentiments, and am not I a prodigy of insensibility, if in considering all this, I am still unmoved? Ah Lord!

can I think of all this, and at the same time reflect, that it is a God who suffered this fearful sadness, in which His Heart was plunged at the sight of so much insult and dishonour, that it is a God who willingly accepted and bore this opprobrium and this disgrace for me, and not die of grief and love? If a man or a slave, had suffered the hundredth part of what Jesus Christ has endured, and still bears daily on our Altars, for the love of us, we could not refuse to love Him, to be grateful to Him, to give Him at least marks of compassion, and to say sometimes: That poor unhappy man really loved me, and he would not have borne so much, if he had not loved me so dearly." Shall it be only the proofs of the love of Jesus Christ, still daily forgotten and despised in the Adorable Eucharist, ill-treated for the love of us, to which we shall be insensible, and what is more, which we shall repay only by ingratitude and coldness? Can it be that the heart of man is capable of such an excess of hardness and insensibility? Alas! Lord, it is but too capable of it, and it will soon give proof of it, if that love which has obliged Thee to expose Thyself to such indignities and outrages for it, does not force Thee to soften its hardness, and warm its coldness, to make it feel its injuries to Thee, and render it capable of Thy love. For of what use would be all the miracles Thou hast wrought, and all the torments Thou has endured, but to harden and make me more guilty, if I were not touched by them, if I did not feel grateful, and if I did not love Thee more in consequence? As I hope, oh Lord, that Thou wilt not refuse me Thy grace, I make at this moment a strong resolution, to give Thee in future undoubted proofs of my love, and of my just gratitude. I have been until now, insensible to Thy benefits, insensible to Thy sufferings, indifferent towards Thee, though I know that Thou art continually with us. I have great reason, my loving Saviour, to feel diffidence in my

Q

promises and resolutions, having been hitherto, so inconstant and unfaithful in Thy service; but it seems to me, that Thy mercy now inspires me with greater courage, and that I shall be in future more constant and faithful, in the promise I make Thee, of showing, by my respect in Thy presence, by my frequent visits, and by my assiduity in attending upon Thee, the sincere devotion I feel to thy Sacred Heart, and the ardent desire I entertain, of repairing as far as possible, during the rest of my days, by my respect, and every kind of homage, all the contempt and the outrages, Thou hast endured in the adorable Eucharist, as also the forgetfulness and the extraordinary indifference that are shown towards Thy adorable Person in the Blessed Sacrament: *Diligam te Domine virtus mea, Dominus firmamentum meum, et refugium meum.* (Ps. xvii. 1.)

Different Subjects of Meditation for the Fridays in each Month.

Besides the Meditation assigned for the first Friday in each month, which is a day more specially consecrated to the honour of the Sacred Heart of Jesus, I have thought it well to assign here various subjects of Meditation for the Fridays in the year, which are also days destined, to honour this Sacred Heart in a particular manner. The subject of these Meditations is taken, from those parts of the Gospel, which relate to the sadness Jesus Christ has felt, during the time of His mortal life, and in which He has testified more feelingly, the excessive affliction with which His Heart was pierced. Let us afterwards consider the sentiments of this afflicted Heart, as applicable to those which He has reason to experience, on account of the coldness, the contempt, and the outrages, that He daily receives in the adorable Eucharist, where alas, wicked Christians, too often, renew the treatment, He has received from the Jews. I have endeavoured as far as possible, that these subjects should be in accordance, with the Gospels of the Sundays in the year.

I will give rather more at length, the two points of the first of these Meditations, but for fear of adding too much to the size of this book, will give only the subjects of the others, making upon each, a few reflections, in conformity with the intention we should propose to ourselves, in these Meditations.

JANUARY.

MEDITATION FOR THE SECOND FRIDAY IN JANUARY.

Si opera non fecissem in eis, quæ nemo alius fecit, peccatum non haberent; nunc autem et viderunt, et oderunt me et Patrem. (Joan xv. 24.)

If I had not wrought amongst them works that no other has ever done, they would not have sinned, but now they have seen them, and they have hated Me and my Father.

FIRST POINT.

CONSIDER, that if the Jews had not been visibly convinced, by the testimony of the Prophets, as they ought to have been, that Jesus Christ was the Messiah, the wonders alone which he wrought, ought to have gained Him the veneration of all, and his most amiable virtues, His indefatigable zeal for their salvation, His excessive meekness, and above all, the wonderful benefits He bestowed on this people, in favour of whom, all these prodigies were wrought, ought to have gained for Him, the hearts of all who knew Him.

All these things however have a quite contrary effect. Jesus Christ is persecuted, hated, and treated worse than the greatest criminal in the world. Have

His benefits and His miracles been forgotten? No, certainly. Men remember them and speak of them: but they almost impute to Him as a crime these benefits and these miracles, and He is only treated so ill by the Jews, because He has loved them too much, and has been too liberal towards them. Conceive, if possible, what must have been the sentiments of Jesus Christ; what was the affliction of His Heart, at the sight of such enormous ingratitude.

SECOND POINT.

But consider, what must His thoughts be now, seeing Himself daily so unworthily treated in the adorable Eucharist by Christians themselves, though He only instituted the adorable Eucharist, to satisfy His excessive love, for these very Christians. If Jesus Christ had not wrought this miracle, if Jesus Christ had not loved us to this excess, should we have any reason for not loving Him? Ungrateful Christians, what do you think of it? Has this loving Saviour done enough to deserve your love? and if His excessive love has moved Him, so to speak, to do too much, ought this excess of love to induce us not to love Him, and to despise Him? This is however what follows from the institution of this adorable mystery. He shall be satiated with insults, said the Prophet. He shall be the last and the most despised of men; and is not this prophecy daily verified towards Jesus Christ, since we have witnessed the miracle He has wrought in our favour, by the institution of the most Blessed Sacrament? The ingratitude and impiety of the Jews excite in us a just indignation against that wicked nation; we see however these impieties and this ingratitude continually renewed, in the insults, to which we know that love exposes Jesus Christ, in the Adorable Eucharist, and shall we never be touched by them?

I have been hitherto insensible, oh Lord, I have been

ungrateful: I have even done what would seem impossible, since, by an unheard of prodigy, and which has no example, except in regard of God, not only have I corresponded with Thy benefits only by outrages, but I have also, if I dare say it, almost made the greatness of my treachery, and of my ingratitude towards Thee, equal the greatness of Thy goodness and mercy for me. Continue oh Lord, this mercy, notwithstanding all my infidelities, but all that I ask now, is, either to die of grief, or to live in a continual repentance, for having so little loved a God Who has loved me to excess, and Who continually gives me, in the Eucharist, the most manifest proof of the greatest love that ever existed.

I will love Thee in future, oh my Saviour; I will begin from this moment, to render Thee my homage in the most Blessed Sacrament, with assiduity and fervour. The modesty and respect with which I will behave in future in Thy presence, my devotion to Thy Sacred Heart, and my ardent desire, of repairing as far as possible, by the help of Thy grace, all the outrages I have been guilty of, and those which Thou daily receivest in the Adorable Eucharist, shall be a convincing proof that I have begun in earnest to love Thee; grant that I may never cease to do so. Amen.

MEDITATION FOR THE THIRD FRIDAY IN JANUARY.

Et scandalizabantur in eo; Jesus autem dixit eis: Non est Propheta sine honore nisi in patria sua et domo sua. (Matt. xiii. 57 *et* 58.)

They were scandalized in His regard. But Jesus said to them: A Prophet is not without honour, save in his own country, and in his own house, and He wrought not many miracles there, because of their unbelief.

IN what could Jesus Christ be a subject of scandal,

if not in concealing Himself too much, and being too cautious and circumspect? The love which He bears us, is excessive and boundless; but this love, which ought to gain Him the hearts of all men, procures Him nothing but contempt. Those, amongst whom He had dwelt longest, are they who know Him the least, and who render themselves most unworthy of His graces; and, as He finds faithful servants only among strangers, it is only amongst them, that He works His greatest miracles, and bestows His benefits most liberally.

It is extraordinary, that a Prophet should be without honour, only in his own country, and his own house, but it is much more extraordinary that Jesus Christ should receive, in His own house, so many insults, that He should be so little known to those, among whom He continually dwells, and so little loved, by those, even, to whom He is known. It is extraordinary, that when He opens to us, all His treasures in the Blessed Sacrament, and gives Himself to us, we feel so little the effects of His presence; and that those who approach Him the nearest, and the most frequently, are not always the most holy, and do not constantly love Him more and more! It is extraordinary, that Jesus Christ, Who is continually amongst us, works so few miracles; that, on the contrary, He should be to many a subject of scandal; but will it not be yet more unaccountable, if, making these reflections to-day myself, I do not love Jesus Christ more, I remain insensible to the insults He receives in this adorable mystery, and do not adopt all possible means to repair them?

MEDITATION FOR THE FOURTH FRIDAY IN JANUARY.

Dixit autem dominus vineæ: Quid faciam? Mittam filium dilectum; forsitan cum hunc viderint, verebuntur. Quem cum vidissent coloni, ejectum illum extra vineam, occiderunt. (Luc. xx. 13 et 15.)

Then the Lord of the vineyard said: What shall I do? I will send my beloved Son; it may be, when they see him, they will reverence him. Whom, when the husbandmen saw, casting him out of the vineyard, they killed him.

THE meaning of this sad parable is too clearly exemplified in the person of Jesus Christ, Whom the Jews treated in this manner; but is not the accomplishment of this parable, renewed daily among Christians, by the unworthy manner in which Jesus Christ is treated, every day, in the most Blessed Sacrament?

Could the Eternal Father make use of a more suitable means of gaining faithful servants, than to send them His only Son? and could Jesus Christ Himself invent a more powerful means, of being honoured and loved, than by instituting the Adorable Eucharist? But is Jesus Christ loved more? Is He not, on the contrary, more dishonoured? Does the ingratitude of the Jews touch us, and are we unmoved by our own? It is a most astonishing fact, that neither the presence of Jesus Christ, His meekness, His benefits, or His miracles have been able to gain the hearts of these infidels; and how long shall the real presence of Jesus Christ in the adorable Eucharist, His abjection, His silence, His benefits, and all the favours He is ready to bestow on us, have no power whatever over the hearts of Christians?

FEBRUARY.

MEDITATION FOR THE SECOND FRIDAY IN FEBRUARY.

Et dixit ad Mariam matrem ejus : Ecce positus est hic in ruinam et in resurrectionem multorum in Israel, et in signum cui contradicetur. (Luc. ii. 34.)

Simeon said to Mary, His Mother: Behold this child is set for the fall and for the resurrection of many in Israel, and for a sign which shall be contradicted.

This prediction transfixed, like a sword, the heart of Mary, but what impression did it not make on the Heart of the Son? Jesus Christ offered Himself to His Eternal Father, for the salvation of all men, and the price which He offered, infinitely exceeded the debt He had to pay. This sacrifice immolated for all, will, however, be useless to a great number, and this infinite price, offered for all men, will be for the ruin, and the resurrection of many. This same victim offers and immolates Himself, still daily, on our Altars, by His Priests, for our salvation, and can we not say, that this same victim is for the ruin of many? and how should it be otherwise, since He is always a sign for the contradiction of men. Some refuse to acknowledge Jesus Christ; others recognize, yet despise Him; the greater number forget Him, and even those who think of Him, are not always grateful. It was not enough, oh my divine Saviour, that this prophecy should be fulfilled in Thy life-time; it must be renewed daily, by the contempt shown to Thy sacred Person, in the Blessed Sacrament. It pierces with grief the soul of the Mother, and shall it never touch our hearts?

MEDITATION FOR THE THIRD FRIDAY IN FEBRUARY.

Assumpsit autem Jesus duodecim, et ait illis: Ecce ascendimus Jerosolymam, et consummabuntur omnia quæ scripta sunt per Prophetas de Filio hominis. Tradetur enim gentibus, et illudetur, et flagellabitur, et conspuetur. (Luc. xviii. 31 et 32.)

Then Jesus took unto Him the twelve, and said to them: Behold we go up to Jerusalem, and all things shall be accomplished which were written by the Prophets concerning the Son of Man, for He shall be delivered to the Gentiles, and shall be mocked, and scourged, and spit upon.

WHAT must then have been the sentiments of Jesus

Christ! Do you see, He said to His Apostles, this people, whom I have so greatly benefited, and in whose favour I have wrought so many miracles? This nation will repay these great benefits, by the most enormous ingratitude; I shall place Myself in their hands, and they will give Me up to the Gentiles; I shall become an object of hatred to the people, the butt of the soldiers, the sport of courtiers, and a victim sacrificed to the malice, and the impiety of the Priests. There will be no insult, that I shall not suffer, no outrage, that I shall not receive, no torment, that I shall not be made to endure. But what would this loving Saviour have answered, had He been then asked why, foreseeing all this, He would place Himself in their hands; if not, that His love was still greater than these outrages, and that He exposes Himself, with pleasure, to all these insults, to show us the excess of His love? All this is daily renewed in the Adorable Eucharist. Jesus Christ has still the same sentiments in our favour; but, my God, what are my sentiments in regard of Jesus Christ, Who is so little loved, and so much ill-treated?

MEDITATION FOR THE FOURTH FRIDAY IN FEBRUARY.

Omnibusque mirantibus in omnibus quæ faciebat, dixit ad Discipulos suos: Ponite vos in cordibus vestris sermones iostos: Filius enim hominis futurum est, ut tradatur in manus hominum. (Luc. ix. 44.)

But while all wondered at all the things He did, He said to His disciples: Lay you up in your hearts these words, for it shall come to pass that the Son of man shall be delivered into the hands of men.

IT required an authority as great as that of Jesus Christ to convince His disciples, who were the witnesses of His miracles, that these prodigies, which gained Him the admiration of all, would not prevent men from ill-using Him. The Jews would not love Jesus Christ, and to be at liberty to ill-treat Him, they shut their eyes, that they might not know Him. Heretics follow in this the example of the Jews, but who would ever have believed that men would be found, who would treat Jesus Christ, with the highest degree of insult and contempt, in the Adorable Eucharist, while they professed to believe, that it was Jesus Christ, Whom they were treating so unworthily?

Lord, Thou didst command Thy disciples to lay up in their hearts these truths, grant they may penetrate deeply into mine.

MARCH.

MEDITATION FOR THE SECOND FRIDAY IN MARCH.

Tristis est anima mea usque ad mortem; sustinete hic et vigilate mecum . . . et venit ad Discipulos, et invenit eos dormientes, et dixit Petro: Sic non potuistis una hora vigilare mecum? (Matt. xxvi. 38 et 40.)

My soul is sorrowful even unto death; stay you here and watch with Me.—And He cometh to His disciples, and findeth them asleep. And He saith to Peter: What! Could you not watch one hour with Me?

WE must be very little touched by the affliction of a friend, when we repose tranquilly, at the time that we see him plunged in the greatest sadness. But how painful is this indifference, to a man in deep affliction! There were then only three Apostles with Jesus Christ, and the pitiable state to which this divine Saviour is reduced, cannot induce them to remain in His company, and to watch only one hour with Him. Jesus Christ is ordinarily neglected in the Eucharist, and how few, even of those who profess to follow Him, and love Him, are touched by the injuries He receives. Jesus Christ is continually about to be betrayed, into the hands of His mortal enemies, and how few, even of those, who flatter themselves they are faithful to Jesus Christ, come to the foot of our Altars, to spend some time in His company; and to how many, might Jesus Christ make daily this reproof: Could you not watch one hour with Me? What answer could I make, oh Lord, who lose so many hours in foolish amusements, and diversions of vanity?

MEDITATION FOR THE THIRD FRIDAY IN MARCH.

Et confestim accedens ad Jesum, dixit: Ave Rabbi, et osculatus est eum: dixitque illi Jesus: Amice, ad quid venisti? (Matt. xxvi. 46.) *Juda, osculo Filium hominis tradis?* (Luc. xxii. 48.)

And forthwith coming to Jesus, he said: "Hail Rabbi, and he kissed Him. Jesus said to him: Friend, whereto art thou come? Judas, dost thou betray the Son of man with a kiss?"

IT is very painful to see an ungrateful man adding deception to malice, trying to deceive us with false appearances, and making use of familiarity, and the marks of the greatest friendship, to destroy us. My divine Saviour, what must be Thy sentiments, in seeing that crowd of Christians, whom Thou so eagerly invitest to Thy banquet, and admittest with so much love to Thy table? Thou givest them in this, the strongest proof of excessive love, and they perform an action, which is in itself, a visible mark of the affection they ought to have for Thee; but to how many of them couldst Thou say: Friend, why camest thou hither? dost thou thus betray Me with a kiss? To how many impure souls art Thou given? to how many hearts stained with vice? How many sacrileges are committed under a false appearance of piety? Shall I, oh my God, be always insensible to this?

Meditation for the Fourth Friday in March.

Milites autem duxerunt eum in atrium Prætorii, et convocant totam cohortem, et cœperunt salutare eum, Ave Rex Judæorum, et percutiebant caput ejus arundine: et conspuebant eum: et ponentes genua adorabant eum. (Marc. xv. 16, 18 et 19.)

And the soldiers led Him away into the court of the Palace, and they call together the whole band, and they began to salute Him, Hail King of the Jews, and they struck His head with a reed, and they did spit on Him, and bowing their knees, they adored Him.

Could the most infamous, and the most wicked among men receive worse treatment? But these painful insults, these outrages, this unheard of cruelty, which the Jews exercised towards the adorable Person of Jesus Christ, at the most lasted only a few hours, and they have been accompanied by the tears, that compassion and love have drawn, from so many faithful servants of Jesus Christ, in many centuries. But is not this sad tragedy daily renewed, in the outrages that are offered to Jesus Christ, in the most Blessed Sacrament. And what is this contempt, but what has been renewed a hundred times by infidels and wicked Christians? How many seem only to enter the house of God, to insult Him? How many dishonour by their ill-behaviour, the sanctity of our most tremendous mysteries? Oh my Saviour, that there were at least many faithful servants who would be truly grieved, to see Thee every day so greatly dishonoured, so little loved, and so ill-used!

APRIL.

Meditation for the Second Friday in April.

Pilatus autem iterum respondens ait illis, Quid ergo vultis faciam Regi Judæorum? At illi iterum clamaverunt: Crucifige eum. (1 Marc. xv. 12 et 13.)

And Pilate again answering, saith to them: What will you, then, that I do to the King of the Jews. But they cried out the more: Crucify Him, Crucify Him.

It might be said, that they know not what to do with Jesus Christ, that He is become useless. To hear Pilate and the Jews, Jesus Christ is fit for nothing, but to be despised, outraged, and crucified. Unhappy people! dost thou not know what to do with that Divine Saviour, Who has been specially given to Thee? This Saviour shall be taken from thee, and given to the Gentiles and to the barbarous nations, who will know how to profit, by that mysterious stone, which thou hast rejected. Jesus Christ is still really present in the most Blessed Sacrament; but is Jesus Christ in the Blessed Sacrament more useful to us? Do we know the treasure that we possess? Are we well aware of the value of this precious victim, and do we profit by the benefits we therein possess? Unhappy countries! Unfortunate kingdoms, in which heresy rules with so much tyranny, your abuse and contempt of this august Sacrament have reached the utmost height, you have not known what to do with this divine Saviour, and this divine Saviour has been taken from you, and carried at the same time, to the Indians, and savages. But my God! have I known how to profit by the presence, and dwelling with us, of this divine Saviour?

MEDITATION FOR THE THIRD FRIDAY IN APRIL.

Pilatus autem cum audisset hos sermones, adduxit foras Jesum, et dixit Judæis: Ecce Rex vester; illi autem clamabant: Tolle, tolle, crucifige eum: tunc ergo tradidit eis illum ut crucifigeretur. (Joan xix. 13, 15, 16.)

Now when Pilate had heard these words, he brought Jesus forth, and he saith to the Jews. Behold your King: but they cried out: away with Him, away with Him, crucify Him. Then therefore he delivered Him to them for to be crucified.

Jesus Christ was no longer to be recognized: the rage of the Jews had reduced Him, to so horrible a condition, that it was necessary, that the judge himself should tell them, that it was Jesus Christ, Whom he was presenting before them. This spectacle would have touched the hearts of the most barbarous: the Jews themselves would have felt compassion, they would have been touched by it, had He been any other than Jesus Christ. Behold then this divine Saviour, given up to the rage of these furies. Behold Thee then satiated with torments and opprobrium, my adorable Saviour! Thy love has carried things to the last extremity. Was not this enough, without again exposing Thyself daily in the Blessed Sacrament to similar treatment! Was not this too much? Yes, He will answer, it is too much to appease My Father, too much for extinguishing the hatred of My enemies, too much for cancelling the sins of the whole world, too much for extinguishing all the fires of hell: but it is not enough, to show Christians the excess of My love. This sufficed to soften My judge and My executioners, and to split rocks asunder; but, neither the remembrance of My past torments, nor the view of the outrages I continually suffer, are sufficient to move the hearts of Christians. Oh hardness! oh insensibility! In effect, all these excesses are incapable of overcoming my indifference. I daily see Jesus Christ insulted in the Adorable Eucharist, and I daily see it with carelessness and coldness.

Meditation for the Fourth Friday in April.

Venit Jesus januis clausis, et stetit in medio, et dixit: Pax vobis; deinde dixit Thomæ: Infer digitum tuum huc, et vide manus meas, et affer manum tuam et mitte in latus meum, et noli esse incredulus, sed fidelis. (Joan. xx. 26, 27.)

Jesus cometh, the doors being shut, and stood in the midst, and said, Peace be to you: then He saith to Thomas, Put in thy finger hither and see My hands, and bring hither thy hand and put it into my side, and be not faithless, but believing.

How attractive is this condescension! and how much must He have loved this incredulous Apostle, to convince him by such persuasive and powerful means! the mere sight of this opened side, inflamed with love the heart of this Apostle. Jesus Christ comes daily to us in the Blessed Sacrament; He gives us therein, the same Body, and in this sacred Body we find the same wounds: lastly, He gives us His Heart. He makes us touch It; and all the fire with which It burns, has not yet had power to inflame ours. With what coldness do we depart from Communion? we are wholly frozen at Jesus Christ's feet. The faith and the new fervour of St. Thomas, greatly rejoice the Heart of Jesus Christ, but what sentiments must He have of my insensibility and want of faith? what sentiments ought I to have of it myself?

MAY.

Meditation for the Second Friday in May.

Tanto tempore vobiscum sum, et non cognovistis me. (Joan xiv. 9.)

So long a time have I been with you, and have you not known me?

It seems as if it were impossible, to know Jesus Christ well, and not to love Him with tenderness: I know not therefore, if we can know Him well, and only love Him indifferently. The complaint which He makes to His Apostles, manifests to us the sentiments of His Heart. Though they had left all to follow Him, they did not yet love Him very fervently, because they did not know Him perfectly. But has not this divine Saviour more reason to give us the same reproof, and to say to us, I have been amongst you so long, I have been day and night with you, I am with you, only, for the sake of the love I bear you, and still you do not know me. If you knew Me, would you leave Me alone the greater part of the time? Would you care so little about visiting Me? Would you show so little modesty in My presence? Would you have so little confidence in Me, in your wants? Would you not immediately have recourse to Me, in all the misfortunes of life, and could you easily separate yourselves from me, during the whole of your lives? What answer should I be able to give?

MEDITATION FOR THE THIRD FRIDAY IN MAY.

Dormite jam, et requiescite: Ecce Filius hominis tradetur in manus peccatorum. (Marc. xiv. 41.)

Sleep ye now and take your rest: behold the Son of man shall be betrayed into the hands of sinners.

It is very painful to a person that loves much, to see himself forsaken in misfortune, by his best friends; but it is no less afflicting, to see that the few friends, who profess to remain faithful, are not at all touched by his misfortunes, and even take no part in his distress. Jesus Christ in the most Blessed Sacrament, is outraged by the greater number of men, He is daily given up therein to the hands of sinners, and the greater part of those who profess to love Him are not at all touched by the outrages He suffers, and do not even think of testifying any grief to Him, in seeing Him so unworthily treated. You sleep, devout souls; religious persons, you repose, whilst Jesus Christ is contemned, and insulted on every side, in the Adorable Eucharist! Here heretics profane the sacred vessels, and tread under foot the consecrated Hosts; there, sinners daily commit the most horrible sacrileges; He is forgotten by all; He is everywhere despised, and you do not feel this contempt, and you do nothing to show Him that you feel it? It is in our power to repair these outrages in some degree, and are we indifferent to them, do we forget them?

MEDITATION FOR THE FOURTH FRIDAY IN MAY.

Et cœpit pavere, et tædere. (Marc. xiv. 33.)

Jesus began to fear, and to be heavy.

A GREAT soul, a truly generous heart seems not to suffer, in any extraordinary degree, at the sight of the injuries, the torments and the death it has itself chosen, and to which it submits spontaneously. But this Heart, which resists all torments, cannot be insensible to the ingratitude of those for whom it suffers, and this is certainly the affliction that causes the grief of Jesus Christ in this Mystery of His agony. I do not so much complain, He might say, of being dragged through the streets of Jerusalem, of being lacerated by scourges, of dying on an infamous cross; all this is my free choice; My love towards men would not allow Me to choose any other means; but what does grieve Me is, that I should receive such ill-treatment in the Eucharist, the most excellent work of My love, and which I regarded as the most efficacious means of being more loved by men, and of thus obliging Myself to love them continually more and more, of receiving their homages, and the reparation they would make by their adorations for the terrible outrages I have received from the Jews; that this should be the place where I receive the greatest insults, where I am continually forgotten, ill-treated, and despised even by those who make a profession of piety!

JUNE.

MEDITATION FOR THE SECOND FRIDAY IN JUNE.

Ego sum panis vitæ: qui venit ad me, non esuriet; et qui credit in me, non sitiet unquam: sed dixi vobis quia et vidistis me, et non creditis. (Joan. vi. 35 et 36.)

I am the Bread of Life; he who cometh to Me shall not hunger, and he who believeth in Me shall never thirst; but I have said unto you, that you also have seen Me, and you believe not.

A REPROOF is terrible after a benefit of such a nature. It is as if Jesus Christ had said: My children, I have not been satisfied with giving My Blood for your ransom; I give you My Body also to be your food: to die for another is the greatest proof of love, but it would not be for Me, the greatest proof of love, unless I renewed this sacrifice every day, and a hundred times every day: unless, being unable to die more than once, I placed Myself continually, for the love of you, in a state of death in the Blessed Sacrament. Yet, I have already said it, you have seen Me, and you love Me little, because your faith is so lamentably weak. Ungrateful Christians! You see what this loving Saviour has done for you, you see what He does daily in the Eucharist, and do you love Him more? If you are so little touched by what He does for you, might you not at least be moved, by what you yourselves do against Him?

MEDITATION FOR THE THIRD FRIDAY IN JUNE.

Et misit nuntios ante conspectum suum: et euntes intraverunt in civitatem Samaritanorum, ut pararent illi; et non receperunt eum. (Luc. ix. 52 et 53.)

And He sent messengers before His face, and going they entered into a city of the Samaritans to prepare for Him. And they received Him not.

WHAT opinion do we entertain of these unhappy Samaritans? what a happiness would it have been for them had they known Who it was, that presented Himself at their gate, and to whom they refused an entrance into their town! But what were then the sentiments of the Heart of Jesus Christ, when the disciples related to Him, the manner in which they had been treated, and the contempt that was shown for His Person? These unhappy people are not, however, alone: there have been at all times Samaritans of this kind, who have refused the disciples of Jesus Christ an entrance into their city, who have even driven from it Jesus Christ Himself. Besides almost the whole of Africa and the Eastern countries, many others have chased Him away. In how many countries of Europe, miserably buried in heresy, is He not refused to be recognised in the Sacrament of His love, and this adorable Saviour sees Himself, so to speak, banished from them? Oh that He were at least better received by the rest of Christians! That He were a little more loved, and less unworthily treated even by those who receive Him!

MEDITATION FOR THE FOURTH FRIDAY IN JUNE.

Et exierunt Pharisæi, et cœperunt conquirere ab illo signum de cœlo, tentantes eum; et ingemiscens spiritu, ait: Quid generatio ista signum quærit? (Marc. viii. 11 et 12.)

And the Pharisees came forth, and began to question with Him, asking Him a sign from Heaven, and tempting Him. And sighing deeply in spirit, He saith: "Why doth this generation ask a sign?"

THIS sigh conveys a reproof, and such a reproof is

well founded. This Sacred Heart feels most deeply,
the insensibility and the malice of the Pharisees.
There was not a city or a town, through which Jesus
Christ had passed, that had not published His miracles.
They might themselves have witnessed them a hundred
times. But he who does not love those that work these
wonders, is little touched either by what he sees or
hears. We must feel little love for Jesus Christ, when
the greatest and most loving of all miracles, that of the
Eucharist, moves us so little. But, oh my loving
Saviour, is not our insensibility itself, a miracle
capable of touching our hearts? it is a prodigy, oh my
divine Saviour, capable of drawing sighs continually
from Thy Heart, if it were still in a condition to be
pierced with sorrow and grief. But, my God, mine is
capable of grief and sadness; grant that it may at least
feel strongly in future, the little honour it pays Thee,
and the injury it does Thee.

JULY.

MEDITATION FOR THE SECOND FRIDAY IN JULY.

Clamaverunt ergo rursum omnes, dicentes: Non hunc.
(Joan. xviii. 40.)

Then cried they all again, saying: Not this man.

WHENCE could arise so extraordinary a hatred, and
what could render Jesus Christ so odious to them?
What sick person was ever presented to Him that, He
refused to cure? what person in distress, ever turned
to Him, whom He would not relieve? This hatred and
this fury of the Jews terrify us, and certainly grieved
the Heart of Jesus Christ. But, my Saviour, are there
not even now hearts, which nourish a similar hatred,
against the most august, and the most loving of all
Thy sacraments? How many heretics are there, who,
refusing to recognize Thee, in this excellent work

of Thy love, cry out still daily, "We will have nothing to do with this man?" how many bad Catholics, who, refusing to receive Thee under some vain pretext, or receiving Thee unworthily, cry out, "We will have nothing to do with this man?" Lastly, how many persons, who are considered to lead a very regular life, show evidently, by their forgetfulness, their indifference towards Thee, and the difficulty they feel in visiting Thee in this adorable mystery, that they do not know how to value Thee? Have I not been, am I not now, of this number?

MEDITATION FOR THE THIRD FRIDAY IN JULY.

Ego veni in nomine Patris mei, et non accipitis me; si alius venerit in nomine suo, illum accipietis? (Joan v. 43.)

I am come in the name of My Father, and you receive Me not; if another shall come in his own name, him you will receive.

How reasonable is this reproof? but how penetrating, and of what a profound grief, in the heart of Him Who makes it, does it give evidence? What would be the feelings of a Prince, if he saw the lowest servant of his Father received with honour, while he was treated with the utmost contempt? We respect a man, whom we know to be sent from God; the relics of those, who have given their blood for Jesus Christ, inspire us with the veneration due to those generous martyrs; long journies even, are undertaken at great inconvenience to render them the honour which they deserve, and this piety is solid and praiseworthy. But is our devotion reasonable, when Jesus Christ Himself, really present at all times in the Holy Eucharist, cannot gain our respect? We feel no devotion towards the Blessed Sacrament; we feel only disgust for this divine food; we carry our dissipation even to the foot of the Altar;

we never find time to pay Him a visit; can we not resolve to attend upon Him more assiduously?

MEDITATION FOR THE FOURTH FRIDAY IN JULY.

Qui manducat mecum panem, levabit contra me calcaneum suum: cum hæc dixisset Jesus, turbatus est spiritu, et protestatus est, et dixit. (Joan xiii. 18 et 21.)

He that eateth bread with me, shall lift up his heel against Me: when Jesus had said these things, He was troubled in spirit, and He testified and said . . .

It required a great cause of affliction, to disturb a Heart as intrepid as that of Jesus Christ. But the contempt, that is shown for the Blessed Sacrament of the Altar, is to Him a motive of the most sensible grief, which He cannot conceal. This Divine Saviour was about to institute the Blessed Sacrament; His love presses Him, urges Him on, but His mind brings clearly before Him, all the outrages, to which this mystery would expose Him. This sad view plunges His Heart into an abyss of grief; He sees that heretics, refusing to believe that He has loved us to such an excess, will make use of this excess of love, to outrage Him most cruelly; and also those impious men, professing to believe in Him, will commit horrible sacrileges. If this Divine Saviour had done for demons, the hundredth part of what He has done for men, would He have been so ill repaid? O my Divine Saviour, these insults and this ingratitude have had power to trouble Thee, and shall I never be touched by them!

AUGUST.

MEDITATION FOR THE SECOND FRIDAY IN AUGUST.

Ex hoc multi discipulorum ejus abierunt retro: et jam non cum illo ambulabant; dixit ergo Jesus ad duodecim: Numquid et vos vultis abire? (Joan vi. 67, 68.)

After this, many of His disciples went back and walked no more with Him. Then Jesus said to the twelve: Will you also go away?

This question came from a Heart so inflamed with love, and was in itself so strong a proof of excessive tenderness, that it could not fail to oblige those, to whom it was directed, to love Jesus Christ yet more ardently. It had also all the effect that this Divine Saviour desired; and this increase of fervour in the Apostles, consoled Him a little, for the affliction He felt, at the departure of those who had forsaken Him. Jesus Christ often asks us the same question, and for the same reason. How happy should we be, if it had the same effect! Every day this loving Saviour sees Himself forsaken by those unhappy creatures, who, tired of His benefits, withdraw themselves from His service. He is left alone. Faithful servants, fervent Christians, hear the question put to you by Jesus Christ: And you, He says, will you abandon Me? Are you disgusted with this divine food, and tired of My service? will you act like those who go away, and come only with the crowd, to offer Me their homage mechanically, or to pass the time?

MEDITATION FOR THE THIRD FRIDAY IN AUGUST.

Dixit illi Jesus: Vulpes foveas habent, et volucres cæli nidos: Filius autem hominis non habet ubi caput reclinet. (Luc. ix. 58.)

Jesus said to him: The foxes have holes, and the birds of the air, nests, but the Son of man hath not where to lay His head.

With what feeling did not Jesus Christ make this complaint? but did He at all exaggerate in complaining thus? Is it true that Jesus Christ was everywhere persecuted, everywhere ill-treated? Alas! the time of

His birth was anticipated by persecution : scarcely was He born, than He was obliged to fly, and seek an asylum amongst idolators. He Himself complains of the bad treatment He received at Nazareth ; He was driven out from Jerusalem ; He was refused an entrance into the villages of Samaria ; He was several times obliged to make Himself invisible, to escape the fury of those, who wished to procure His death, before the time had come which He had chosen. But lastly, did this period of persecution and contempt, end with His mortal life ? Yes, it would have ended, if He had not instituted the most Blessed Sacrament. How so? Because Jesus Christ, in this adorable mystery, is not safe from the insults and outrages of the impious. No one can doubt the fact. Savages, Canadians, and Idolaters might indeed doubt it, and never could believe it, if they did not know any Christians. But it is but too plain to Christians who are witnesses of the contempt shown to Jesus Christ in the Adorable Eucharist, even though they perhaps may have no feeling of grief at all on account of it.

Meditation for the Fourth Friday in August.

At ipse nihil illis respondebat ; sprevit autem illum Herodes cum exercitu suo : et illusit indutum veste alba, et remisit ad Pilatum. (St. Luke xxiii. 9 et 11.)

But He answered him nothing. And Herod with his army set Him at nought, and mocked Him, putting on Him a white garment, and sent Him back to Pilate.

How heroic is this patience, and how attractive this meekness ! how admirable and eloquent is this silence, and how many beautiful lessons, it teaches us ! But, my God, how great was the contempt with which He was treated on account of these great virtues, which were alone manifest proofs of His Divinity, and which should have gained Him the love and veneration of all! Thy marvellous patience, oh my loving Saviour, and Thy admirable silence at the sight of all the outrages Thou sufferest in the Adorable Eucharist, have not an effect entirely similar? If the smallest irreverence, if a single unworthy Communion, was at once severely punished, we should not be so immodest and so wicked. But this divine Saviour, Who has so rigorously punished even in this life, the least injuries done to His servants, Himself endures, without opening His mouth, the contempt shown to His Adorable Person in this mystery, and prefers to expose Himself, to the outrages of sinners by His great patience, rather than keep just souls away from His holy table, by inspiring them with fear. My God, what beautiful lessons does this silence of Jesus Christ, in the Adorable Eucharist, teach me!

SEPTEMBER.

MEDITATION FOR THE SECOND FRIDAY IN SEPTEMBER.

Jesus dixit: Nonne decem mundati sunt? et novem ubi sunt? non est inventus qui rediret, et daret gloriam Deo, nisi hic alienigena. (St. Luke xvii. 17 et 18.)

And Jesus answering, said: Were not ten made clean? and where are the nine? There is no one found to return and give glory to God, but this stranger.

IN the world, we cannot endure ingratitude. It is only when God is in question that we do not concern ourselves about being ungrateful. This wonderful cure, this miracle, had been extended to ten persons, and of them all, one only was found who thanked his Benefactor. Of all the benefits we have received from Jesus Christ, we cannot doubt that the Blessed Eucharist is one of the greatest: and even the greater part of the blessings we daily receive, are derived from the same source. But who thinks of often thanking Jesus Christ for this great benefit? Who returns thanks to this loving Saviour, who, in abolishing all the other sacrifices, has left us a Victim that cannot but be pleasing to God, an offering equal to all the other benefits we have received from Him, and to those that we may ask of Him ; a Host capable of cancelling all the sins of men ; a Host which is truly a sovereign remedy for all kinds of evil; a tree of life that has power to communicate to us, not only health, but even immortality ? So sinful a forgetfulness, such enormous ingratitude, touched the Heart of a Man-God, and shall it not move mine, even when I myself am of the number of these ungrateful wretches?

MEDITATION FOR THE THIRD FRIDAY IN SEPTEMBER.

Et ut appropinquavit, videns Civitatem flevit super illam dicens: Quia si cognovisses et tu, et quidem in hac die tua, quæ ad pacem tibi, nunc autem abscondita sunt ab oculis tuis. (St. Luke xix. 41 *et* 42.)

And when He drew near, seeing the city, He wept over it, saying : If thou also hadst known, and that in this thy day, the things that are to thy peace ; but now they are hidden from thy eyes.

How well do these tears of the Son of God, express the sentiments of His Heart ! Unhappy Jerusalem ! Unfortunate people, into what misfortunes does not thy blindness precipitate thee ! What wilt thou say, when thou shalt see that thy happiness was in thy own hands, and that it depended on thyself, to be the happiest of all nations, if thou wouldst have recognized on that day, the best of all Masters, and the meekest of Kings ? If Jesus Christ were still capable of grief and of shedding tears, loving us as He does, could He see us without weeping ? But can He at least, behold the indifference we feel for Him, in the Adorable Eucharist, the contempt we show Him, and the misfortunes that this indifference and this contempt draw down upon us, without saying to us, as He did to that unhappy people; Ah slothful Christians! ungrateful men! If you would recognize at least, on this day which is given you, Him who is in the midst of you, Who alone can give you peace, and make you eternally happy! But now all this is hidden from your eyes, you will not know Me. How would it ever be possible for you to be so unhappy, if you knew Me and loved Me?

MEDITATION FOR THE FOURTH FRIDAY IN SEPTEMBER.

Ecce venit hora, et jam venit, ut dispergamini unusquisque in propria, et me solum relinquatis. (St. John xvi. 32.)

Behold the hour cometh, and it is now come, that you
    shall be scattered, every man to his own, and shall
    leave Me alone.

WHAT were the sentiments of the Heart of Jesus Christ, when preaching to His Apostles, regarding their baseness and ingratitude, their flight and their forgetfulness! But could these Apostles persuade themselves, that they would ever be capable of abandoning so good a Master? Nevertheless, it has so happened. But my Saviour, this time is past: but how can I say this time is past? The time came when Thou wert left alone: and wert Thou then left more alone, than Thou art at this time? Jesus Christ is day and night on our Altars, and who is there, that is earnest and assiduous in visiting Him? Was a palace of a prince ever without a crowd of courtiers, though the number is so small of those that are able to speak, to the prince? Jesus Christ is the only one Who is always ready and Who receives all equally: the only one, Who has an excessive desire to do good to all, and Jesus Christ is almost always alone.

OCTOBER.

Meditation for the Second Friday in October.

Amen dico vobis, quia unus ex vobis tradet me, qui manducat mecum; væ autem homini illi per quem Filius hominis tradetur. (St. Mark xiv. 18 *et* 21.)

Amen I say to you, one of you that eateth with me, shall betray me: but woe to that man, by whom the Son of man shall be betrayed.

It is not surprising, that the Scribes and Pharisees, that impious and wicked men should have conspired against Jesus Christ, for they were His mortal enemies, and what else can be expected from an enemy? But that Jesus Christ should see Himself betrayed by an Apostle, that is, by a man whom this Divine Saviour had chosen in preference to so many others, and to whom he had given such manifest proofs of the most ardent love! But, my Saviour, since it is Thou, that choosest Thy servants and Thy favourites, how long wilt Thou find ungrateful men, even traitors, among those Thou hast chosen? Out of so many Christians, whom Thou hast selected, by a pure effect of Thy love, in preference to so many infidels; with whom Thou condescendest to dwell, on whom Thou so liberally bestowest Thy benefits, to whom Thou givest Thyself; how many are there who abuse Thy benefits! how many ungrateful men, who refuse to communicate! how many traitors, even among those who communicate! Shall I oh Lord, be always insensible to all this.

Meditation for the Third Friday in October.

Populus hic labiis me honorat: cor autem corum longe est a me; in vanum autem me colunt. (St. Mark vii. 6 *et* 7.)

This people honoureth me with their lips, but their heart is far from Me. And in vain do they worship Me.

TRULY, this honour, which was rendered in appearance to Jesus Christ, must have been most insincere! the heart could indeed, have had little share, in the praises, that were bestowed on Him, from time to time, since all these homages terminated, by His being made to endure the greatest outrages, and finally, to expire on the cross! To how many slothful Christians, may not Jesus Christ address the same fearful reproof at the present day! That want of recollection in the Churches, that disrespect in presence of the Blessed Sacrament, that disgust for this divine food, all this clearly proves that our homage does not proceed from the heart. We have some appearance of devotion : but in this sort of devotion, there is much affectation : ah Lord! can my heart be near Thine; and not be wholly inflamed with Thy love; can it love Thee so little!

MEDITATION FOR THE FOURTH FRIDAY IN OCTOBER.

Jerusalem, Jerusalem . . . Quoties volui congregare filios tuos, quemadmodum gallina congregat pullos suos sub alas, et noluisti. (St. Matt. xxiii. 37.)

O Jerusalem, Jerusalem . . . how often would I have gathered together thy children, as the hen doth gather her chickens under her wings, and thou wouldest not?

WHAT answer can this unhappy people make to this reproof? But what answer can we ourselves make, when it shall be addressed to us also? The figure which Jesus Christ here makes use of, shows our ingratitude so much the more clearly, as it expresses more forcibly the love of Jesus Christ for us. This loving Saviour has placed Himself in the Blessed Sacrament, to enable us to find in Him at all times, a powerful protector, a physician, a Father. He is continually in the midst of us, because He wishes to have us constantly with Him. But do not the reluctance, and the forgetfulness of the greater number of Christians, oblige Him to say to us: My poor children, how often would I have gathered you, as a hen gathers her chickens, and you have gone away, and you have refused! Do you wonder that you are so long afflicted, so often overcome, so often mortally wounded! For this reason, there are many among you that are sick and languishing, and many sleep the slumber of death. Shall I have any feeling in future, oh my loving Saviour, of the charitable reproof Thou givest me, or of the contempt I have hitherto had for it?

NOVEMBER.

MEDITATION FOR THE SECOND FRIDAY IN NOVEMBER.

Procidit in faciem suam orans, et dicens: Pater mi, si possibile est, transeat a me calix iste; veruntamen non sicut ego volo, sed sicut tu. (St. Matt. xxvi. 39.)

HE fell upon His face praying and saying; My Father, if it be possible, let this chalice pass from me. Nevertheless, not as I will, but as thou wilt.

JESUS Christ had always passionately desired to give His Blood, for the salvation of men, and had a hundred times testified this desire. It is not then death, which terrifies Him, and makes this chalice so bitter, but the ingratitude of those very men, who will not profit by His death. I have desired, Eternal Father, and more than ever I desire, to give liberty to slaves, but I have never desired to make ungrateful men. The outrages I am about to endure from my enemies, do not alarm

Me, but the contempt, that I foresee my own children will show Me, afflicts Me, the blindness of the first moves Me, but the enormous ingratitude of these last, pierces My Heart with grief. Jesus Christ passionately desired, that the time were arrived, for instituting the most Blessed Sacrament of the Altar; but were not the abuse and the contempt of this august Sacrament, which He foresaw, a great cause of sadness to Him? and had He not reason to say, that if it were possible He desired this chalice might pass from Him? In very truth, this chalice must be very bitter, but do we not know, that it depends on us, to remove this chalice from Him, for it is we ourselves, who by our contempt and unworthiness, constitute all its bitterness, we who offer it to Him? How is this Oh Lord! It is in my power to sweeten this chalice by my homage, and shall I not do it?

MEDITATION FOR THE THIRD FRIDAY IN NOVEMBER.

Conversus autem ad illas Jesus dixit: Filiæ Jerusalem, nolite flere super me, sed super vos ipsas flete, et super filios vestros. (St. Luke xxiii. 28.)

But Jesus, turning to them said: Daughters of Jerusalem, weep not over Me, but weep for yourselves, and for your children.

WAS love ever witnessed equal to that which Jesus Christ shows us on this occasion? His body is all lacerated with scourges, He has scarcely a few drops of blood remaining; He is become the laughing stock and the butt of a whole nation, and in this pitiable state, He is not at all touched by what He Himself suffers, He feels nothing, but what we are about to draw down upon ourselves, by our want of gratitude. Alas! if we have a heart capable of feeling, what can move it, if this cannot? Jesus Christ forgotten, despised, outraged in the adorable Eucharist, feels, so to speak, more deeply the misfortunes we draw upon ourselves by this contempt, than the contempt itself. Weep, He says to us, weep, my children, over your forgetfulness of your Redeemer, of your Father. Weep over that enormous ingratitude, that you have carried to the highest pitch; over those irreverences, that you have committed so boldly, in My presence. Weep for so many sacrilegious Communions, weep for the great loss you have suffered, by refusing to acknowledge Me; or by knowing Me, and refusing to love Me. In what, oh my beloved Saviour, can my tears be employed, if I can think of my ingratitude without weeping?

MEDITATION FOR THE FOURTH FRIDAY IN NOVEMBER.

Regina Austri surget in judicio cum generatione ista, et condemnabit eam; quia venit a finibus terræ audire sapientiam Salomonis; et ecce, plus quam Salomon hic (St. Matt. xii. 42.)

The queen of the south shall rise in judgment with this generation and shall condemn it: because she came from the ends of the earth, to hear the wisdom of Solomon, and behold a greater than Solomon here.

THERE have been newly converted Christians, in the Indies and in Japan, who have travelled more than a hundred leagues every year, to have the consolation, of once adoring Jesus Christ, in the most Blessed Sacrament, of hearing one single Mass; and they thought nothing of the fatigue, of so difficult a journey, that they might have the happiness, of spending half an hour with Jesus Christ. My God! how many will rise up at the day of judgment, and will condemn us! We have Jesus Christ in our town; religious persons have Jesus Christ in their own house; and this benefit is esteemed as nothing! and some value it so little, that they only visit Jesus Christ with indifference, many even with repugnance, and almost all, without devotion. Will not the Queen of the South rise up on the day of judgment against this people? and will she not suffice to condemn them, because she came from the extremity of the earth, to hear the wisdom of Solomon? and yet, He who is here upon our Altars, is greater than Solomon.

DECEMBER.

Meditation for the Second Friday in December.

Hoc est autem judicium; quia lux venit in mundum, et dilexerunt homines magis tenebras quam lucem. (St. John iii. 19.)

And this is the judgment: because the light is come into the world, and men loved darkness rather than the light.

How deplorable is the blindness of the Jews! and what will these unfortunate men be able to say, when they shall be reproached, for the misfortunes they have drawn upon themselves, by their blindness? You had the light in the midst of you, will it be said to them, and you have shut your eyes, because you preferred darkness. The Sun of justice so long expected, had risen amongst you, and you would not profit by the brilliant light which would have made you happy. This same light is still with us in the Blessed Sacrament, but are all Christians wiser than the Jews? do all Christians profit by this light? and is there no reason to fear, that the presence of Jesus Christ in the Blessed Sacrament, His Heart open to all men, His Heart always ready to pour out upon us all the treasures of grace It encloses, and of which It is the source, may be the cause of our condemnation? Do we have recourse to Jesus Christ in the Blessed Sacrament? Do we go to Him with confidence? Do we expect from Him, the lights and helps that are necessary for us, in the various circumstances of life? Alas! we despise this light, because we love the darkness, and this contempt will be, without doubt, the cause of our condemnation.

MEDITATION FOR THE THIRD FRIDAY IN DECEMBER.

Respondit eis Joannes dicens: Medius autem vestrum stetit, quem vos nescitis . . . cujus ego non sum dignus, ut solvam ejus corrigiam calceamenti. (St. John i. 26 et 27.)

John answered them saying . . . but there hath stood one in the midst of you, whom you know not . . . the latchet of whose shoe I am not worthy to loose.

WHAT a misfortune for the Jews not to have known Him who was in the midst of them! But do we know Him who is amongst us? Great ones of the world, do you know Him? You, who punish so rigorously, the least omissions of the respect due to you, and who are so little touched by the outrages offered to that Monarch, whom you profess to acknowledge? People, do you know Him who is in the midst of you, you, who are so assiduous in attending upon those, from whom you hope for some favour, and so circumspect in the presence of those you fear, while you show no respect in the Church, and never find a moment of time, to come and pay your homage, to Jesus Christ, in the Blessed Sacrament? Lastly, ministers of our Lord, religious persons, do you know Him who is continually in the midst of you? For, if you do know Him, whence comes it that you are so seldom near Him? No Lord, we do not know Thee; I confess that hitherto I have not known Thee; but my devotion towards Thee shall show in future, that I begin really and truly to know Thee, because I will begin really to love Thee.

MEDITATION FOR THE FOURTH FRIDAY IN DECEMBER.

Factum est autem cum essent ibi, impleti sunt dies ut pareret, et peperit Filium suum primogenitum, et reclinavit eum in præsepio ; quia non erat ei locus in diversorio. (Luc. ii. 6 et 7.)

And it came to pass, that when they were there, her days were accomplished that she should be delivered. And she brought forth her first-born Son, and laid Him in a manger, because there was no room for them in the inn.

THERE is room for all, and none for Jesus Christ! This divine Saviour begins, even before His birth, to be rejected and despised. A Man-God is reduced to be born in a stable, whilst mere men are born in palaces. What were then the sentiments of Jesus Christ, on seeing Himself so wretchedly lodged, and what must they be at the present day, seeing Himself ill-received, when Christians dwell in magnificent houses? Do all the sacred vessels, in which Jesus Christ is continually enclosed, do all the holy places where He dwells, correspond with that sumptuous magnificence, that we witness, in the apartments and furniture, of persons in the world? Oh that, at least, this loving Saviour did not often find Himself received in impure souls, and hearts stained with a thousand sins! I know, my loving Saviour, that Thy delights are to be with a pure heart; purify mine then, that Thou mayest find Thy delight in it. Grant that in future, I may have the happiness of receiving Thee less unworthily. Inflame this heart with Thy pure love; may Thy Sacred Heart come and take the place of mine; may mine in future be so intimately united to Thine, that it may have no other sentiments. Amen.

EJACULATIONS.

Good Jesus, too late have I known Thee, too late have I loved Thee! I will love Thee, because Thou hast loved me first. Grant me a heart that may think of Thee, a soul that may love Thee.

I will know Thee Lord, Who knowest me, I will know Thee, the strength of my soul: show Thyself to me, oh my comforter.

Grant that my heart may desire Thee; desiring Thee, may seek Thee; seeking Thee, may find Thee; and finding Thee, may love Thee.

O love, which burnest always, and art never extinguished, inflame me wholly with thy fire, with thy love, with thy sweetness!

O my joy, draw my heart to Thee! Sweet food of my soul, may I feed upon Thee!

Thou hast loved me, Lord, more than Thyself, for Thou hast been willing to die for me; that Thou mightest redeem a servant, Thou hast delivered up Thyself.

Grant to my heart repentance; to my spirit contrition; to my eyes a fountain of tears.

Extinguish in me the desires of the flesh, and inflame me with the fire of Thy love.

Look down, oh holy Father, on the torments of the Redeemer, and forgive the sins of the redeemed.

O Lord Jesus! I am the wound of Thy torments, and the cause of Thy death; I am the bruises of Thy passion, I am the burden of Thy anguish.

I entreat of Thee, oh my hope, through all Thy mercies, to forgive all my iniquities.

I could offend Thee, oh holy Father, of myself, but I could not appease Thee; behold in Thy Son what will cause Thee to show mercy to Thy servant.

He is a Priest and sacrifice for us to Thee; and He is a sacrifice, because He is a Priest.

I should despair, on account of my exceeding great sins, unless Thy Word, oh my God, had been made Flesh, and had dwelt amongst us.

O charity! oh mercy! oh my Redeemer and my hope! in Thee I breathe, to Thee I sigh.

I, whom Thou lovest, am not worthy, but certainly Thou, Whom I wish to love, art not unworthy.

Hope of my heart, if I have not as yet deserved to love Thee as much as I ought, at least I desire to love Thee as much as I ought.

Grant that I may see Thee, the joy of my heart; grant that I may love Thee, the life of my soul.

Be in my mind, be in my heart, because I languish with love, because without Thee I die; it is better for me not to exist, than to be without Jesus.

O Lord Jesus, light of the hearts of those who see Thee, and life of the souls of those who love Thee, come into my heart, I beseech Thee!

Come into my soul, that Thou mayest possess it, and that I may place Thee as a seal upon my heart.

Be with me, Thou, Whom I seek, Whom I love, Whom, with my heart and mouth, as well as I am able, I praise and adore.

EJACULATIONS.

Oh my God, my Jesus, whom shall I love, if I love not Thee, my sovereign Good?

Place me within Thy wounds, unite me to Thy Heart, that I may never more separate myself from Thee.

Oh most merciful Jesus! I weep for the time when I did not know Thee, I weep for the sins by which I have offended Thee. Ah, how many years have I lost, in which I might have loved Thee!

I weep for my sins, and I will always weep for the outrages that are committed against Thy love, and against Thy most sweet Heart.

Accept, oh holy Father and my God, the most sweet sentiments of the Heart of Thy blessed Jesus: I offer them to Thee in satisfaction for my sins, and those of the whole world.

Oh my Beloved, my Lord, why do men forget Thee! why do they not love Thee, Who didst die to love us!

What can I give Thee to repay some little of the great debt I owe Thee?

I offer my heart to Thy love, Thy love to Thyself.

My adorable Saviour and my God, I hope in Thee, in Thee I will live and die.

O Heart wounded through love of me, wound mine with Thy holy love.

O may my heart burn with Thy most sweet love, and melt with contrition for having so much offended Thee.

May I live in grief and contrition, to die loving Thee, in Thee, and with Thee.

When, my Jesus, shall I see Thee, to love Thee always.

When shall I cling to Thy adorable feet, embrace Thy sacred side, and wholly unite myself to Thy most loving Heart?

O my Saviour, my mercy, show now what Thou canst do in me; help me in my sorrows, in my afflictions, in my fears.

In Thy mercy watch over me in life, defend me in dangers, save me at my last hour.

I consecrate to Thee my life for ever, to Thee every breath I draw, to Thee all the motions of my poor heart.

I offer and unite, to Thy life and passion, every action, every good work I do; help me to do much that I may love Thee more.

Glory be to Thee, oh my God, as it was, as it is, and as it ever shall be, world without end.

FINIS.

INDEX.

	PAGE
The Author's Preface	i
Notice	viii

MOTIVES OF THE DEVOTION TO THE SACRED HEART OF OUR LORD JESUS CHRIST.

FIRST PART.

CHAPTER I.—What is meant by Devotion to the Sacred Heart of our Lord Jesus Christ and in what it consists .. 1

CHAPTER II.—The means employed by Almighty God to inspire this devotion 6

CHAPTER III.—How just and reasonable is the devotion to the Sacred Heart of our Lord Jesus Christ 10

    I.—The excellence of the Adorable Heart of our Lord Jesus Christ 11

    II.—The amiable qualities which are found in the person of Jesus Christ 13

    III.—The sensible proofs of the immense love that Jesus Christ has for us 16

    IV.—The extreme ingratitude of men towards Jesus Christ.. 21

CHAPTER IV.—How useful the devotion is for our salvation and for our perfection 25

    V.—How much true sweetness there is in the devotion to the Sacred Heart of Jesus 30

    VI.—Of the devotion that the Saints have had to the Sacred Heart of Jesus Christ 34

SECOND PART.

CHAPTER I.—The dispositions requisite for a tender devotion to the Sacred Heart of our Lord Jesus Christ...... 42

    I.—First Disposition.—A great horror of Sin .... ib.

    II.—Second Disposition.—A lively Faith 43

III.—Third Disposition.—A great desire of having an ardent love of Jesus Christ..................................	45
IV.—Fourth Disposition.—Interior Recollection	47
CHAPTER II.—What are the obstacles which prevent us from gathering all the fruit we ought from the devotion to the Sacred Heart of Jesus Christ	56
I.—First obstacle.—Tepidity	58
II.—Second Obstacle.—Self-love	65
III.—Third Obstacle.—A secret Pride	69
IV.—Fourth Obstacle.—Some unmortified Passion ..	73
CHAPTER III.—The means of overcoming the obstacles that hinder us from gathering the fruit we ought from the devotion to the Sacred Heart of Jesus Christ	76
I.—First Means.—True mortification	77
II.—Second Means.—Sincere Humility	81
III.—The joy and true sweetness that are inseparable from the exercise of true mortification and of sincere humility...	83
CHAPTER IV.—The particular means of acquiring the perfect love of Jesus Christ and this tender devotion to His Sacred Heart	89
I.—First Means.—Prayer	ib.
II.—Second Means.—Frequent Communion	92
III.—Third Means.—Visits to the Blessed Sacrament	98
IV.—Fourth Means.—Fidelity in accomplishing with exactness some practices of this devotion	99
V.—Fifth Means.—A tender devotion towards the Blessed Virgin	101
VI.—Sixth Means.—A special devotion to St. Aloysius Gonzaga	106
VII.—A Day of Retreat every month	110

THIRD PART.

CHAPTER I.—What are the motives and sentiments with which we should practise this devotion	112
CHAPTER II.—Visits to the Blessed Sacrament	119
I.—The motives that should induce us to visit the Blessed Sacrament	ib.

	PAGE
II.—Method of visiting the Blessed Sacrament	124
III.—Practice for spending every day, a quarter or half an hour, in prayer before the Blessed Sacrament, suited to all sorts of persons	131
IV.—A few words of advice on frequent Visits to the Blessed Sacrament	135
CHAPTER III.—Practice for celebrating and hearing Mass	138
I.—Reflection on the Sacrifice of the Mass	ib.
II.—Practice for the celebration of the Sacrifice of the Mass	142
III.—Practice for assisting at the Sacrifice of the Mass	147
CHAPTER IV.—Practical Reflections on Communion	151
CHAPTER V.—What are the marks of the perfect love of Jesus Christ and of true devotion to His Sacred Heart	159
I.—Character of one who has a true love of Jesus Christ	160
II.—Effects of the perfect love of Jesus Christ	167
CHAPTER VI.—Practice of devotion to the Sacred Heart of Jesus for the day of the Feast	174
CHAPTER VII.—Practice of devotion to the Sacred Heart of Jesus for every month, for every week, for every day, and for certain hours of each day	180
I.—Practice of devotion to the Sacred Heart of Jesus for the first Friday in each month	ib.
II.—Practice of devotion to the Sacred Heart of Jesus for every week	183
III.—Practice of devotion to the Sacred Heart of Jesus for every day	184
CHAPTER VIII.—The Exercises of this Devotion	188
Preparation of honour to the Sacred Heart of Jesus Christ	189
Act of Consecration to the Sacred Heart of Jesus Christ	191
Offering to the Sacred Heart of Jesus Christ	193
Act of Love to the Sacred Heart of Jesus Christ	195
Act of adoration of the Sacred Heart of Jesus Christ	196

INDEX.

	PAGE
Offering, that may be made at the time of Mass	196
Act of Contrition	197
Prayer, that St. Gertrude used to recite every day, in honour of the Sacred Heart of Jesus Christ	198
Act of love	ib.

MEDITATIONS FOR THE FEAST OF THE SACRED HEART OF JESUS,

For every Friday in each month, and for certain days of the year, more especially consecrated to the honour of the Sacred Heart of our Lord Jesus Christ 199

For the first Friday after the Octave of Corpus Christi, on the incomprehensible love shown us by Jesus Christ, in the most Blessed Sacrament of the Altar .... ib.

1st Point.—The ardent desire Jesus Christ feels to be with us 201

2nd Point.—The excessive desire of Jesus Christ to make us partakers of His blessings 205

3rd Point.—The excessive desire of Jesus Christ to be united with us 210

Meditation for the first Friday in each month, on the sentiments of the Heart of Jesus Christ at the sight of the ingratitude of men, and of the outrages, to which His excessive love for these very men, has exposed Him 217

1st Point.—The sentiments of the Heart of Jesus Christ at the sight of the torments He would have to endure from the cruelty of the Jews .... ib.

2nd Point.—The sentiments of the Heart of Jesus Christ at the sight of the outrages He would endure from the malice of Heretics 220

3rd Point.—The sentiments of the Heart of Jesus Christ at the sight of the ingratitude of the greater number of the Faithful 222

Subjects of Meditation for every Friday in the year .. 226

January.—Meditation for the 2nd Friday 227
1st Point .... ib.
2nd Point 228
For the 3rd Friday 229
For the 4th Friday 230

	PAGE
February.—For the 2nd Friday	231
For the 3rd Friday	232
For the 4th Friday	233
March.—For the 2nd Friday	234
For the 3rd Friday	235
For the 4th Friday	236
April.—For the 2nd Friday	ib.
For the 3rd Friday	237
For the 4th Friday	239
May.—For the 2nd Friday	ib.
For the 3rd Friday	240
For the 4th Friday	241
June.—For the 2nd Friday	242
For the 3rd Friday	ib.
For the 4th Friday	243
July.—For the 2nd Friday	244
For the 3rd Friday	245
For the 4th Friday	246
August.—For the 2nd Friday	ib.
For the 3rd Friday	247
For the 4th Friday	248
September.—For the 2nd Friday	249
For the 3rd Friday	250
For the 4th Friday	251
October.—For the 2nd Friday	252
For the 3rd Friday	ib.
For the 4th Friday	253
November.—For the 2nd Friday	254
For the 3rd Friday	255
For the 4th Friday	256
December.—For the 2nd Friday	257
For the 3rd Friday	258
For the 4th Friday	259
Ejaculations	260

4 JU63

www.ingramcontent.com/pod-product-compliance
Lightning Source LLC
Chambersburg PA
CBHW031939230426
43672CB00010B/1975